WITHDRAWN
NDSU

CONSCIENTIOUS CAVALIER

COLONEL BULLEN REYMES
artist unknown

HELEN ANDREWS KAUFMAN

CONSCIENTIOUS CAVALIER

Colonel Bullen Reymes, M.P., F.R.S.
1613 - 1672

The Man and his Times

HARVARD UNIVERSITY PRESS
CAMBRIDGE, MASSACHUSETTS
1962

© 1962 BY HELEN ANDREWS KAUFMAN

PRINTED IN GREAT BRITAIN

CONTENTS

	FOREWORD	9
I	THE REYMESES AND THE PETRES	13
II	SPLENDOUR ON THE STRAND	26
III	LIFE IN THE EMBASSY	36
IV	BULLEN STARTS HIS DIARY	45
V	PARIS ON ONE'S OWN	57
VI	THE EDUCATION OF A COURTIER	67
VII	DISCOVERING VENICE	81
VIII	BY BOAT, COACH, AND SADDLE	90
IX	CONSTANTINOPLE AND RETURN	101
X	AUTUMN IN FLORENCE	113
XI	THE NEW AMBASSADOR	120
XII	COURTESANS AND BANDITS	132
XIII	FIGHTING FOR THE KING	143
XIV	PAYING THE ROYALIST PENALTY	158
XV	THE NEW WORLD OF THE RESTORATION	176
XVI	MISSION TO TANGIER	190
XVII	SERVANT OF THE SICK AND WOUNDED	199
XVIII	THE CROWDED YEARS	216
XIX	YE MARINERS OF WEYMOUTH	229
	NOTES	241
	INDEX	251

ILLUSTRATIONS

COLONEL BULLEN REYMES *Frontispiece*
From the portrait by an unknown artist in the possession of Mrs G. V. Troyte-Bullock, Zeals, Wiltshire

YORK HOUSE AND THE WATER GATE *facing page* 34
as seen from the river. From a drawing by Hollar in the Pepysian Library, Cambridge

'VUE DE WESTMINSTER'
A rare seventeenth-century drawing by Jacob Esselens in the Graphische Sammlung Albertina, Vienna. It shows a view along the Thames, with the Water Gate and the east side of York House in the foreground
(Reproduced by permission of the Österreich Nationalbibliothek, Vienna) 34

FACSIMILE OF THE SIGNATURE OF THE DUCHESS OF BUCKINGHAM *page* 35

FACSIMILE OF REYMES'S SIGNATURE *facing page* 44
in a letter to the Duchess of Buckingham

FACSIMILE OF A PAGE OF REYMES'S DIARY 45

IL PALAZZO GIUSTINIANI 128
Residence of the English Ambassador, Basil, Lord Feilding. From a photograph taken about 1900
(Reproduced by permission of Böhm, Venice)

REYMES'S HOME, WADDON, NEAR PORTESHAM, DORSET 172
A photograph of a painting made some time between 1700 and 1704 in the possession of Mrs B. O. Corbett. A glimpse of the west wing which Colonel Reymes built can be seen through the trees. It was later destroyed, probably by fire
(Copyright *Country Life*)

WEST SIDE OF WADDON AS IT LOOKS TODAY 172
The grassy area in the left foreground was the old bowling green

FOREWORD

Because Bullen Reymes kept a diary, wrote many and voluminous letters, and because he carefully preserved the scores of papers relating both to his public activities and his private life, there remains an unusually full and exact account of the man himself and of the background and personalities of the seventeenth century. In fact it would be difficult to find, in the first half of that century, an individual who has left so complete a record of himself.

For a great many years all of Colonel Reymes's papers and books were stored in the attic at Waddon, 'left to the mercy of anybody and cats and mice'. It was not until July 28th, 1859, that William Chafyn-Grove, to whom Reymes's property had descended, removed them to his home in Zeals, Wiltshire. There, in 1955 and 1958, through the courtesy of Major G. V. Troyte-Bullock, their late owner, I was able to examine these books and manuscripts.

The story of Reymes, his family, and his friends is based primarily on his own papers, for the most part unpublished (some documents relating to events in the later years of his life appeared in *Somerset and Dorset Notes and Queries*). Additional information has, however, been derived from such sources as the *Thomason Tracts*, letters and other documents in the Record Offices of Devonshire and Dorset, in the Public Record Office, and in the National Maritime Museum. The references to these and to secondary sources which have been used are given in the notes.

Reymes's diaries and his many letters given in their entirety would fill a book of more than 600 pages. I have, therefore, selected for verbatim reproduction only what seemed to me to be the most salient and characteristic passages, reducing the rest to a narrative account of his activities and ideas, as found in both the diaries and letters, trying at the same time to design an appropriate setting for his words and actions.

Because the old spelling helps to preserve the atmosphere of a period and even reflects the pronunciation, I have, with the

FOREWORD

exception of a few changes, such as, for example, the substitution of a *v* for a *u*, a *j* for an *i*, and an *F* for an *ff*, retained the contemporary spelling. But I have amended the punctuation when it was so erratic as to confuse the sense.

My first debt of gratitude is to the late Major Troyte-Bullock for his generosity in allowing me to examine and use the Reymes papers, for his permission to reproduce the Colonel's picture and to have certain of the documents microfilmed, and for the gracious hospitality of Major and Mrs Troyte-Bullock during the many days I sat in their home reading and copying the words of Bullen Reymes. I am also indebted to Mr and Mrs Corbett, with whom my husband and I stayed in beautiful Waddon, not only for their hospitality but for their information concerning Reymes and the house in which he once lived.

For the grant which made possible my trip to England for the perusal of the Reymes papers, I have to thank the American Philosophical Society. I wish also to acknowledge my indebtedness to Dr E. S. de Beer for his interest and help, and to Dr I. F. Burton of Bedford College for reading my manuscript and for his pertinent advice. To Dr C. V. Wedgwood I am particularly grateful not only for reading the manuscript but for her encouragement and valuable suggestions.

Among others to whom my gratitude is due are Professors Wallace Notestein and Caroline Robbins; Brigadier Peter Young; Messrs. A. L. Raimes; H. G. Tibbutt, F.R.HIST.SOC.; E. L. C. Mullins, M.A., Secretary of the History of Parliament Trust, and P. H. Hulton, Assistant Keeper of Prints and Drawings of the British Museum. Appreciation for my husband's constant help is greater than can be expressed.

University of Washington H. A. K.
Seattle

For
George and Peggy

CHAPTER ONE

THE REYMESES AND THE PETRES

1. A Gentleman of Seventeen looks back upon his Youth

ONE day late in May of 1631, Bullen Reymes, a gentleman in the service of the Duchess of Buckingham, was standing on the stairs of the Water Gate of York House waiting for a wherry to carry him to Greenwich. As on any summer day the Thames was crowded. Heavy barges and eight-oar wherries were making their way slowly down stream, while white-sailed pinnaces and the tilt boats, gay with their bright awnings, slipped quickly by, some on their way to the 'City' and others sailing south to Westminster. For York House, with its gardens, its water wall and lion-adorned Water Gate, stood just at the bend as the river turned south past Northampton House, Whitehall, and Westminster.

The boat for which Bullen was waiting would carry him to Lord Dorchester, the Secretary of State, from whose hands he was to receive a letter for Sir Isaac Wake, the English ambassador in France. This letter was the open door to a career in the embassy in Paris.

Like any lad of his years, Reymes was no doubt eager enough to be off and on his way. But for the moment his thoughts may well have been caught up with the past and all that he was leaving. Perhaps he was remembering the gaiety of York House, the kind and gentle Duchess, and the handsome gentleman usher — Bullen's own father. Or possibly he was thinking of the lovely lady-in-waiting, Mistress Priscilla Hill, and reliving the hours he had spent with her in 'the sweete walke next Durram house'. A dozen pictures could have flashed across his memory: the fun and bustle at the New Exchange on the Strand just behind Durham House; the familiar lodgings of his beloved uncle, Robert Petre, at Castle Court Yard near Holborn; or his mother and sisters living amid the decaying grandeur of Old Buckhurst in Sussex. Had his memory travelled further back across the years, he might have caught glimpses of the luxurious London home of another uncle, Sir George Petre; of the many-acred farm of his Coker cousins in Mapowder; of the mansion house of his grandfather in Exeter, where he had been born; of his mother's home near the little Devonshire village of Torbryan, or of the sea-swept town of Overstrand where his father and all the Reymes kin had lived. But by this time the picture would have blurred and merged with the stories he had heard so often, tales of the Petres of Devon and the Reymeses of Norfolk, and of the deeds of ancestors who lived long ago — the heritage of the past which had become an unconscious part of himself.

II. *The Reymeses of Norfolk*

One of Bullen's ancestors was a Norman baron, Roger de Rames, who, as early as 1086, held land in Norfolk. By the beginning of the thirteenth century, descendants of Roger de Rames were living in Overstrand on the Norfolk coast, where for almost five hundred years they were to be lords of the manor and patrons of the church.[1]

Today in the coastal village of Overstrand the sound of the sea is muted. The church and most of the houses lie a little way from the shore. On the seaward side the land ends abruptly in a steep bank which rises some fifty feet above the narrow strand at its base. Strong winds blow across the top of this precipitous bank, while below, the North Sea slowly but ceaselessly eats away at its very foundation.

This stealthy invasion by the sea has been going on for centuries. Once the church, the manor house, and much of the village stood on the high land overlooking the water. Shortly after 1400, however, when the church, on the very edge of the crumbling bank, was in imminent danger of falling into the sea, John Reymes, the lord of the manor, decided to build a new church — or to re-erect the old — in another and safer place. It was to escape the sea that he chose for its new site the half-acre of land on which stands the present St Martin's. This St Martin's is the one clear link with the past and with the Reymes family. More particularly it is a memorial to the same John Reymes who, in 1411, was buried under the large stone which now lies just outside the chancel.

As the years went by, the Reymeses continued to prosper. They had many important friends and made many advantageous marriages. Important folk visited Overstrand. From neighbouring Southrepps came the Cotterell family, and from Aylsham, less than ten miles away, came the Boleyns.

It was Queen Anne Boleyn's cousin, Elizabeth Boleyn,[2] who brought the name Boleyn (or Buleyn) into the Reymes family. In 1571, Elizabeth's daughter Mary became the wife of William Reymes, the lord of the manor at Overstrand. William and Mary were both prosperous and prolific. They had thirteen children — four daughters and nine sons. When, in 1586, her eighth son was born, Mary, in honour of her mother, named him Bullen.[3]

By 1600, all but the three youngest sons of Mary and William Reymes had settled in or near Overstrand. As was so often the case with younger sons, these three, Francis, Bullen, and Barney, had to seek their fortunes elsewhere. London, the home of their uncle Clement Reymes, was the logical choice.

Just when the boys left Overstrand it is impossible to say, but by 1602 they were living in London, either with or near their Uncle Clement. Of Bullen Reymes of Overstrand and his life in London we shall hear more. Now the story moves to Devonshire and the home of Mary Petre whom this Bullen, Bullen the first, is to marry some ten years later.

III. *The Petres of Devonshire*

Mary Petre was born in 1585 at Tor Newton House near the village of Torbryan in southern Devon. Some fifty years earlier her great-grandfather, John Petre, had purchased the manor of Tor Newton, and here his descendants continued to live until the early years of the seventeenth century.

Of the Petres born in Tor Newton House the most famous was John's son, Sir William Petre. Associated with Thomas Cromwell in the suppression of the monasteries, he was knighted by Henry VIII and made Secretary of State. Sir William served not only Henry but his three successors — Edward, Mary, and Elizabeth — as well.

CONSCIENTIOUS CAVALIER

But it was a less famous son, Sir William's elder brother John, who inherited Tor Newton House which he, in turn, left to his son William. This William Petre, in 1571, married Cecily Southcott of near-by Bovey Tracey. Of the couple's six children only four reached maturity — Thomasine, George, Mary and Robert.

Torbryan has changed but little in the last three hundred years. The valley in which it lies, miles away from the busy highway, is quiet and isolated. In some ways the quiet may be more pervasive today than it was in Mary's time, for there are fewer people about. Some two miles to the north of the stately old church with its battlemented tower and thirteenth-century arch, the grey stone manor of the Petres, Tor Newton House, lies almost hidden in a deep, tree-shadowed hollow. Although the sixteenth-century house where Mary was born lacked the high front wing of the present structure, it included the two low wings and the ancient stone outbuildings which encircle a court at the rear.

Except for its setting, we know little of Mary Petre's childhood beyond the fact that from 'both her parents' and from the rector (John Herle) she learned the doctrine of the Church of England to which she was to adhere so faithfully all her life. In 1600 Mary's mother died. Six years later William Petre left Tor Newton House and, with his daughter Mary and his new wife, Grace Spicer, moved into the mansion house of Petre Hayes in the parish of St Thomas the Apostle, just across the river from Exeter. Petre Hayes is important in the annals of the Petres and the Reymeses. It was to be Mary's home for eight years and the birthplace of her son, Bullen Reymes the second.

IV. *In Stuart London*

Queen Elizabeth died early on Thursday morning, March 23rd, 1603. By Tuesday, April 5th, her kinsman, the waiting James Stuart, had left Edinburgh and was on his way to London.

The sense of loss, the spectre of change which had gripped all England at Elizabeth's death, was mingled with a vast sense of relief. At last the succession was settled. The country was eager to believe that James could bring it what it wanted — peace, stability, and economic progress. Englishmen, troubled by the threat of religious changes, pushed into the back of their minds their uneasy fears, hoping that somehow this son of a Catholic mother, reared in a stronghold of Presbyterianism, would be able to resolve the brooding religious antagonism in his new kingdom.

As if a threat to the country's high hopes, the first year of King James's reign was clouded by an outbreak of the plague. It had come almost simultaneously with the King's arrival in London. By the time of the coronation on June 25th the disease was raging, and all who could left the city.

But by the spring of 1604 the pestilence had almost subsided. Already people were beginning to forget. James and his retinue were back in London, the theatres had reopened, the streets were crowded, and the pace of life quickened. All in all, 1604 promised to be a good year. The new King was sitting securely on his throne, albeit he preferred the back of his horse. The Puritans may have smarted from his jibes at their pride, but they were mollified by the prospect of a new translation of the Bible; and the Catholics, who had enjoyed a relaxation of the laws against recusants, were not yet disturbed by a slight tightening of those rules. The mood of the country was optimistic.

Among those who were to profit by the accession of King James I was Mary Petre's brother George. George was a Catholic now. During his years at Exeter College, Oxford, he had been converted to the old faith by his Essex cousin, young William Petre. No doubt George, like other Catholics, had welcomed James, believing that he would remit the recusancy fines and tolerate private worship. The King's statement acknowledging 'the Roman Church to be our Mother Church' had aroused extravagant hopes. So little did the Catholics understand James's curious attempts at tolerance that they thought this could mean but one thing — a promise of the King's own conversion. These high hopes were, of course, not realized, but for a time James did relax the laws against Catholics and rewarded many of them for their support. On July 23rd, 1603, George Petre was knighted, and that same year William's father, John Petre of Ingatestone, was made a baron.

Two years later Sir George went abroad, in all probability accompanying the Earl of Nottingham to Spain for the ratification of the peace treaty with Philip III. By August of that same year he was in Florence with Tobie Matthew and had laid the first stone in that young man's conversion to Catholicism.[4] Although Sir George's association with the Jesuits may not have been widely known, Sir George Cornwallis, the English ambassador in Spain, was convinced of his sympathies for that order, calling him 'a man that carryes an infected Harte ... an Impe of the Jesuiticall Tree'.[5]

By 1610 Petre was back at his house in White Friars. His circle of friends included such men as Sir John Digby, Richard Sackville, the Earl of Dorset, Sir Clement Cotterell and Tobie Matthew, as well as less important persons like Clement Reymes and his three nephews. Just how Sir George and Clement Reymes became acquainted is not clear. Possibly they met at Whitehall, for Clement, who held a post at Enfield House, one of the King's hunting lodges, moved on the fringes of the Court circle. Moreover, the two had a mutual friend in Sir Clement Cotterell, the King's groom porter. In any case it was to Clement Reymes that Sir George Petre first broached the subject of his sister's marriage. The prospective bridegroom was Bullen Reymes.

Reymes held some minor clerical post in the household of James. Possibly he was an assistant to one of the King's comptrollers, for among his son's papers is a small MS. pamphlet, inscribed 'M. Bulleyn Reymes. his boock. Anno 1613', and entitled 'An accompt of severall Fees belonging to places'. 'M. Bulleyn Reymes' must have received the education of a gentleman, for he could read Latin and French. He also seems to have had his share of good looks and charm, advantages without which few could survive in the Court at Whitehall. And survive Bullen did. He continued to serve in the Royal Court during the King's lifetime and, at the same time, to win the favour of Buckingham, whose servant he became after the death of James in 1625. How well Reymes knew the slovenly, good-natured pedant, King James, it is impossible to say, but very few of the personable youths about his Court managed to escape the notice of that oddly amorous monarch.

In spite of the lavish display, funds in the household of James were often dangerously low. Regular salaries often turned out to be only regular promises, and many were in attendance merely for the prestige that went with their offices. Reymes probably received a fee for his services and at least some of his meals.

But he apparently had no regular quarters at Whitehall, for he lived with his brother Francis in the parish of St Martin-in-the-Fields. He was perennially hard up.

It was in 1611 that the twenty-five-year-old Bullen entered into the negotiations for his marriage. Whether at this point he had ever seen Mary Petre we do not know. But she was of good family, the sister of Sir George, and — she had a dowry of £1,000. In any case, late in the year Reymes set out for Devon and the manor of Petre Hayes, lying close to the bank of the river Exe, and on February 23rd, 1612, 'Bulline Reymes, gent. and Mrs Marie Peeter, d. of William Peeter, Esquier' were married in Holy Trinity Church in Exeter.[6] Less than ten months later their daughter Elizabeth was christened.

Despite her changed status and despite the fact that her husband's duties kept him in London much of the time, Mary continued to live at Petre Hayes. Men who held any sort of public office in those days were away from home a great deal. Distances may not have been great, but roads were often almost impassable. There was, however, a sort of unwritten law that spouses should be together at the birth of their children. As a rule the husbands stayed on long enough after the event to ensure a similar trip the following year. So, if Reymes followed the approved custom, he would have been back at Petre Hayes on December 28th, 1613, when his son and heir, Bullen Reymes the second, was born. Three months later, however, when her father died, Mary, with two family servants, Richard and Patience Adams, and with her two babies, left for London, her husband, and her new home 'at the upper end of St. Martin's in the Fields'. Within the next six years there were three more children: Mary, William and Judith.

Great changes were taking place at Court, changes which were to have a marked effect on the fortunes of the Reymes family. As early as 1614 there had been reports of a divinely handsome youth in an old black suit 'broken out in many places', hanging around the race-course at Newmarket. It was whispered that certain of Somerset's enemies saw in this handsome newcomer a chance to supplant the high-handed favourite, and were planning to invest money in the future of this obscure young man, George Villiers. Villiers' rise to fame was due in part to the powerful enemies of

Somerset; in part it hinged on the timeliness of his appearance, for by 1614 James was growing weary of the peevish Somerset and wanted someone with whom he could relax; in the main, however, it depended upon George Villiers himself — upon his charm and magnetic beauty. But although Somerset's power was waning, he still had a hold on the King. For everyone at Court it was an anxious time — a nervous, tightrope-walking sort of existence.

When, therefore, the soup episode occurred, the Court held its collective breath. One of the gentlemen waiters, a friend of Somerset, pretending clumsiness, spilled a bowl of soup over Villiers' elaborate costume. The hot-tempered Villiers jumped up and hit the man on the head. Since the blow was delivered in the presence of the King, the law demanded that Villiers lose his right hand. As Lord Chamberlain, Somerset pressed for the punishment, but James overruled him. Villiers' future looked bright.

It was probably through their friend Clement Cotterell that Francis and Bullen Reymes succeeded in catching Villiers' attention. Clement Cotterell, the King's groom porter, was, says Chamberlain, 'a creature of the Lord of Buckingham'.[7] By 1620 Francis and Bullen had also become 'creatures' of Buckingham. Francis was his haberdasher. What office Bullen held is not clear, for he is simply referred to as Buckingham's servant.

In the service of Villiers, Reymes got to know some of the most influential men of the Court as well as members of Buckingham's family — his sister (Lady Denbigh), and his ambitious mother, who, with Villiers' successes, grew more arrogant than her son and quite as unscrupulous. So notorious was her power that Gondomar, the Spanish ambassador, wrote home saying, 'There was never more hope of England's conversion to the Roman faith than now; for there are more prayers offered to the mother than to the son.' Not that the son failed to take advantage of any opportunity to line his elegant pockets. Villiers may have expected to be paid in the coin of smiles and adulation, but he also expected and got more than his share of the coin of the realm. Other courtiers profited from traffic in offices, but none on so grandiose a scale. Buckingham was, to quote Pym, 'their broker-in-chief'.[8]

But of all the family it was Villiers' young wife Kate whom Bullen was to know best. When, early in 1620, Buckingham married the seventeen-year-old Lady Katherine Manners, the whole Court fell captive to her charms. At first James had violently opposed the match. Katherine's religion — she was a Catholic — was the stumbling-block. It was only when she agreed to accept the Anglican faith that the King gave his consent.

James's objection to a Catholic wife for Buckingham may seem strange in view of the fact that even then he was considering a Catholic Princess for his son. But the Spanish match was primarily a diplomatic project. The King may well have convinced himself that, for the sake of world peace, for the sake of the Palatinate, and for some badly needed Spanish gold, a properly restricted Catholic daughter-in-law might not be too great a price to pay.

Bullen Reymes the first, though a member of the Anglican Church, had apparently adopted the sophisticated Court attitude towards Catholicism. Not so his wife. Mary, fiercely loyal to the Church of England, looked with suspicion on any brand of Catholicism, especially upon the Jesuits who owed their first allegiance to the Pope. Many shared her views, and when, in 1619, Tobie Matthew refused to sign the oath of allegiance to the English King, he was ordered to leave the country.

By 1622, however, the climate of opinion had changed. Now that the marriage of Prince Charles and the Infanta seemed certain, many of the restrictions against Catholics were forgotten. Tobie Matthew, in high favour now, was back in England and, in company with George Petre, had resumed his nightly visits to Count Gondomar. Many persons, including King James and Buckingham, were under the spell of this brilliant Spaniard. But, clever though he was, Gondomar underestimated the strength of Protestantism in England. He firmly but mistakenly believed that the Spanish marriage would result in the conversion not only of Charles but of all England. James, for his part, was just as deluded in believing that Spain would fight to restore the Palatinate, and that the Jesuits would cease to advocate the assassination of Protestant rulers.

The dismal failure of the story-book adventure of Prince Charles and Buckingham travelling incognito to Spain to win and bring home a beautiful bride, of course, put an end to all talk of a Spanish marriage. The wind of opinion shifted once again and began to blow against Spain and, to a lesser degree, against Catholics. Both Buckingham and Charles, bitterly anti-Spanish now, were acclaimed by the people because they had failed in their mission and no Spanish-Catholic Queen was to rule over England.

In the midst of this growing antagonism towards all things Spanish, it is little wonder that Thomas Middleton's *Game of Chess* should have drawn such crowds. The villain of the piece, the Black Knight, was none other than Gondomar. On August 21st, 1624, John Chamberlain writes to Sir Dudley Carleton:

> I doubt not but you have heard of our famous play of Gondomar which hath ben followed with extraordinarie concourse and frequented by all sorts of people ... rich and poor ... papists & puritans ... churchmen and statesmen ... and a world besides.

He goes on to say that they counterfeited Gondomar to the life

> with all his graces and faces, and had gotten (they say) a cast sute of his apparell ... and his Lytter, wherin the world says lackt nothing but a couple of asses to carrye yt and Sir G. Peter or Sir T. Matthew to beare him companie.[9]

Everyone was busy trying to identify the chess-men. The white King James, black King Philip and black Knight Gondomar were easy enough to place—the others, more difficult. Possibly the white Knight was identified as Charles and the white Duke as Buckingham. And some may have guessed that the white King's pawn, who wore black under his white garment, was Sir George's friend, Tobie Matthew.

The year 1624 was a good one for Buckingham's 'servants'. The Duke had never been more powerful, for the King, tired and sick, had turned over to his beloved favourite virtually all control of affairs. But when King James died on March 27th, 1625, Buckingham's friends feared, and his enemies hoped, that the favourite's power had at last come to an end. Luckily for his friends, the accession of King Charles I gave the Duke even more scope than he had had before. He was still the 'principal verb' of the realm. Actually he had won the confidence and devotion of Prince Charles even before their journey to Spain, and once Charles made up his mind about an idea or person he seldom changed.

THE REYMESES AND THE PETRES

Less than three months after the death of the old King, the new King took a wife. In June of 1625 King Charles's bride, the tiny, fifteen-year-old Henrietta Maria, sister of Louis XIII, arrived in England with her horde of Catholic followers. Almost simultaneously with the Queen's arrival came a recurrence of the plague. Reminded of the dreadful epidemic in 1603, the superstitious shook their heads in apprehension. Perhaps they were right. In spite of the French marriage, England at the beginning of the following year was not only at war with Spain but on the brink of a conflict with France. For all the country's woes Parliament put the blame on Buckingham. They demanded his impeachment, and the King, to save his friend, dissolved his Parliament. Buckingham's power had increased, but so had his enemies.

All these events, especially the career of Buckingham, were part of young Bullen Reymes's background. Of the boy's early years in London, however, we know nothing save that he lived in the parish of St Martin-in-the-Fields and visited from time to time the home of Sir George Petre, his 'howse at the White fryers', and the 'logings' of his other uncle, Robert Petre, in Castle Court Yard just beyond the city wall. But when Bullen was twelve there was a change in the Reymes household. It was because of his Uncle George. Sir George Petre had always moved in expensive circles. The Petre fortune was a substantial one, but he had been chipping away at it steadily ever since his father's death in 1614. Tor Newton House and other property in and about Torbryan had long since been sold. Now Sir George needed money for a new project — a country estate within a reasonable distance from London.

It was no modest little farm but Old Buckhurst, the oncesplendid estate of the Sackvilles, which was tempting Bullen's extravagant uncle. It came to the Sackville family about 1200 and was their principal residence until Thomas Sackville moved to his new manor of Knole, the gift of Queen Elizabeth. When his grandson Richard, notorious even in the lavish Court of James for his wasteful life, died in 1624, his bankrupt estate went to his brother Edward, fourth Earl of Dorset. The new lord, a much thriftier gentleman than his late brother, set about repairing his battered fortunes. To raise the needed money he leased Old

Buckhurst to his friend George Petre. In turn, Sir George, to raise the money for the lease and to pay off his own accumulated debts, sold Petre Hayes and all his remaining property in Devon.[10]

Close to the village of Withyham in Sussex, Buckhurst lies about halfway between East Grinstead and Tunbridge Wells, and less than forty miles from London. Today all that remains of the old estate of the Sackvilles is one high battlemented stone tower and a small section of the original house with its base of yellowish tinted stone. But at the beginning of the seventeenth century the mansion of Buckhurst was spacious, perhaps even larger than Knole. Approached by a drawbridge, the building was in the shape of a rectangle built round a large courtyard, its long, wide hall communicating with a lower level on which stood a chapel and a tennis court. There were six battlemented towers then, one at each corner and one guarding either side of the broad entrance.[11] Unfortunately, some time between 1609 and 1624, part of the house was torn down to build a college at East Grinstead for the relief of '31 unmarried persons, 21 men and 10 women'.

There must, however, have been more of the old house standing in 1626, the year Sir George took possession, than is generally believed. For, in the inventory of Petre's goods and chattels, the numerous rooms referred to suggest a still commodious dwelling.[12]

Young Bullen learned to know Buckhurst well. Some time during the summer of 1626 Mary Reymes and her five children moved to Sir George's new estate in Sussex. Evidently Mary, in return for food and lodging for her family, acted as a sort of supervisor of her brother's extensive household. Whether she lived in the house proper or in the comparatively new keeper's lodge, we do not know. Robert Petre had a chamber of his own in the big house and it is possible that at least some of the Reymes occupied the '2 next Chambers' where there were '3 old bedsteads and ... one little bedsted and quilt of woll'.

Old Buckhurst, with its rolling acres of wheat and pease, its barns stuffed with grain, the oxen, the sheep and lambs, and horses — 'the bay with a bald face, the cropp-eard nagy, the grey herriot mare, the bay gelting' and a dozen more — must have been a delight and wonder to the city-bred Reymes children. Then there was the house itself: the dining-room with its '6 redd lether chayres and 6 green velvett stooles', and Sir George's luxurious chambers boasting damask 'curteins', 'a blew rugg' and three pairs of Douai hangings. There were the cheese-presses and vats in the dairy, the huge copper kettle in the brew-house, and the bolting-trough in the 'old' kitchen. And against the background of everyday life were everywhere reminders of the past — just a stone's throw away: the old church at Withyham with its monuments of the dead Sackvilles, the ancient oaks of near-by Ashdown Forest, the ruined chapel on the lower green, the lone stone tower and the broken foundations of its demolished companions — enough to stir the fancy of anyone, young or old.

Mary Reymes and part of her family were to stay on at Buckhurst for a good many years. But after that first summer, Bullen lived in London, riding down to Sussex only during the holidays. During the next two years he attended a small school run by a Master Hebert and his wife, possibly as a boarder.

Events of vital importance to the Reymes family occurred during these two years. In the summer of 1627 Buckingham set forth to rescue the Protestants of La Rochelle. The mission failed miserably, and late in October the Duke sailed home, leaving the Huguenot city in worse straits than he had found it.

A less buoyant nature would have been crushed by a defeat so overwhelming and by an England so bitterly hostile. But Buckingham, undismayed, now bent every effort to organize another expedition to relieve starving Rochelle. It was to speed up this new expedition that he travelled down to Portsmouth where, on the morning of August 23rd, 1628, he was stabbed to death by one John Felton. The King, the Duchess of Buckingham and the Duke's many followers were stunned and saddened by the loss of this spectacular man. But the assassin, who proudly confessed his crime, became a national hero. To many Englishmen, George Villiers had become the symbol of their country's woes.

The death of his friend and patron brought to Bullen's father not only grief but a threat to his hopes for advancement. Yet he was more fortunate than many of the late Duke's creatures. He was able to stay on at York House as gentleman usher to the Duchess Katherine. Young Bullen, like his father, was to know York House well, for by the next year he too was living there, a member of Lady Buckingham's 'family'.

CHAPTER TWO

SPLENDOUR ON THE STRAND

1. *The Famous House*

TODAY all that is left to remind us of the once resplendent York House are its stone Water Gate and the names of the near-by streets — Buckingham, Villiers, Duke, George Court, and 'Of' Lane (now rechristened York Place) — which spell the name of the famous Duke.[1] Lying in the Embankment at the foot of Buckingham Street, the Water Gate is now several hundred feet from the river which once washed up and down its grey stone steps. Whoever its architect may have been, George Villiers himself was ultimately responsible for this beautiful gateway to the river and for all the changes wrought in the old Palace of the Bishops.

York House had originally been the town house of the Bishop of Norwich, and later of the Archbishops of York. In 1621, however, when the Marquis of Buckingham tried to get possession, the estate belonged to Sir Francis Bacon. Bacon loved the old turreted palace[2] where he had been born and at first refused to sell. In fact it was not until the spring of 1622, and after considerable pressure had been brought to bear, that he finally agreed to give up York House.

The Duke of Buckingham's palace was only one of a number of great houses which lay between the Strand and the river. To the west was Northumberland House, and to the east Durham House, separated from York gardens by a pathway, or 'common passage', which led from the waterside to the Strand and the New Exchange, one of Bullen's favourite haunts.

Along the Strand side of Villiers' property were the servants' quarters and the tall iron gate over which lived young Reymes's friend, Cuthbert Feilding, the porter of York House. It was his duty to 'take care what sort of people he let in and out ...

especially mean people or such as have burdens going out'. He had to watch lest some slippery character carry out a piece of silver plate, or wood or coal 'hidden under cloaks, or secretly wrapped, or in baskets'. He had to close the gate when the plate was brought up and keep it shut until the meal was over and the precious plate safely stowed away. At 9.30 in the evening he was to 'rid the house of all strangers and idle persons' and shut the gate and allow none of the household to enter after 11 p.m. Apparently he liked Bullen, for he relayed his messages, looked after his mail, and gossiped with him, discussing 'how business goes and what newse is sturing or what new ballet is come out'.

The beautiful gardens of York House fell by an easy slope to the river and commanded a view as far south as the famous Lollard Tower and as far east as London Bridge. Among the trees and flowers were 'a great white marble table' and 'a great marble bowle', and 'on the mound' stood 'A Neptune and a Dolphin', 'One great figure of Pallas', and Giambologna's magnificent 'Cain and Abel'. There, in the garden's 'sweet little walkes', Bullen poured out his youthful confidences to Mistress Mosly, the 'mother' of the ladies-in-waiting, and there on summer nights he walked with 'sweet Mistress Priscilla Hill', whose song was like 'the melodiousness of a sweet nittinggell'.

Such was the external setting for the incomparable splendour within. For much of this, Balthazar Gerbier was responsible. As collector and keeper of the treasures, he probably made the list of paintings and other objects which served as a basis for the later inventories.[3] These inventories describe the contents of the rooms (fifteen, in addition to the passage-ways and the numerous unnamed 'Upper Roomes'). They list 'those Roman Heads and statues which ... belonged Sir Peter Paul Rubons';[4] the medals, stones and objets d'art; some 387 paintings, and, in some cases, the furnishings of the chambers in which the treasures were stored.

In 'the Hall' were a portrait of the Emperor Charles by Titian and 'one great piece being Scipio' by Van Dyck, and, in 'the comeing above', some twenty-two paintings — one by Raphael, and a full-length portrait of the Marquis of Hamilton by Mytens. There were paintings in the 'Vaulted Roome', the 'Sumpter Roome', and in the long 'Passage by the Ladies Closett' —

Holbeins, Bassans, Tintorettos, and more than a dozen by Rubens.

'The Roome call'd the King's Bedchamber' was done in green. The French bed was 'hung' with embroidered green velvet curtains; the table was covered with a 'Carpett of Green Velvett, embroidered suitable to the Bedd', and there were '6 great chares of the same' and '2 Brasse Armes for lights'. All nine pictures hanging on the wall were by Bassan.

The colour-scheme in 'The Withdrawing Chamber next the King's Bed Chamber' was red. The room was 'hung with crimson velvett, being lac'd above with gold and silver lace', and there was a 'Pavilion with a car'vd and guilt head' and 'two curtaines of Crimson Velvett ... lyn'd with Crimson Satten'. Under it was one 'Court chare of Crimson Velvett'. On the walls were paintings by Titian, Tintoretto, Andrea del Sarto and Paul Veronese.

In 'My Lords Closett' the only furnishings listed were: One green marble table, a crystal candlestick, and ten gilt stools. But the walls were adorned with twenty famous paintings, among them Titian's great 'Ecce Homo'.

'My Lady's Redd Closett' must have been large, for there were seventy-six pictures on the walls, more than in the Gallery itself. Besides the paintings there were a great looking-glass, eight feet square, a large ebony cabinet, a crimson velvet couch with two 'elbow cushions', and eight crimson velvet stools.

'My Lady's Green Closett' seems to have been used as a sort of museum. There were boxes of medals, and twelve cases full of 'Antiquities of ... diverse stones', and on four shelves against one wall were objects of rare beauty fashioned from agate, crystal, and gold. Twenty paintings hung on the walls, among them a portrait of the Duchess of Chevreuse by Nicholas Lanier. And, in addition to all the shelves and cases, there were two ebony cabinets, two trunks, a red velvet mirror, a white satin embroidered looking-glass, two crimson velvet back stools, thirteen great books with blue ribbons, and 'one embroidered psalm'.

In 'The Great Chamber', the new, thirty-five-foot-square room at the east end of the house said to have been built by Gerbier, there were twenty paintings and fifty-eight pieces of statuary. The latter were of various sizes and subjects — 'The Emperor Trajanus at length', 'a little laughing Boy', 'A little head with a bald pate'. Among the paintings was Rubens's famous equestrian portrait of Buckingham, 'My Lord Duke on Horseback'. Few furnishings are listed — only 'two great Brass Andirons', 'A christall candlestick', and 'seaventeen guilt stooles' — probably because the room was used for dining, with boards set up at meal-time and afterwards removed. Two doors led from 'The Great Chamber' to the Chapel (probably the peak-roofed building to its north), for in the list of statuary are 'a man's head above ye chapel dore', and 'a head of Plaister of Christ at the other Chappell Doore'.

Duchess Kate must have heeded Gerbier's plea, begging her 'for the love of Paul Veronese ... to dress the walls of the gallery: poor blank walls they will die of the cold this winter',[5] for the walls were hung with more than sixty paintings. The furnishings of the gallery were sparse — seven 'Italian Painted' chests, twenty-five gilded stools, and an 'Organ and a Harpsichord' — but there were thirty-one statues, Roman statesmen for the most part. Just as the 'Great Chamber' seems to have been the room most frequently used for banquets and masques, so was 'the Gallery' the popular setting for the ballets. It was, no doubt, the room which Bassompierre, the French ambassador, says they entered through a 'turnstile such as they have in convents' and where he saw the Duke dance in a 'superb ballet'.[6]

Buckingham spent a fortune upon his paintings alone, an indulgence which to his enemies among the Puritans seemed a wanton extravagance. Anent their criticism Gerbier wrote to the Duke:

> Let enemies say what they will they cannot deny that pictures are noble ornaments, delightful amusements and histories that one may read without fatigue ... I know they will be pictures when those ignorants will be less than shadows.[7]

II. *Kate's Book of Rules*

It was in this Thames-side palace, whose walls were covered with priceless paintings and huge 'panes of glass', as the famous York House mirrors were called, that Bullen lived for the two years before his journey to Paris in 1631.

CONSCIENTIOUS CAVALIER

York House was a miniature court, resembling in many ways the royal household at Whitehall. Although the Duchess had for many years been familiar with the informal and licentious Court of King James, the household over which she reigned was closer to the well-ordered Court of Charles. At least Kate did her best to conduct the York household in a seemly manner. In a small calf-bound book she set down the rules of her establishment:

> To the end that all my servants may live togeather under a commendable forme of regular Civility ... I have established generall orders ... The care thereoff ... I have comitted into the trust of Peter Golding, my steward.

Following the 'Direccons ... to my Steward' and her own signature, 'K. BUCKINGHAM', written in bold letters across the bottom of the page, the Duchess outlines the duties of nine members of her household: the 'Steward', the 'Gentleman Usher', the 'Clarke of the Kitchen', the 'Usher of the Hall', the 'Pantlre', the 'Keeper of my Linnen', the 'Yeoman of the Wardrobe', the 'Porter', and the 'Butler or Botleman'. She also refers to the chaplain, the housekeeper, the cooks, the grooms, and to an indeterminate number of gentlewomen, gentlemen and yeomen, as well as to 'chairewomen', scullions, boys, and 'other inferior servants'.

Young Reymes knew York House well, from the great rooms that housed the treasures to the cellar underneath where the barrels of wine were stored, and where, in spite of the butler's attempts to obey orders, the gentlemen used to congregate and drink. He seems to have made friends with practically everyone in the house, both above and below stairs. Although his formal studies must have taken a good deal of his time — Bullen continued his Latin and Greek under Master Hebert, his lessons in drawing from Signor Marrane, and his lute lessons from 'Master Boner, loging near St. Martin's Church' — he apparently had plenty of leisure to live and learn in York House. Uncritical of the principles of that aristocratic household which so sedulously drew its lines of class demarcation, he was proud to be one of the 'Gentlemen of the family' and to be taken up by Master Thomas Freeman and others of the older gentlemen. He took as a matter of course the deference shown to the 'Upper Officers' and, no doubt, approved of the rule that 'noe Yeomen or under officers ... speak to the Steward but [he] shall be uncovered and hee that shall disobey shall have his hat taken and nailed to the skreene', and of the Duchess's insistence that at meal-time 'everyone be sett according to ranck and qualitie'.

To take part in the ceremony of meal-time was an education in itself. Kate bent every effort to see that decorous behaviour was maintained, but she obviously had her difficulties. In addition to the members of her household permitted to sit at the elaborately covered 'boards', there was a constant stream of visitors, many of whom had to be carefully watched lest they carry food or dishes away from the table. To prevent such an occurrence it was the special duty of the yeoman of the wardrobe not only to look to the hangings in the room and 'to brush the chairs, stooles and carpetts there', but 'to see that noe meate be conveyed away'. This despite the fact that 'noe stranger' be allowed to 'sitt at table' unless permitted by the steward, gentleman usher, or clerk of the kitchen. Although the Duchess welcomed 'no inferior servants' or 'strangers unfitting' to her table, she did not wish her 'service to be neglected', and stipulated that none of the privileged members of the household be absent from meals without the consent of the steward. Apparently, however, these members of the family had to be watched as well as strangers. None were 'to carie foorth of the dyning roome any ... spoones, table napkins, case knives or aught else ... neither shall they sett or leave [them] in the windows, odd corners or other places from where it might be stolen.'

With all their elaborate manners and graceful speech, the gentlemen of the household, as well as the inferior servants, occasionally got out of hand. On such occasions it was the duty of the usher of the hall to reprimand 'any hee shall noate to live riotouslie, Lycentiouslie, to be a blasphemer or prophaner of god's holy and sacred name'. It was also upon the usher of the hall that the responsibility for much of the ritual and deportment at meal-time devolved. When the tables in the 'Great Chamber' were covered and ready, it was he who warned those serving under the gentleman usher to bring up the plate, glasses and meat, and to command all persons waiting in the hall 'to be uncovered, and to goe before them to the great Chamber doore with a white wand in his hand and uncovered'. It was his duty to see 'that during the tyme Grace is a saying ... sober and reverent behaviour be used ... ' He was responsible for the delivery of the plate, glasses, and napkins from the pantler and for their safe redelivery after the meal was over, and it was he who gave notice to the porter 'to keep the gates close shutt' while the plate was on its perilous journeys. He was also the guardian of the hall itself, where he was 'to suffer noe gameing at unseasonable howers, as neither brawling, quarrelling or other Disorders ... ' Nor was he to allow 'Doggs or Hawks to be kept in the Hall'.

All played their parts in the management of the intricate household. The 'Bottleman' was not only responsible for the quality of the liquor he served, but 'must use curteous speeches ... ' and 'must deliver no Bottles to anyone's Chamber with wine, beer or ale but to such as are allowed by the Steward'. As for the 'Yeoman of the Wardrobe', he more than had his hands full. At least once a week he must 'goe through all the chambers ... and see that all the beddings and Bedds and furniture ... be neither abused, torne or be sluttislie amisse.' He was responsible for the airing of the rooms and the care of the pictures and statues, and was expected from time to time 'to give an inventory of all the household stuffs, pictures and curiosities in his custody'. It also fell to his lot to keep track of the keys of the various rooms, tying 'to each key a lable of parchment signifinge to what chambers they belong'. This was an attempt to do away with an annoyance which had long plagued the Duchess. Whenever she left York House for a sojourn at some of her other estates, there was, she says, great disorder and negligence:

> soe that some lock their Chambers and carie away their keys, others carelessly lose them, soe that Lockes and Doores are broken open. My will is that everyone ... deliver up their keys to the Yeoman of the wardropp ...

The steward, Peter Golding, to whom full power had been granted, was, of course, first in command. Not only was he the final arbiter in matters of protocol and discipline, but he held in his hands the purse-strings of the establishment. It was he who doled out the 'moneys' needed in the several departments, and received from each of the 'Officers' his weekly or quarterly account. Even the powerful 'Clarke of the Kitchen', who was responsible for the buying and the preparation of the food and the safe keeping of the precious 'plate', was dependent upon Peter Golding.

Although the gentleman usher was also technically subordinate to the steward, he seems to have enjoyed almost complete independence in the management of his affairs. His duties were varied, but he was to 'give his continuall attendance in the great Chamber', accompanied there by the gentlemen and the liveried yeomen. He had authority to demand that they and all the gentlemen and yeomen of the household perform their services, and it was his privilege 'to receave and give entertaynment to all strangers that may come'. It was to Bullen's father, as gentleman usher, that the Duchess told her daily plans — when she was 'going a broade' or, if at home, in what room she wished to dine. The Great Chamber generally served as the dining-room, though other 'fitting rooms' were sometimes used. The 'boards' were brought in and set about the room wherever the gentleman usher decided. He appointed the gentlemen and yeomen who were to wait at the tables each week; he made sure that all were 'orderlie sett at meals', and commanded any unwelcome stranger who might 'intrude into the table' to be put out of doors.

With the 'Great Chamber' where his father presided Bullen was thoroughly familiar. It was there that he ate his meals and took his turn at serving, and there that masques were performed and important guests entertained. Many of these Bullen knew — Viscount Dorchester, the Secretary of State; Lord and Lady Denbigh and their two sons, Basil, Lord Feilding, and George, Earl of Desmond; Olive and Endymion Porter and dozens of others, including the painter, Orazio Gentileschi who, Reymes says, 'with another Italian lived long at York House'.

Apparently the ladies in attendance on the Duchess had taken the young son of the gentleman usher under their collective wing. Among these gracious gentlewomen to whom the homesick boy in Paris was to write so often, his warmest friends were Lady Elizabeth Feilding and Mistresses Frances Mosly, Priscilla Hill and Anne Smedley.

Mistress Mosly, the attendant of the Duchess's little daughter, Lady Mary Villiers, was also the 'mother of the maids'. It was customary in large households for an older woman to act as confidante and adviser to the younger ladies-in-waiting. She was their 'mother' and they were her 'daughters'. Seventeenth-century gentlefolk loved to make relatives out of friends, and Bullen was not one to lag behind in this fashionable pursuit. Mistress Mosly was his 'loving mother' and he her obedient son; Mistress Smedley was his 'loving sister'. There are even some obscure references in his letters to 'wives', 'husbands' and 'fathers-in-law'.

In fair weather Bullen walked with his 'sweet Mother' in York House gardens; on 'tedious winter nights' he sat by the fire in her chamber, where Mistress Mosly, among a group of young gentlemen and gentle ladies, was the centre of York House gossip, discussing 'who is now in favour with you know who and who is not'. With his adopted mother and his 'sweet sister, little Anne Smedley', Bullen eschewed all pretence and spoke frankly of his practical difficulties, especially of the 'shortness' of his father's means. Anne was closer to the Duchess than were any of the other ladies of the household and, therefore, better able to help her 'brother'.

It was upon the good will of the Duchess of Buckingham that Bullen's future rested. The elder Reymes had ambitious plans for his son. He was to fit himself, by study and travel abroad, to act as chief attendant to Katherine's son, George Villiers, the second Duke of Buckingham (at the moment only three years old). For such a programme both money and influence were needed. Bullen's father may never have learned the lesson of thrift, but he did know how to cultivate important people. Now he sought their aid for his son, help in securing a post in the English embassy in Paris, and in providing funds for the journey. Two of his friends, the Secretary of State, Lord Dorchester, and the generous Endymion Porter, were apparently able and willing to use their prestige on young Bullen's behalf; Gentileschi and others wrote letters of introduction to their Parisian friends; several persons, including Peter Golding, gave small sums of money; Robert Petre agreed to send his nephew an annuity of £20, and Reymes and his wife promised an equal amount. But best of all, the Duchess was to be Bullen's sponsor. Young Master Reymes's future seemed assured.

YORK HOUSE AND THE WATER GATE FROM THE SOUTH AND EAST

SPLENDOUR ON THE STRAND

There was one person, however, who disapproved of the whole undertaking. Mary Reymes's distress over her late brother George's conversion to Catholicism had long since been translated into fear that her son might follow the same course. Already troubled by the Catholic atmosphere of York House, she was now full of misgivings about the dangers ahead. But by the end of May, Mary had finally sent her blessing, all the preparations for the journey had been completed, and we rejoin Bullen on the steps of the Water Gate.

FACSIMILE OF THE SIGNATURE OF THE
DUCHESS OF BUCKINGHAM

CHAPTER THREE

LIFE IN THE EMBASSY

It was Friday, May 29th, 1631. The wherry for which Bullen was waiting pulled up to the stone landing-stairs of York House Gate and he stepped aboard. The boat moved down stream, past Durham House, past the Savoy and Somerset House and the Temple Stairs, through the swirling waters under the bridge, on past the Tower and Traitors' Gate, and finally across to Greenwich on the south side of the river.

Even with the ebb tide and the steady motion of the oars the ride down stream to Greenwich was a long one. To Reymes it must have seemed endless. But finally he was there and in the Palace, and had received from the Secretary of State's own hands the letter he was to carry to England's ambassador in Paris, Sir Isaac Wake. By five the next morning Bullen was on his way to Paris via Rye and Dieppe. After spending the night at Rye he sailed on Sunday morning for France. The weather must have been good and the winds favourable, for by Wednesday night, June 3rd, Reymes was in Paris and had delivered to Sir Isaac the precious letter from Lord Dorchester:

> Beeing to write yor Lp agayne so soone ... I will say no more to you for present, save only that the bearer thereof is the gentleman the Duchesse of Buckingham hath, by my meanes, recomendide unto you: & because you accept him so willingly ... I doe so much the more readily send him unto you ... [1]

On June 4th, Wake replied:

> By Remes I receaved last night a letter wherin Yor Lp. was pleased to honour mee dated at Greenich the 29th of May, for which I do return unto yor Lp. most humble thancks, as likewise for sending mee this gentleman who shall reape

as much fruites of your recommendation as may lye within the possibility of my power ... [2]

Less than a month after he left London Bullen was a member of the ambassador's household, one of the fourteen gentlemen 'who doe dayly eate at Sir Isaac Wake's Table'.[3] He ate at the embassy but he did not sleep there, at least not at first. Since, at the moment, Wake and his staff were living in temporary and crowded quarters, arrangements had been made for Reymes to lodge in the home of Monsieur Naudine, an apothecary who, with his wife and three daughters, lived over his shop at the Sign of the Golden Mortar in the Rue de Seine. There Bullen lived during his first two months in Paris. But most of his waking hours were spent at the embassy, where he learned to know the ambassador and the members of his 'family', and where he heard the good sound of English. A foreign embassy of the seventeenth century was, in many ways, a little world unto itself. To Bullen it was an oasis of familiarity in an alien city full of strange, hurrying people and ringing with the unintelligible cries of the street venders.

Sir Isaac's household was comparatively small — only forty-three persons all told — and its daily routine was, in many ways, less pretentious than life at York House. Nevertheless, the cost of maintaining the embassy was considerable, and Wake was hard-pressed to get the necessary funds from England. A letter sent to Dorchester gives

> A list of Sir Isaac Wake's expenses for three monethes beeing only in Diet, Hors meate & hows rent: From the 14th April to the 14th July he hath spent for diet which is above the rate of £6 a day   £550
> For a Quarter's rent from our Lady day in March to St John the 24 June   £75
> For expence of 7 Coach horses with eight saddle horses & mules in hay & oars   £130
>   Som. £755

In the same letter Wake says, 'I have always tryed to bring the ordinary expenses within the compasse of six pound a day but I do not find it possible' ... [4] In view of the elaborate menus expected at an ambassador's table and of the numbers of English visitors who drifted through Paris and made a point of dining at the embassy, it is little wonder that Sir Isaac had difficulty in making ends meet.

Reymes did not start his diary until January of 1632, but his expense account and letters tell a good deal about his first six months in Paris. Thanks to the lists to which this meticulous young man was so addicted, we know that in the months between June 13th and December 25th, 1631, he wrote 108 letters. One ambitious record, entitled 'A Table to finde each letter by observing in which number it stands and then in a direct line you may find the page', is accurate as far as it goes. One can easily find one's way up and down the neat columns and quickly locate the desired letter on the proper page in the Letter Book, at least as far as 'Letter 60'. There the author of the imposing table stopped his matching game.

Bullen was lonely during his first six months in France, and waited eagerly for mail from home. Whenever any one of Sir Isaac's staff, any merchant, or chance traveller, arrived from England, there were sure to be letters, but seldom any for young Reymes. Of his many friends who had promised to write regularly, only a few remembered. Even his mother was strangely remiss and his Uncle Robert sent not a single letter. His father was his most faithful correspondent, but his letters were usually long on the way. From August 31st until November 20th, Bullen had no word and — no money.

Reymes brought with him to Paris exactly £12. 4s. 0d. and he spent during the month of June £33. 17s. 9d. This initial burst of extravagance was, however, balanced by comparatively temperate expenditures during the rest of the year. In spite of his penchant for lists and his careful bookkeeping, Bullen was no miser; neither was he a spendthrift. To be sure, he liked fine clothes, but fine clothes were necessary equipment for gentlemen of an embassy where the prestige of the ambassador, and the monarch he represented, depended so largely on the appearance of his entourage. If Bullen expected to accompany Sir Isaac on his visits to the other embassies or to the French Court, he must be properly dressed or, as he puts it, 'goe hansome'.

LIFE IN THE EMBASSY

Fashions in France were far in advance of those in England. As Reymes said in his letter to Giles Porter:[5]

> Our fasions they are all contrary to those in London, for wee wear our hats littell, our bands like nightrails,[6] our dublets short, our breaches long, our spurs littell, our heals greate ...

So he was probably wise in waiting until he reached Paris to buy the green suit lined with red taffeta, and the grey suit and cloak with their blue silk linings. As the expense account for June shows, practically every penny was spent on clothes and accessories:

	lb s d
Imp: for this booke	00-02-05
For the carig of my truncke and lute	00-18-03
For a greane stuf sute and clocke the dublet and the lining of the clocke being red taffe, also being laced with silver lase, with the making and pouints and all things there unto	16-10-00
For 2 last shurts and 2 halfe shurts & 2 last bands and 6 pare of large plaine cufes, also 6 band strings	03-05-00
For a silver hat band	00-08-04
For the barber	00-01-06
For mending of my lute and for strings	00-04-06
For a graye stufe sute and cote lined with blewe taffyte with a silver lase in a seame, and all things theare unto	11-00-00
For the lining of an olde hatt with taffite and a silver lase about the brimes	00-10-00
For washing of my lining	00-02-00
For powder for my head	00-07-00
Spent idelly	00-08-09
Sum for this munth	33-17-09

Wake may have welcomed Reymes because he was a protégé of the Duchess of Buckingham and of his old friend Dorchester, but he soon grew fond of this youngest member of his household.

CONSCIENTIOUS CAVALIER

Perhaps it was the music of Bullen's lute which first drew him to the dark-eyed youth, but there must have been some appealing quality in Reymes himself which won for him the ambassador's affection and confidence. Certainly no parents could have chosen for their son a wiser or kindlier guide than Sir Isaac Wake. Bullen wrote to his troubled parent:

> I must give your motherly love notise, that god hath blest me ... with a lord no lesse good, then your counsil which you gave me at partinge, for he is both religiose, wise and learned in all things. He nether loves cardes, nor dice, nor long haire, in so much that he hath made me cut of mye locks by his perswation, where of I have sent you parte; I make no question but to learne in a shorte time, that, that will staye by me longer then either lute or danceing ...

Sir Isaac Wake's name has been linked with those of Sir Henry Wotton and Lord Dorchester as one of the three great English ambassadors of the seventeenth century. He had entered the world of diplomacy in 1610 as secretary to Sir Dudley Carleton, and in 1624 had been appointed ambassador to both Savoy and Venice, a position which he held until the spring of 1631, when he took up his duties in Paris. Well aware that his long tour of duty at the Court of Savoy, which had so recently sided with Spain, made him *persona non grata* in France, Wake was not surprised at the lukewarm reception he received. The hostility he met because of alleged Spanish sympathies was, however, soon dispelled by his 'honest face', which had so impressed King Louis that 'he durst and would' trust the new ambassador. The difficulty with Richelieu, a thorny problem of protocol, was not so easily solved. Sir Isaac might have adopted the realistic solution of other Protestant ambassadors by bowing to Richelieu, not as Cardinal but as supreme dictator of affairs of state, had not King Charles refused to sanction such a course. As a result he could get no audience with the Cardinal who declined to make the necessary bow.

The famous 'Day of the Dupes' in November of 1630, when young King Louis XIII had wisely turned from his domineering mother, Marie de Medici, to the Cardinal, had raised Richelieu to new heights of power. Now, in the summer of 1631, when the

LIFE IN THE EMBASSY

talk of the Queen Mother's discomfiture was just beginning to die down, Marie slipped away to Brussels. Probably a good many besides Richelieu were glad to see her go, for the arrogant daughter of the Medicis was a constant troublemaker. She was to live in Brussels for many unhappy years. No country wanted her. The once-powerful regent of France, in spite of her three royal sons-in-law, Charles I of England, Philip IV of Spain and Victor Amadeus, Duke of Savoy, was probably Europe's most unpopular mother-in-law.

Richelieu was now in a stronger position than ever. Not only had he outmanoeuvred the intriguers at home, but he had successfully concluded a treaty with the Duke of Savoy, who agreed to give surety against any new league with Spain. In the light of all these developments, it is remarkable that Wake, in spite of his defiance of the King's great minister, managed to gain the good will of Louis and, perhaps, the respect of the Cardinal himself.

* * *

About the middle of August the ambassador 'changed his house'. Beyond the fact that it was in the Faubourg Saint-Germain, that popular suburb on the left bank, Reymes says nothing about the location of the new residence, and little about its appearance. All we know is that it had a large audience chamber and — a room for Bullen. This was important, for it meant not only free lodging but closer contact with Sir Isaac and the members of the household. At the same time the new room posed some problems. It had a fireplace but nothing else. As Reymes wrote to his father:

> My Lord ... bestode a chamber upon me (and indeade but a chamber). It was without any thing belonging to it, in so much that I could not tell what to doe for mony to bye my household stuf, namely beding, sheats, tabell, stoule and many ... things. That 5 lb furnished me with only a bede and scarce that ... it is a littell one & without curteyns. And for the ... rest ... I shall furnish myself littell and littell.

More important than a room in the embassy was the growing interest Sir Isaac took in the 'new young gentleman' and his lute. Sometimes after supper Wake sat with others of the household listening to the music of Reymes's lute-strings, and sometimes, after he had gone to bed, he sent for Bullen and asked him to play on the stairs outside his chamber door. More and more often Reymes, dressed in his new clothes, attended his lord on formal visits to the other embassies, or to the homes of such distinguished ladies as the Princess of Condé or the Duchess of Soissons. But the greatest honour came early in September when

> My lo: Ambassador was pleased to let me and my lute waite on him to the Courte, which was at Mont Sose [Montsauche], now at Compreane [Compiègne], where he intends to goe within two dayes and follow the King till he come to Paris ...

When the ambassador left for Compiègne on September 10th, Bullen was again one of his attendants. For almost two months they rode back and forth, following the zigzag course of the restless King from one city to another. They had been in Compiègne for little more than a week when Louis decided to ride south to Fontainebleau, Wake and his train following wearily on behind. In describing this rambling autumn journey to his father Reymes says:

> My Lord Ambassador was pleased to take me with him to Courte wheare I have not only seene faire howses and townes by the way, but a country no lesse delectable then fruitfull ... Wee have traverst the country to and frow, not knowing (indeade) wheare to find the King, for he no sowner came to a place but he was as sowne gone. But when he came to Fowntaneblow (the finest howse he has) it was supposed he would stay theare at least a mounth, which provde som 7 days, and then to Sedan which is thence 70 leage ...

Riding through the French countryside on those golden autumn days, stopping at the strange old towns where the roving Louis held his Court, catching glimpses of the story-book figures who surrounded the King — all this must have kindled the imagination of the young Englishman who so suddenly found himself a part of the spectacle of the great. On those evenings when he and his lute brought moments of peace to the weary and frustrated ambassador, Bullen may well have seen opening up before him a career brighter than he had dared to hope for. The guarded statement to his father, 'I hope in time to be one whome he [Wake] will put sum trust in, for he imployes me more and more in his occations every daye ... ' covers a multitude of dreams.

Paris on a chill, rainy day in November, its streets covered with layers of filth and sticky black mud, the air heavy with its unpleasant sulphurous odour, must have been a gloomy contrast to the 'delectable and fruitfull' country Reymes had so recently 'traverst'. And Bullen back in 'the very cold and raine' of Paris was depressed and worried. For days he had looked forward to the letters from home that would be waiting for him — and there were none. He had been in France five months now, and had received not one letter from his mother or his Uncle Robert, and none from his father 'this 3 mounths, nor from any body ealse, which makes me marvell very much'.

There were no letters and there was no money. And Bullen was deep in debt. He had not finished paying for the new clothes he had bought so blithely four months before and new bills were piling up. Since there was no way of asking his father's advice, Reymes took matters into his own hands and did the only thing he knew — he borrowed, 'thow with some lose', ten pounds from Mr Burlamachi,[7] promising him 'it should be payd in Ingland shortly'. But no sooner had he done so than he was filled with consternation lest his father disapprove. He sat up until well after midnight writing an involved letter of explanation. Very respectfully he points out that his father's failure to send 'the parte of my annuity the beginning of October ... hath forced me to take up 10 lbs'. He continues:

> I beseach you not to thinke amisse ... for it was not my ill husbandry forsed me ... but I knew not how soune my Lorde might goe to Courte againe, wheare he might send me to and frow, as he hath alredy done.

Finally he begs his father to remember that he lives

> in an Ambassador's howse, wheare I cannot but goe something reasonable or ... stay home allways, and never goe

with him to see either courte or fasion ... If you please but thinke over it, you will find it better bestow 3 or 4 pounds extraordinary to goe hansom, whearby I may see that, which hereafter I cannot, if I would pay twise as much.

The letter is affectionate and reasonable and, like many of those to his dilatory parent, gives the impression of an older and wiser head explaining a difficult problem to an engaging but irresponsible youth. And yet young Reymes seems deeply fond of his father, discusses his problems with him, is eager for his approval and always ready to obey. We might hope that the elder Reymes appreciated his son's dilemma and applauded his resourcefulness, but apparently he did not. For months Bullen's letters are full of apologies for his bold act.

In the summer when the sun shone, and the flower-pots and bird-cages in the windows brightened the streets, Paris was gay enough. But now that the dark came early and the winter rains had filled the gutters with dirty brown water, it was sombre and chill. It was hard to keep one's footing on the slippery, mud-covered stones, or to jump over the roaring water in the gutters. Bullen was young and probably little bothered by the dark and cold of December. Still, it is possible that the chilly weather and wet streets may have been responsible for his last purchases of the year:

For a red bayes weaskote	00-08-06
For a cape of knite yearden	00-03-02
For a pare of knite sockes	00-01-00
For a pare of waxt shoes with leaden soles	00-04-06

> To the high and mighty Princes
> Katren Duches of Buckingham
> my singguler good lady
>
> May it please your exilency
>
> As my servis tyes me to present my humblest duty, so
> my obligations seactifyes my thankefullnes for
> those noble incorragements which your Grace has bin
> pleas'd to bestow upon those fews qualityes which I
> desiered to serve you in; your Grace hath not oly heather
> to loused vertues in strangers but alsr contributed
> sumthing to the maintinance, thearof, which I hope
> will now to the perfitting of those alredy begun
> of one whose greatest endeuors shall be to attains
> sumthing worthy your patronage; Madam if you
> be but pleased to thinke it is not much that I desier
> nor for but a yeare or two and to charatable a deade
> as for the making of a man who will one daye direct
> them to your sirvise, and in the meane time your
> grace shall not have any that shall pray more feruen
> tly for your health and happynes then
>
> your Graces obedient
> seruant
>
> Bulyn Reymes
>
> Paris the 12 of
> July 1631

**FACSIMILE OF REYMES'S SIGNATURE IN A LETTER TO
THE DUCHESS OF BUCKINGHAM**

A iournale of my voyage with the Right ho:ble the Earle of Desmond beginning on the 5t of May 1636 when wee both set out togethor and continewed as fodoy--th my lord taking with him onely one man, and my selfe;

| Thursday 5 | Wee departed from London about 5 of the clock, in a coach which cost 18s, and wee ouertooke the messenger at Bromly 7 miles from London, where he stayd for vs here we tooke a ..., and went out the rest of that iory, which was to Chipsted 10 miles from Bromly, thence to Flamwell 22 miles, where we dyned, thence to Rye 20 miles, where we came about 8 of the clock; we lay at the marmaide, this night wee shewed our licence to the officers. I gaue the messenger 18li to defray vs to Paris, I payd it him at Bromwell, in the presents of my lord and Captayne Hiders sonns, who went with the messenger also. at Chipsted wee ouertooke Sr Alexander Seton with 6 or 7 Scots in his Company, and at Rye many others, french Duch and the like which stayd for the messengr passage |
| Friday 6 | The winde being easterly, we imbarked altogether paying the ordinary rates to the officers, which was 5 shillins to him that coppied our Licence, 2s 6d for copping the licence, 2s each one to |

FACSIMILE OF A PAGE OF REYMES'S DIARY
actual size [see page 132]

CHAPTER FOUR

BULLEN STARTS HIS DIARY

ON the first day of the new year Bullen started his diary:

>   Heare beginneth my Diere it
>   being the first of Janewary
>   in the yeare of our lord
>   1632 ...

I rise in the morning about 10 of the clock, when afterwards I heard prayers, and then theare dined with us Mr. Gosling and Mr. Barker and Courteane. After dinner La Peare came to see me and about eavning prayer Sr. Thomas Wharton came from Charington[1] whear thear was kept a proclamed fast. And about supper I betoke me to my chamber for to writ into Ingland and came nomore downe that nite and sat up till 12 of the eavene writing.

Anxious to give his letters to a gentleman bound for England, Bullen was up at '7 the clock' next morning 'and writ till eleven at nowne'. After the elaborate midday dinner, enlivened as usual by unexpected guests — this time a Madame le Cole and her daughter from 'Fountainblow' — he walked across the busy Pont Neuf to Paris's favourite shopping centre, the stalls in the arcades of the Palais de Justice, where he bought 'a quire of paper and an almanack with 8 ... graven pictures'.

During the rest of that pleasant, idle, Twelfth-Night holiday, Reymes wrote nine more letters; played on his lute; watched his friend La Peare 'louse a partie at tennis'; went with him to visit 'the nunnire'; heard prayers twice each day; on Sunday rode with 'my Lord Rich' to hear a mass; and on the sixth, 'being Twelve day', played games until midnight.

And then we made colation with a twelve cake, whear there

was Mr. Parker, king. And after, wee drank three helths in a great basin of white wine, drest like our wasils in Ingland. And then our king went to bed ... leaving the rest of the company at cards, where we plaid till eyght of the clock the next morning. And then I went to bed after we had drunck our morning draft in beare and sugar.

No wonder Bullen stayed in bed until four in the afternoon. At that, he did better than most of the household, for when he went down to supper 'thear was no body but Mr. Parker and my selfe ... and we talked till 9 of the clock, this day being my bearthday, now 18 years ould, for which I prayse god.'[2] This is the only reference to his birthday. If it were not for his letter to his mother there would be no way of knowing how homesick young Reymes was on this first Twelfth-Night celebration and first birthday away from home. He was worried about his mother. He had been in France almost six months now, and though he had written many times there had been no word from her. Puzzled and hurt, he wrote once more to his 'deare Mother Mrs. Mary Reymes':

> ... it is almost halfe a year that I have bin expecting to heare from you, which hath not a littell caused me to wonder, for when I was in London I receved then, every other weeke, a letter from you ... I humbly beseach you ... to let me hear from you ... For I assewre you I never knew the want of a mother before now, in so much that I have vowed god, if ever it be my fortune to come into Ingland againe ... that I shall not only be more dutiful to you but seeke to repaye my former neglect by my dilygent observance ...

Reymes had another worry, the same one that had been troubling him for weeks — lack of money, or what he called 'the prinseble verbe'. He had long since discovered that his £40 a year was barely enough to pay for clothes and daily expenses. If he expected to pursue his 'studies and exercises' he must somehow get additional funds. He had written to his father in November of his plan to ask help of the Duchess of Buckingham:

> Unles she dose I know not what will become of my exercises. Learne I cannot upon the lute, under 2 pistols[3] a munth of

Mr. Mesantir ... As for dancing I cannot learne till I have paid him for what is past, and for fencing I have not undertaken it as yet. But if I cannot learne anything, I beseach you assewre your selfe I will forget nothing. I desired you already to send me a grammar of London print.

Apparently the elder Reymes had approved of his son's decision, for Bullen sat up half the night writing his difficult letter. After thanking the Duchess again — he had written to her in November — for 'graceing' him 'with so singuler a honor' as to make him an attendant of Sir Isaac Wake, he gets to the heart of the matter:

> Now most gratious lady I must humbly beseach your Grace to pardon this presumption if ... this great cost heer ... and the weekeness of my father's purse ... cause me to implore your Grace to bestow some annuytie on me during my absence out of Ingland. The which ... Noble Act ... I will wholly imploye to make my selfe fit ... to serve your Grace and your ... posterity.

After finishing this embarrassing task, Bullen wrote his 'Sweete Sister, Mrs. Ann Smedly', asking her to intercede for him with the Duchess, 'assewring my selfe you can frame these contents in a more winning way than my pen can suppose, I leave it to you.'

Now that Sir Isaac was away (he was at Metz, where Louis was holding his Court), the gentlemen of the embassy had time on their hands. Hours were consumed playing gleek,[4] a popular three-handed game which quickly emptied the purses of the inexperienced. 'I went to gleake till supper and then again till 12 and so to bed,' is a typical entry. Then there was dancing.

> When the taylor broght home my new graye cloth sute and cote I went to dancing scole before dinner. And after diner I dansed with Mo. Nodins daghters, and then to the dansing scole againe, wheare I herd a man play very well on the lute ... After supper I plaide at gleake and on my lute, being the first day of my new clothes.

One wonders about the people who appear on the pages of the diary. Some are well-known personages, but the identity of many is lost with the years. Beyond Reymes's own references there is no information about the Huguenot apothecary, M. Naudine, his wife 'Madam Anne', and the three daughters, 'Amy, Margret and Luise', nor about Mr Rowland who preached on Sundays and said prayers each morning and evening. He must have been very human, this chaplain with whom Bullen walked in the fields, played tennis and gleek, and with whom he carried on long discussions. 'After supper I plaide gleake and then I talked in Mr. Rowlands chamber of surgery till 2 in the morning.'

Others are better known. Sir Thomas Wharton,[5] a frequent visitor, was one of the young Englishmen studying in Paris whom Wake seems to have felt responsible for. Sir Henry Rich, the Earl of Holland, was a great favourite of Queen Henrietta Maria, whom he kept informed of affairs at the French Court. The Earl of Desmond and Basil, Lord Feilding, the two nephews of the late Duke of Buckingham, Reymes had seen often at York House, where their sister, Lady Elizabeth, was in attendance upon Duchess Katherine. Their mother, Susan Villiers, the late Duke's sister, had married Sir William Feilding, who had been created Earl of Denbigh and Master of the Great Wardrobe. Lady Denbigh herself was the Queen's first Lady of the Bedchamber.

George Feilding, the Earl of Desmond, who appears so frequently in Reymes's diary, was the Denbighs' younger son. In 1628, when he was still a lad in his teens, George succeeded to the Earldom of Desmond (an Irish peerage), and two years later married Bridget, the daughter of Sir Michael Stanhope. Like many young bridegrooms, Desmond was sent abroad to pursue his studies, while Bridget, like many young wives, stayed in England with her husband's family.

Writing to the Earl of Denbigh, early in 1632, Lady Denbigh says: 'Your sonne Desmond hath bin in an academye at Pares this halfe yeare, wheare he profitteth him selfe very much in his exersises.'[6] Apart from this hopeful comment of his mother, our knowledge of 'My Lord Desmond', during his years abroad, must depend upon Bullen Reymes's more realistic observations.

King Charles had a warm spot in his heart for any and all of the relatives of the Duke of Buckingham, but of Basil, Lord Feilding, he was particularly fond. Basil was not only a handsome, dashing youth, with much of the charm of his late uncle, but he had won the King's gratitude by his chivalric devotion to Buckingham in those last dangerous days before his assassination. In January of 1632, Lord Feilding was about twenty-four, a clever, well-educated young man, 'exceedingly affable and gay'. He must have taken a fancy to Bullen, for the two spent hours playing chess, walking on the Pont Neuf, and dancing together. One night during the carnival season, Reymes went to a party where he danced 'till two of the clock in the morning'. Feilding was there too, and

> did dance with so much grace and activity that he did get the prize from all the French, and foyle all strangers, the voice of the court running that he is the most compleat Cavalier ... in this Court as his noble uncle was the nonpareille of all.[7]

Bullen, undoubtedly flattered by the attention of so 'compleat' a Cavalier, must have been overcome by embarrassment at his own performance the night Feilding came to the embassy to say goodbye. 'My Lord Filding toke his leve this nite, being to part for Ingland the morn. When I kist his hand my nose bled. I did not supe.'

The ambassador had returned to Paris on Saturday, February 21st, just in time for dinner. That very night Reymes 'played on the lute to my lord after he was a bed', and the next day — it was the height of the carnival when folk went wandering from house to house, dressed in gay costumes and accompanied by masked entertainers — 'Mo. Nodeins daghters and him and his wife was heare with theare maskers, and my Lord made them a colation of swet meats. I told my Lord of theare coming.' That last appealing sentence reveals both Bullen's hesitant hope that his friends will be courteously received, and Wake's never-failing understanding.

Within a few days Bullen, dressed in his new clothes, was once more accompanying the ambassador on his official visits. They called on the 'Holland Ambassador extraordinary "Mr. Usberg",' on the Venetian ambassador, Giovanni Soranzo, and on 'Madam Cheaveris wheare I saw her sick a bed'. Sick or well, the dramatic Duchess of Chevreuse was a person to be reckoned with. She was the confidante of the Queen of France, the moving spirit of the Spanish faction and the enemy of Richelieu. Clever, conscienceless and fearless, she was notorious for her intrigues and her lovers.

'My lord Rich' had first succumbed to her charm when he was in France making arrangements for Henrietta Maria's journey to England; even Walter Montagu is reported to have once fallen into her net. And, although no one caused him more trouble than this amazing woman who so deftly used her lovers as tools in the game of politics, Richelieu himself may not have been completely impervious to the seductive Duchess of Chevreuse. Little wonder that she fired the imaginations of the young blades in Paris, or that Bullen refers to her so often.

On March 13th, word came of Lord Dorchester's death.[8] Denise, the traveller who brought the unhappy news, told Reymes that there was talk in England 'as thow my Lord Ambassador should be sent for to sucsede him', and that Sir Thomas Roe[9] 'was thoght to be in my Lords place'. Denise's prognostications did not materialize. Wake was not given the Secretaryship. But Denise was right when he said there was talk of Sir Isaac's appointment to Dorchester's post. Probably Wake expected it. For years he had stood high in the King's favour and, like Dorchester, had patiently climbed the career ladder. To have looked towards the highest rung would have been only natural.

The ambassador had not heard of his friend's death until Denise brought the news. Since his departure for Metz, early in December, he had had no word from the English Court, and was to receive none until May. Beset with problems that could not wait, Wake had been forced to rely on his own judgment. His chief worry was Canada. Some time after the surrender of Quebec in 1629, Richelieu, convinced of the importance of New France, demanded its restoration. And Charles, told that the payment of the remainder of Henrietta's dowry hinged on Canada, readily agreed to give it back to France. Sir Isaac, eager 'to renounce my kingdom of Canada ... a croune of thorns',[10] did his best to goad the French into action, and finally, on March 28th, the treaty was signed. Now surely the ambassador had reason to hope that a grateful King would send word of his appointment to the Secretaryship. When, however, the long-awaited letter arrived it brought neither praise nor reward, but a sharp reprimand from the King. One wonders what connection there may have been between this crushing letter and Wake's death a month later.

BULLEN STARTS HIS DIARY

If Reymes was aware of the ambassador's anxiety, he gives no indication. He still played 'on the lute to my lord'. Sometimes he stood at 'the chamber dore', sometimes 'on the stares', and, when the evenings were warm, he played while 'my lord supped at his garden'. In fact life went on as usual. The embassy table was still crowded with visitors — two young soldiers, Henry Wilmot[11] and William Legge;[12] Lord Grandison,[13] a nephew of the Duke of Buckingham; and Sir John Suckling, the handsome poet, soldier and diplomat who, with another part-time diplomat, Peter Paul Rubens, had brought messages from Sir Henry Vane in Vienna.

For Bullen the world was a pleasant place in the spring of 1632. The combination of warm weather, letters from home, and thoughts of lovely Priscilla Hill wrapped him in a cloud of romance. He read the *Arcadia*; wrote a poem to his 'best friend', Giles Porter; walked 'alone in the felds' and dreamed of York House garden, filled with 'those sweet thouts' which his 'mother', Mistress Mosly, had once said 'did spring in him about this time of year'. One of the letters was from Mistress Hill, now 'Maide of honor to the Queene of Greate Brittaine'. Priscilla had been slow in writing, but Reymes, grateful for even a tardy letter, answered at once. He is excessively apologetic, fearful that the mere reading of his epistle may hinder 'her sweet pastimes at hide parke'. With great humility he begs 'for som show-string or other thing that you have worn'. The letter ends, however, with a characteristic flourish. Taking advantage of a fire in his room to build one of the rhetorical figures in which he delighted, Bullen concludes:

> As I am now writing the candell hath taken fire in my closett, wheare I did not perceave it, till allmost to late, having attempted to tast this paper also, but finding it sacredly inriched with your name, it then blushing shamfully dyed, by whose death you are made an Ayre of this assewrance, that whilst I live I shall ever seeke by my greatest power to shew my selfe really to be
>   Sweet Mrs. Hill   Your most obedient faithful servant
>   BULLEYN REYMES

On almost any evening, but more particularly on Sundays, the young gentlemen of Wake's 'family' sat about 'discoursing'. Sometimes they contented themselves with current gossip, but more often they discussed political events in France and England. News from England was hard to come by — even for Sir Isaac. In almost every letter Reymes begged his father for news.

> Sr, I beseech you to write me some newse every time that you write becase there is nothing so wellcome to my lord as newse, for he dothe all he can to get intelligence as well in private affairs as publicke. Thearfor I pray send me somtimes the Corant wch coms out weakly and in exchange I will send you the Gaset which comes out every Friday morning heare.

The *Gazette* may have been Richelieu-controlled but it was the best source of information available, and Bullen undoubtedly profited by reading it. In a letter to his Uncle Robert, he says:

> I have heare sent you our weekly Gaset which, althow they be printed, yet I asieure you thear inteligence is very good and seldom faulce and weare it my fortune to know wheather you like it or no, you should not faile to have them every weeke and as much other newse as I dare send you (living in my lo: Ambassadors) wheare I would not willingly be taxed for giving intelligence.

Reading the *Gazette* served a double purpose: it kept Reymes abreast of current events and increased his knowledge of French. He could read the language and doubtless spoke it after a fashion, but months were to pass before he could compose a passable French letter. Well aware of this shortcoming, Bullen, on Monday morning, May 3rd, 'began at Mo. Mince to learne French at 8s. the munth'. Faithful M. Mince must have worked hard with his new pupil, for five days later Reymes begins to write his diary in French — and he keeps it up for three whole years. With dogged determination, in the face of sickness, sorrow, and catastrophe, that conscientious young man valiantly spells out his curious brand of the Gallic tongue. His spelling is frankly phonetic and when he does not know the French word he handily substitutes its English equivalent. At the start the sentences are short, simple, and comparatively easy to understand.

> Je joue de lute. Jay escrite dans mon livson. Mon. Mesantir estoit avec moy et Mo. Mince. Mon. Jarvis a prye conge de

moy pour aller en Anglataire. Voicy le fin du second moy avec Mo. Mesantir. Le Ambassador Extraordinary de Savoye estoit icy.

It takes only a few weeks, however, for the phrases to become freer, less laboured, and, unfortunately, for the handwriting to grow careless.

By May of 1632 Reymes had been in France almost a year. In all those eleven months he had heard from his mother only once and from his Uncle Robert not at all — this despite the fact that he had written to them both again and again. Now, just a few days after he had started his French lessons, Bullen learned from an English traveller 'that my unckle was extreame sicke which was a greate greafe unto me, having ever found him to love me as his oune childe'. It was to Patience Adams, his old nurse and good friend, that Reymes poured out the full measure of his anxiety:

> I will only desire you for the love of me ... to have a greate care of my deare unckle Petre ... for I vow to god that next my father and mother, his life is all my hopes and desiere ... And I pray you, if he does not lye in your house, to visit him often at his loging ... I desire you (rather with tears then with inke) that you be with him often, for I know your presents is a greate comforte to any body that is sicke.

If Bullen was troubled by the fact that Sir Isaac had not asked for him and his lute since the middle of May, he fails to record his worry. The first reference to Wake in more than a week is on May 29th: 'Mo L'Ambassador estoite malade tout aujiourdue.' Almost every day from that time on there is some statement about Sir Isaac's health. On May 31st, after he was bled, the ambassador apparently felt better, but on June 6th he was 'encore malade'. No one in the embassy, however, seems to have been especially worried by Wake's illness, and, at the moment, Bullen was too upset by the news of his uncle to think of much else. On that very day a letter from Patience Adams had told of Robert Petre's death. It also must have spoken of Petre's legacy to his nephew, for in his reply Reymes writes:

> ... I could wish your newse of my unckles deth had ben the asswrance of his helth, because [you] know how he ever loved

me ... I vow to god I did love him with all my harte ... and should have more rejoyced to have seene him living then my selfe the posessor of his kind legacy ... And I think my father has forgotten me quite, for I have sent him many letters and I have never heard one from him this 3 mounthe. I pray put him in mind of my Quarterly for I want it very much.

Three days later Reymes is again concerned about Sir Isaac, for he writes: 'Mo L'Ambassador estoite extremamant Malade,' and the following day, June 10th, in inch-high letters, the words, 'MO L'AMBASSADOR ET MORT.' Beyond the size of the letters, there is nothing in that fateful day's entry to indicate the impact of Wake's death. But that night, in a letter to his father, Bullen reveals his distress.

May thes lines (or rather) my teares testifye unto you of the greate ... lose which is befalen unto us ... this very morning about eleven of the clocke, 10th day of June, 1632, by the death of my good lord Ambassador, who dyed now in the time of his hoped harvis, having spent the best of his yeares in his Kinges ... servis. And now to be cute of ... before he had receved the frutes of his labors ... His life was never esteamed dangerous but with in som 3 oures before his death, his sicknes being ever since the 28 of May last ... both of a retention of his water and a inflamation of the liver and the lungs. His nephew (Mr. Wilkinson) being to parte to morrow for London, I beseach you to visit ... being the only joy my Lord had in his lifetime, and one whose swetnes and good disposition would make his enemies love him ... I desire you ... that you will please to write ... how I may dispose of my selfe, whether to returne for Ingland (as I desire) ... I beseach you to send me 30 lb sterlinges ... Ealce it will be as littell as I can doe to gette out of toune ...

That same day de Vic wrote to Coke of the ambassador's death, saying that Wake, in his sickness, was 'desirous to be alone' and 'avoided discourse'. As for Wake's official family, 'wee doe understande that it is the custome ... that it shoulde continue together as longe as the body remaines in the howse ... ' The following day de Vic wrote again, telling Coke that they had embalmed the body that morning and 'purposed this night to bury his bowels in the Protestant churchyard nearest to these parts. The rest we purpose to keepe and dispose of according to orders out of England ... '[14]

Reymes witnessed the embalmment, but his only comment was 'Ieu veu Mo: L'Ambassador oufert.' All the entries during these troubled days are brief and impersonal. Beyond the fact that he does not touch his lute for five whole days, the diary gives little indication of Bullen's feelings. Perhaps, carried along by the atmosphere of morbid excitement, he had not fully grasped the significance of Wake's death. At the moment all he wanted was to go home. Even in his letters to his father, where he usually shows so much more of himself than in the diary, it is 'going home' that he talks of continually. That he will go, he takes for granted, the only question is when and how.

In the meantime, Reymes, like the rest of Wake's 'family', continued to live at the embassy. It must have been a strange and macabre household those days, with the body of the ambassador waiting patiently while all the arrangements were being made for an impressive exit from this land of protocol and ceremony. It was to be a long wait, almost a month, for the funeral procession did not start on its journey until July 9th.

Meanwhile, on June 22nd, a letter had come from Bullen's father telling him not to come home. Beyond this command there was nothing, no suggestions and no money. The first words in the next day's entry, 'Je feu malade tout le matin,' give the only hint in the tight little statements of the last days in June which even suggests the disappointment which must have overwhelmed this homesick young man.

In the five days which followed Reymes did a good deal of growing up. By the 27th he had himself in hand and wrote a restrained and dignified reply, saying that since it had always been his study and delight to make his desires obedient to his father's will, he would make his 'aboad heare in Paris' until he heard to the contrary. He continues:

> As yet I have not determined wheare to bestow my selfe, wheather in pention or to dyet my selfe ... In the meantime

I doe intend to take up 20 lb sterlings ... which are due me ... to maintaine me till I heare furder from you ... The dead body of my lord is to part from Paris to morrow senite with all the hole houshold with him.

There was some difficulty about getting persons of quality to accompany the corpse out of the city, since most men of ambassadorial rank were with the King in Lorraine. But finally, on Friday, July 9th, the body, according to plan, was laid upon a chariot covered with black velvet and drawn by six horses. It was attended 'before and behind' by the under-servants of the household, while all the gentlemen of the 'family' followed on horseback. In addition there were six coachmen in attendance upon the chariot, and as many persons of importance as could be found to augment the pomp and ceremony of the occasion. Bullen, unlike the other gentlemen of the household, did not follow on horseback, but rode in a carriage with the Earl of Desmond, accompanying the procession only as far as Saint-Denis.

Reymes fails to explain why he did not ride with the other gentlemen, but it was probably because he was no longer an official member of the ambassador's household, having moved to his new lodgings on Wednesday, two days before the funeral procession. The ride to Saint-Denis was his last formal tribute to the man who had given him so much understanding and affection. But on Sunday Bullen went alone to the embassy and, climbing the stairs to the hallway where he had so often played on his lute, for a little while walked back and forth before Sir Isaac's door. 'Ie me promene devan la porte de Mon. Lord Ambassador.'

CHAPTER FIVE

PARIS ON ONE'S OWN

Reymes's new home was a furnished room over a 'Sempster's' shop on the left bank of the Seine. His 'loging' cost £1. 10s. and his 'dyet' £3 a month. For the monthly three pounds, one of the servants in the house went each day to the market, bargained for the food, prepared it, and climbed with it up two dark flights of stairs to Bullen's chamber.

Eating alone in his sparsely-furnished room was not as pleasant as 'going in pention', but it was considerably cheaper. Even so, Reymes spent a great deal more than when he lived at the embassy, where everything — food, heat, candles — was provided. He was certainly far less comfortable. But more than the comparative luxury of the embassy, Reymes missed the excitement of the ever-changing procession of visitors, the good talk in the evenings after supper and the companionship of his friends. Not only had he lost Sir Isaac but the members of the household whom he knew best. Sir Thomas Wharton, Richard Browne, William Parker, Robin Jacob and Wake's nephew, sweet Mr Wilkinson, had all gone back to England. The embassy itself had been dismantled and the furnishings sold to pay outstanding debts.

Reymes spent the whole of the first lonely week in his new quarters writing letters. The first was in reply to one from his mother. Mary Reymes, who was to outlive her husband and most of her friends, enjoyed dramatizing her poor health. This time she has apparently outdone herself, for Bullen in his reply writes:

> ... I find you write in such a maner as though you weare but to live a munth ... Whearefore in my conseyte ... you [should] retire yourself from that beastly ... and unwholsom ayre, since it no wayes agreas with you ... For it hath pleased god not to give you a boddy able and strong to tumble and toyle in the world. Thearfore I beseach you, for

gods sake, for the pitty of all your children, that you will seake the best place ... you can to preserve your health ... I know your care is but to leave us well, which makes you to hunt from post to pillour, whearby you may at last find the best advantage. But I beseach you ... that you let those cares passe ... this I bege with teares ...

The letter to his 'sweete sister', Anne Smedley, strikes a happier note. In answer to her good news that the Duchess has promised to help him 'sometime', Bullen urges her to 're-speak' in his behalf, for, as he points out:

... if ever I needed her Graces bounty it is now, being in a country wheare not the least courtise is to be purchesed without mony, and wheare all things are in such an exces of dearnes, as I will undertake ... to live better in London for 6 pence than heare in Paris for 18 pence. But, being this is the only place wheare all good exearsises are to be obtained, I must stretch for a yeare or 2, the highest string I have ... My fathers estate is allredy knowne unto you and the desire he hath ever had to make me fit to serve so sweet a prince as my lord Duke [George Villiers, the second Duke of Buckingham, then four years old]. Thearfore I can say no more in my behalfe but this — her Grace will eternally oblege him who shall ever pray for her prosperity.

Although the long letter to his father — almost 1,600 words — was 'frayghted' with the old problem of money, it spoke of other things as well. After asking again about his uncle's legacy, and after pointing out once more that his quarterly payment is long overdue, Reymes describes his new lodgings, 'right against Mr. Mervilles of whome I intend to learne of ... on the lute ... (who plays best of any one in Paris).' Then, apparently, in answer to some question of his father, Bullen turns to his diary, or rather, to his reason for keeping a diary. He does his best to explain this almost universal urge. Unlike many, he did not write with a wary eye on a possible reader. His scribbled, blotted, and well-nigh illegible entries, with their careless spelling and syntax, were obviously meant for no eye but his own. The reason he gives is neat, to the point, and completely characteristic. His diary is an expense account of his time. 'I keepe a dayere ... for the expense of my time, as I doe for that money I spend ... '

That same week he wrote to his old nurse and 'loving frend', Patience Adams. Patience had dictated her last letter to her husband, and Bullen, who knew Richard almost as well as his wife, can't resist a bit of teasing:

> Before I opened your letter I perceved who was your Secratary, and ... the more willingly, reade it through with much trobble, his Inglish being worser then mine, in so much as I found many sillables with out a vowell. But, at length, I partly knew what he mente.

He goes on to congratulate Patience on her new position as assistant to Mrs Mountny at St James (Mrs Mountny had left York House the year before to care for young George and Francis Villiers, who were being reared with the sons of King Charles), and then turns to his uncle's legacy. In brief, what he wants Patience to do is casually to question his father about the legacy without letting him know that she has been prompted. As always, Reymes begs her to

> write oftner to me ... tise only that, that gives me content, to heare from my frinds. And, indeade, sometimes (when I am weary) ... I goe to my Cabynet and reade all those letters which I receved out of Ingland, over and over, though I have read them 100 times before ... Thearfore I earnestly desire you to neglect no occation ... and asseure your selfe that whilst I live and have anything, you can lacke nothing ... so, god bless you, good Mrs. Adams.

Shortly before Bullen had moved to his new quarters, his old friend and drawing master, Signor Francesco Marranc, had arrived from England. More than anyone else Signor Marrane helped to fill the place of the ambassador and the friends Reymes had learned to know so well at the embassy. He stopped by often. The 'Sempster's' shop was conveniently located on the busy Rue Dauphine, at the south end of the Pont Neuf and less than three hundred yards from the 'City' itself, that long narrow island lying between the arms of the river. Sometimes in the late afternoon the two walked across to the island where the bridge widened into a plaza, flanked on one side by Henry IV astride his great horse, and on the other by the Place Dauphine, named in honour of Louis when he was still the Dauphin of France. Often they made their way through the crowded 'Place' to the Galerie Marchande in the arcades of the Palais de Justice, where they bought paper and 'chocke' for limning, and where, on one occasion, they purchased a variety of trinkets for Bullen's father. For five pounds they bought more than fifty 'toys' — masks, chains, pendants, beard brushes, bottles of essences, glasses of orange, 'citteron' and 'jessament' oils, pots of orange-flower butter, sprigs of artificial flowers, gloves and books. Just what the elder Reymes hoped to do with these 'toys', which he periodically commissioned his son to purchase for him, is never made clear. Perhaps he planned to sell them at a profit; perhaps they were intended as gifts.

On other days they went to the gallery of the Louvre where Marrane was painting a 'full-length' portrait of Reymes. There was a surprising amount of activity going on in the Louvre. All day people passed on their way to and from the gardens, stopping now and again to watch the artists at work or to examine the volumes spread out on the book stalls. Once, Reymes and Marrane saw a comedy acted in the garden of the Louvre, and another time they examined a 'woman without arms, made of marble'.[1]

In September Bullen was very ill. On the 2nd, there is but one line in the diary, 'I limned — very sick with a cold.' Three days later he started a letter to his father but laid it aside half finished. The burden of this doleful note was a plea to pay the merchants from whom he has borrowed money. 'I humbly beseach you ... that you keep the worde which I promised them ... otherwise you ... may be ill spoken of and I may want if — ' There was good reason for Reymes's concern. One of the merchants, Mr Draper, annoyed because he had not yet been reimbursed for the £20 he had given Bullen early in July, had said that he would make no more loans.

But by the next day Reymes was too sick to worry about money or anything else. He probably had a chill, for, though the weather was still warm, he had a fire going in his room all day. On Thursday, September 9th, 'very sick of the fever continually', he sent for Dr Davison,[2] and the treatments began in earnest.

Bullen must have had an iron constitution to have withstood those treatments — enemas and bleedings almost every day. There was a special surgeon, Mr Alloset, to adminster the bleedings. Once he pierced his patient twice, before he could find the vein. On Saturday night Reymes almost died. Signor Marrane was with him all that day and all night, and the doctor came twice. But, miraculously, by the 13th, Bullen was able to write, 'I was in a little better health,' and three days later, 'I commenced to eat again.'

Callers had come during the first days of his illness, when Reymes was too sick to know or care, then, having done their duty and satisfied their curiosity, they ceased their visits. Only Marrane was faithful. Writing to his father of his illness, Bullen says:

> I could not for a fortnight stur out of my bed, being so weakened by the want of bloud and, ever since, trobled with a lightnes in my hed and weeknes in my eyes ... He [Marrane] is the only frind I have heare in Paris, and espetially in my sicknes ... he hath begat such a trewe frendshipe in me by his love and care ... and I am so far from [for]geting it, as I shall ever hearafter esteame him as my brother and best frend ... He was never from me night or day.

Reymes was always loyal to his friends. Although he was impressed by rank, and well aware of the importance of cultivating persons in strategic positions, it is usually of the less pretentious among his friends that he speaks with the greatest warmth and gratitude. He refers many times to his 'very good friend', Richard Browne,[3] asking his father to thank him for the love Browne had given him; to Wake's nephew, whom he always called 'sweete Mr. Wilkinson', and to the steward, William Parker, 'a good, wise and honest gentleman' to whom he was more indebted than to anyone in the household. It is significant that neither in his diaries nor his letters does Reymes say anything disparaging or unkind about his friends. A tendency to expect from others the same loyalty and affection as he so readily gave them, though tempered by years of experience, was to remain with him to the end of his life. Actually the tempering had already begun. Some of Bullen's buoyant expectations had been dampened by the failure of his friends in England to write as often as he had confidently expected, and by the sudden falling off of his acquaintances in Paris, now that he no longer enjoyed the prestige of the English embassy. But it was the neglect he had suffered during his illness which disturbed him most and brought forth the melancholy statement that Signor Marrane was the only friend he had in Paris. It was to be a good many years before Reymes acquired a measure of that amused and tolerant detachment with which Sir Isaac Wake had learned to accept the failure of friends and fortune.

As his fever abated and his head cleared, Bullen began to worry about his finances and about the Duchess of Buckingham. When 'littell Anne' had written in July of the Duchess's promise of help, she intimated that Lady Buckingham would be pleased to have Reymes send her some 'essences and sweet waters' as well as an account of the Court gossip. It was the latter commission which had filled Bullen with dismay. He had put it off, partly because he found it so difficult to write, and partly because the Royal Court was so seldom in Paris, and news, now that he was no longer at the embassy, was hard to come by. The task must have weighed heavily upon his conscience, for, during the first days of convalescence, he summoned all his strength and resources and wrote the difficult letter to 'the Duches of Buckingham, her grace'.

> ... according unto these [commands] I receved by littell Anne from your grace, I, in the trewest of obedience, doe present ... the news of thes parts, though my intelligence (by reson of the kings being so littell in Paris) will be of so narrow an extent ... Yet may your Grace be pleased to know that the last time the Court was heare in Paris, there was an Italian gentleman, named Signor Lazarine, who had the honor to kise your la[dyships] hand latly in Ingland, [who] told the Queene so much of your Grace's merit and princely goodnes, which was then second[ed] by the Duches of Cheverous, as her Magstie hath ... a desire to see your la[dyship] heare in her Courte ... He likewise told her ... how much your Grace esteamed and loved her pictor.
>
> She [the Queen] redoubled her speach, saying that she would faine see her of whom she had heard the world speake

so nobly of ... Nether was her Maj[es]tie only contented to question many other perticulers of your Grace, but ... of the Courte in generall and of the fations. In so much ... she resolved to dres her selfe after the Inglish ladyes habit, and the Duches of Cheverous also, who is now the greatest and only lady with the Quene, in so much as her Maj[es]tie had only she and Madam de Hauterive [Hautefort], the Kings Mistris, with her in her Coch when she went to Parlament, which was the 12 of August. And the 16 of the same she parted from heare to meate the kinge at Fountainblow, and then to take her journie with him to Lions ...

The weeks of sickness, with all their extra expenses, had completely emptied Bullen's purse. Dr Davison would wait for his fee, but the six shillings for the surgeon, another six for the nurse, and fourteen for the 'poticary' had to be paid at once — all this in addition to the ordinary monthly expenditures and enough besides to buy the 'essences' for the Duchess and the articles Reymes's father had been waiting for. On September 20th, as soon as he could 'creep about', Bullen had a long talk with Mr Draper, who finally agreed to lend him another £20. A week later, he and Signor Marrane walked across the bridge to the 'Palis' where they bought for the Duchess a box of 'essences, spirites and sweete waters' for 16s., and, for Reymes's father, a 3s. pair of 'cisers', a pair of 'tweese[r]s' for 10s., and the usual assortment of chains, purses, masks and gloves.

Uncertain of Lady Buckingham's reaction to his 'news letter', he wrote to Anne Smedley of his fears. Unless she makes ample apologies for his efforts, he 'will dispare of ever having the same imployment hearafter'. 'It is,' he says, 'the first Corispondence I ever undertooke, which, after a littell practis, will arrive me som better forme'.

On October 8th Signor Marrane left for England, taking with him Bullen's portrait and a letter to his father. Much of the letter was taken up with Reymes's indignation at some uncomplimentary statements that had been made about Marrane in England.

You shall see how he will prove himself to be another maner of man then Signor Gentileschi ... reports him to be. He hath begun my picture ... though not quite finished it by reason of my sicknes ... This hindered him also of coming into Ingland this 5 weekes, because he would not leave me till he saw what would become of me ...

Reymes would have missed Marrane even more than he did, had it not been for the timely arrival of Sir Charles Cotterell, who introduced him to two new friends, William Russell, the future Earl of Bedford, and Richard Boyle, Viscount Dungarvan, the eldest son of the Earl of Cork and brother of the famous Robert Boyle. For more than a month, Bullen, Desmond, William Russell, 'cosin Cotterell', and the gay and generous Dungarvan made the most of life in Paris. Reymes was most often with Dungarvan. One day he rode with him in his carriage to see an exhibition of horses in the Faubourg Saint-Honoré, and then to a tennis court where they watched the matches; another time the two practised 'voltage' (vaulting), and later, with Lord Russell, attended the 'sall' of M. Provost, the dancing master. In the evenings the five young gentlemen were usually together in a cabaret, or in the lodgings of Lord Dungarvan, where they danced, had a collation, and where Bullen invariably played the lute. Pleasant, idle days — more than a month of them — hurried by. Then, early in December, all of Reymes's gay friends left for Orleans and a long holiday.

Bullen was alone again, and the problems he had temporarily pushed aside had to be solved. He had had no letter from his father since summer, no money and no news of his uncle's legacy. The gift from the Duchess was still in the future and his credit with Mr Draper exhausted. Ignorant of his father's plans, Reymes had cast about on his own for some way of staying on in Paris. A post in the household of Wake's successor seemed the only solution. Accordingly he wrote, asking his father to let him know

> who shall come heare Ambassador ... some says one and som another, but the most parte concludes Sir Robert Amstrudder ... [4] Pray be before hand with him for me, in getting some place under him.

Then, worried by his father's long silence, he writes:

> I finde it strange to be 4 munths without one assewrance of

your health ... because not only your silence ... but all the rest of my acquaintances in England buried me likewise in forgetfullnes. The which gives me just cause to imagin some ill fortune befalls me, the which I cannot remove from my fantise.

Christmas was a dreary day. All Bullen did was attend a service at the 'Augustine', write again to his silent parent, and play on the lute. Then, on December 29th, came the long-awaited letter. But, instead of cheerful holiday greetings, his father sent word of Signor Marrane's death.

Reymes's foreboding had been justified — the fear of some 'ill fortune' which he could not remove from his 'fantise'. He sorrowed deeply for his friend. The pleasure he had known in the companionship of this gentle and intelligent Italian, and his gratitude for Marrane's care during his illness, were mingled with an uneasy feeling that he might have been responsible for his friend's death. Between the bare lines of his diary, in which he simply states that he neglected all his exercises, ate no supper, played the lute, and was extremely sad, one can read something of the loneliness and grief which overwhelmed Bullen in his room on the Rue Dauphine. 'Je mance toute mes exersises. Je jouee du lhute estant extremanent trisd. Je ne pas soupe.'

The new year dawned as mournfully as the old had closed. Reymes had no heart and no funds for the season's festivities. On his birthday, January 7th (N.S.) he replied to his father's letter 'whearin the death of Signor Marrana is mentioned'. He is glad that his friend

> shewed him selfe to be an nother man then the wourld reported him to be ... And for my picture, you may get Francisco Gentile[5] to make an end of it ... and as for all the things he leaft me ... it was but a littell looking glas, the which I will keepe for his sake ... I never past Christmas so malingcolly in my life, both without new clothes or mony eather. And even this, my bearthdaye, I must selabreat with empty pockets, a threadbare cote, and a heavy harte, which nether agreese with the time, seson or person ...

Around the middle of January Reymes's finances took several

turns for the better. Another letter from his father brought cheerful news of Robert Petre's legacy and of Lady Buckingham's gift, news which immediately opened the wary Mr Draper's purse. Bullen forthwith purchased a new suit and coat for £2. 4s. 8d.; a 14s. hat with a 5s. plume; a pair of boots and galoshes for 18s.; dancing shoes for 3s. 2d., and a cap of blue satin for 8s. — understandable extravagances if we are to take seriously Reymes's doleful picture of himself in threadbare clothes. The most important result of the more liberal allowance, however, was the increase in Reymes's 'exersises'. And 'exersises' for Bullen meant not only the 'violent exersises of the body' but those 'of the minde' as well. According to his own words, he accomplished more during the first six months of 1633 than at any time during his stay in Paris.

CHAPTER SIX

THE EDUCATION OF A COURTIER

LIVING though he did midway between the fourteenth and twentieth centuries, Bullen was, in many ways, much closer to Chaucer's squire than to the twenty-year-old student of today. The 'exersises' on which he spent most of his time — lute-playing, vaulting, fencing, dancing and limning — were almost identical with those of that lusty fourteenth-century 'bachelor' of whom Chaucer says,

> Singing he was, or floiting al the day ...
> Wel coude he sitte on hors, and faire ride;
> He coude songes make, and wel endite,
> Juste and eek daunce, and wel purtraye and write.[1]

Out of the fusion of the militant, courtly squire and the scholarly clerk of the *Canterbury Tales* there emerged the ideal Renaissance figure — soldier, courtier and scholar — who, with only a few changes, was to become the 'Compleat Gentleman' of the seventeenth century. 'The Compleat Gentleman' was the subject of Henry Peacham's popular treatise on education; it was the term used in describing Basil, Lord Feilding, and it was probably the title for which Reymes, like countless other young men of his day, was striving.

In general the education Reymes received during his years abroad was similar to that of other seventeenth-century youths who were combining travel and study. Most of these travelling gentlemen, however, belonged to wealthy families who could afford tutors and servants to look after their sons. In Paris many of them attended the fashionable Riding Academy of M. Antoine de Pluvinel,[2] where they learned not only to ride the 'Great Horse' but the majority of the other popular exercises as well. Although membership was too expensive for Bullen's modest allowance, he often visited Pluvinel's 'manege'. 'I was with Lord Dongarvan at his "manege", where I saw him "mont a cheval" '; and 'I was at the Academy Honoré with Desmond', are typical entries.

But if Reymes did not ride at the Academy of M. Pluvinel, he danced at the 'salles de danse'. As the guest of his friends he visited the dancing schools of several masters — Messieurs Alexander, Arnavill, Noyes and Brunen — but he belonged to the Academy of M. Provost. During the winter months the visiting Englishmen seem to have spent half their time at one or another of Paris's famous dancing schools. Some afternoons they made the rounds. Not only was dancing a necessary art, but the 'sall' was a pleasant place to meet one's friends.

Bullen took his dancing seriously. 'My dansing', he wrote to his father, 'the quality I love best ... will cost me £12 the yeare, besides a great deal of flatery.' M. Provost must have been a good-natured soul, for out of the more than twenty months he taught young Reymes, he received cash payment for only eleven. Possibly he was willing to be lenient because he liked his serious and apt pupil, and also because Bullen had persuaded Lord Russell and others of his influential friends to join the school. Once, in lieu of cash, Reymes asked his father to 'bestow a paire of silke stockins upon me and halfe a dosen of white gloves to present to M. Provost ... being indebted to him for 6 mounths. For which present I know I may be excused.'

As for his lute, Reymes wasted more than a year with M. Mesantir who, as a tribute to the Duchess of Buckingham, had agreed to give the lessons gratis. But he seldom bothered to appear, so Bullen found a new master, M. Merville, who charged £1 a month, but was as conscientious and interested as M. Mesantir had been indifferent and lax. A passable knowledge of music and a modicum of skill on some instrument were necessary parts of a gentleman's training, but music for Reymes was more than a fashionable accomplishment. The strains of his lute, which drew so many to him, grew from his deep love of music. Reymes also learned to play the guitar, although he had no professional instruction, and, until the spring of 1633, did all his practising on borrowed instruments.

Another gentlemanly accomplishment was the art of limning. Of Reymes's skill in drawing and painting there is no evidence beyond a few mutilated pen-and-ink sketches of carts, benches, and other homely objects of Italian life which have somehow managed to survive the centuries. Skill in drawing was, however, but a means to that more important aspect of a courtier's education — a knowledge and appreciation of art. And, in all probability, Bullen's own purpose was to become a connoisseur of art rather than a great painter in his own right, for he says:

> I only learne to lime in black and white ... and I am perswaded a man may judge a picture very well that can lime but indifferently ... (as all men say) thear is more skill in a desine than in the making of it in colors.

Thanks to M. Mince, who came practically every day at a modest fee ranging from 8s. 2d. to 8s. 5d. a month, Reymes's knowledge of French had increased appreciably. He was also indebted to his new surroundings, his quarters in the Rue Dauphine throwing him into daily contact with French-speaking persons, an advantage of which he was fully aware, for he speaks several times of his wisdom in 'absenting my selfe from Inglish'.

Reymes was also aware of the opportunities he was missing. Again and again he had pointed out to his father the impossibility of pursuing even half the prescribed exercises on £40 a year. Yet, in spite of the fact that until 1633 he had been able to pay for only lute-playing, French and dancing, Bullen had worked at his drawing; learned to play the guitar; practised vaulting and tennis, and reviewed his Latin and Greek.

In January of 1633, however, when more money was available, Bullen added four new masters to his list: M. la Franc, who taught fencing at 16s. 8d. a month; M. de Malta, who charged 17s. a month for thrice-weekly lessons in mathematics; Father Francis, who supervised his Latin and Greek in return for an occasional gift; and an unnamed master, who gave lessons in the handling of fire-arms at the rate of £1. 5s. 2d. a month.

The foreign training of English youths may well have been influenced by the views of Henry Peacham. Certainly Reymes's concept of the purpose of his education and travel, and, to a degree, his attitude towards life, were in accord with the ideas presented in Peacham's *Compleat Gentleman*. The 'compleat gentleman' was to be neither a professional scholar, artist, nor soldier, but an accomplished amateur, and one so conversant with the ways of other lands as to be a credit to his King and country. Thus, while not advocating a professional military career, Peacham realized that a gentleman might at any time be called on to defend his King, and must, therefore, be conversant not only with the handling of weapons but with the art of war itself. For this, mathematics was a *sine qua non*: 'Should you,' he says, 'follow the warres ... you cannot without Geometry fortifie your selfe, take advantage of hill or levell ... order your Battalia in square, triangle, crosse ... '[3]

Reymes also seems to have held utilitarian views regarding the study of mathematics. In June he finds the heat

> so extreame as it is imposible for us to doe anything but study Mathematikes, the which, for my part, I have allredy learned as much as will proffit me in all my observations through out my travelles, as well for the situations of Countryes and townes as some littell insite of fortifications.

And, almost as if he were following Peacham's advice, Bullen, during his travels, not only commented on various fortifications but brought home sketches he had made of these and of military formations — squares, triangles and crosses. In fact, the two must have seen eye to eye on a good many points. Peacham commended riding, dancing, leaping, the study of foreign tongues, and not only drawing but also the ability to evaluate works of art.

Apparently with no master but experience to guide him Reymes was slowly improving his style. In his letters — his hastily written and often obscurely abbreviated diary is no criterion of his ability — there are fewer involved and difficult sentences, a tendency to temper the flamboyant extravagances of his earlier epistles, a growing skill in the turning of a phrase, and even a touch of humour now and then. Probably most of his progress was due to sheer practice, but some of it may have been the result of his reading, which, says Peacham, is one way to acquire style in both writing and speaking. As his diaries testify, Reymes read a good deal, but what he read is another question. For the most part the entries simply say 'I read' and let it go at that, though sometimes they grow expansive and say, 'I read French' or 'I read Inglish'. He did read the weekly *Gazette*, but the only

THE EDUCATION OF A COURTIER

books he mentions during his years in France are the *Arcadia*, 'a booke of Shaxper', a French book against Richelieu, 'a french pshalme booke', 'un liver de fense', 'un liver de Sinuc' [Seneca], and Amyot's translation of Plutarch's *Lives*. In this connection it is interesting to note that among the books recommended for 'morality & rules of well living', Peacham puts Plutarch first and Seneca second, while among the 'authors in prose, who speake the best and purest English', he names the *Arcadia*.

Of the serious purpose of his education abroad, Reymes was well aware: 'My coming to Paris,' he says, 'hath not only bin a trew lookingglas to anatimise my weaknese, but rather a meanes to induse me to the perfiting something before my return.' But in spite of this and other protestations of noble purpose, Bullen was disturbed by a nagging worry that he had not taken full advantage of his opportunities. An active conscience and a sense of duty were by no means confined to the Puritan population of the seventeenth century.

Reymes seems to have felt a measure of responsibility for his young brother William, who was living in Delft with Uncle Barnaby Reymes, and, in the spring of 1633, wrote him a letter so heavy with good advice as to be worthy of the most sober-minded grandsire of the century. After telling him to serve God, obey his parents, and pursue his studies, he says:

> For my parte, I have spent my time so ill, as I understand nothing, and tise by you I hope to make my fortune (the more shame mine) ... I neade not tell you the weaknes of my father's estate ... nor the desire he hath to advance our fortunes ... Whearfore ... have a care to your selfe (take warning by me).

Reymes, no doubt, wrote as he thought an elder brother should. Still, his advice is good, if stereotyped, and, although the self-depreciation may be largely a combination of literary convention and a desire to make his brother more receptive to his admonitions, there is also a touch of truth about it. There can be little question that Bullen felt that he had done more than his share of playing, and was genuinely troubled about it. When he refers to his father's efforts to better his sons' fortunes, he speaks with complete sincerity, for, although he was often annoyed by his parent's procrastinating ways, young Reymes was well aware of his affection and interest.

Bullen's relationship with his father was a salutary, if difficult, experience. Like most persons of the seventeenth century he took his filial duties seriously, yet he was forced to recognize certain of his father's less pleasing characteristics. Not only was the elder Reymes dilatory and impractical, but there was a touch of weakness about him that his son could not fail to see.

In the complicated situation which had arisen after Signor Marrane's death, Bullen's father was deeply involved. He was in possession of all of Marrane's papers, among which were bonds claimed at once by Signor Orazio Gentileschi in London and by two Italian gentlemen in Paris. Young Reymes, after months of long-distance negotiating, had finally managed to effect an agreement whereby Gentileschi was to retain certain of the bonds and send the others to the two Italians. Now, to Bullen's dismay, he finds that his father, instead of handing the bonds over to Gentileschi for the agreed distribution, is attempting to sell them. Consequently, in August of 1633, he writes a letter which put an end to this bit of chicanery.

> I desire you, by all means, as a thing in all conciens and reson, that you sell not those papers ... To doe so greate a wrong as to make thes men louse theare bonds of 160 sterlin, who have alredy lost 30 lb by his death, for 20 lb proffet to you, weare to merrit the same iustis in your law bewsnes. Whearfore obleage me with that satisfaction ... as you give them all into Sig. Gentileschi hands without any more adoe. This, I beseach you, do not faille to doe ... And for the lose of your mony layd out, god will reward and blis you ...

Perhaps if Reymes had had more money and less responsibility, life would have been easier. But the chances are that he would have taken longer to grow up and might never have learned so well the lessons of adjustment. As it was, he was already building up a reputation for integrity, dependability, and sincerity which was to remain with him all his life. 'Cencerite,' as his friend Lord Andover[4] 'was pleased to remark', was 'the proheminency' in all Bullen's actions.

Bullen worked hard during the first months of 1633, but not as hard as the letters to his parents indicated. There were too many distractions. One by one his light-hearted companions — Dungarvan, Desmond, Cotterell, and Lord Russell — drifted back to Paris. Meanwhile, new travellers were constantly arriving to join the clique of English gentlemen — Lord Chichester,[5] Lord Andover, Robert Slingsby,[6] Henry Frederick Thynne,[7] Sir Thomas Lyttleton,[8] 'Mr. Digbie',[9] and a dozen or more less well-known persons.

By the middle of February the diary reflects the quickened tempo of Reymes's social life. At the moment the 'Foire St. Germain' was the chief attraction. This famous fair, which had been held every year since 1176, lay outside the city walls, not far from the old church of St Sulpice. In the temporary stalls which had been set up on the cobble-stoned plaza one could purchase, says Bullen, every imaginable sort of article at bargain prices. The fair was popular, not only because of the crowds and the bargains, but because of the numerous games of chance and skill. One day Reymes and Lord Russell won a box of 'confitures' in a throwing contest, and then wandered over to a crowded spot to 'watch the queen and Madam Chevereux play a game'; another day he and Dungarvan entered a contest (a walking version of the one in which a player on horseback removes rings from a pole with a lance) in which Reymes won a bonnet worth 4s. 4d.

In March a new item appears in the expense account: 'pour avoir este rase — 1s.' Thereafter the shilling shave is recorded approximately once a month, while on a separate page, at the end of the 1633 diary, Bullen notes with pardonable pride, 'the number of times I was shaved ... 1,2,3,4,5,6,7,8,9,10'. There are other sophisticated items, 'un trou Madame' and 'un tripot'. It is on March 12th that Reymes first writes, 'J'este dans un Tripot avec M. Dungarvan et M. Digbie.' From that time on, visits to 'cabarets' and 'tripots', where the gentlemen dined, drank and flirted with the young women who served them, are recorded with increasing frequency.

There were healthier distractions. Reymes refers repeatedly to 'walks in the fields' and to games of tennis, usually with M. Dungarvan. They played most often at the Sign of the Three Swans in the Rue de Seine, where Bullen's friend, M. Gournie, was

'The Tenis Court Keeper'. But there were plenty of other places, for Paris boasted well over 250 courts. As early as 1598, Sir Robert Dallington had reported two for every church, and more tennis-players than ale-drinkers or malt-worms with us. 'You would think,' he says, 'that they were born with rackets in their hands.'[10]

In April, with money in his pocket and Easter just around the corner, Reymes purchased a suit for £4. 6s.; 'un chapeau de eastore' for £5. 2s.; a pair of spurs for 1s. 2d.; garters trimmed with ribbons and a rose for 16s., and a 'perruque' for £1. 18s. 6d. Wigs, thanks to Louis XIII who was prematurely bald, had been popular in Paris for some ten years. French gentlemen had long since adopted them and many English visitors copied the current mode. Bullen, who took seriously the pursuit of French fashions, after much thought finally made up his mind to be measured for a wig. On April 7th, 'Je prie mesur pour une periuque.'

Of the members of Sir Isaac Wake's household, only two stayed on in Paris, the French secretaries, M. Augier and M. de Vic. After Wake's death, the latter had been put in charge of English affairs pending the appointment of a new resident ambassador. He had never been popular with the gentlemen of the embassy and made no attempt to keep in touch with them. Augier, on the other hand, like Sir Richard Browne in later years, opened his house to the Englishmen in Paris and was always ready with help and advice. Reymes often mentions his visits to the home of this hospitable gentleman, whose knowledge of French affairs proved a lively supplement to the *Gazette*. Besides his own interest in French gossip and affairs of state, Bullen had another reason for his pursuit of information — news to send the Duchess of Buckingham. The letter he had written in September of 1632, when he was so ill, had met with her approval. Now she wanted more letters.

Alert for news he might send on to Lady Buckingham, Reymes had listened with interest to the affair of M. Châteauneuf. Late in February, on the pretext that this elderly admirer of Madame Chevreuse had been engaged in an intrigue with her and with Henrietta Maria, Richelieu had ordered him to be imprisoned in the castle of Angoulême. Then, on April 3rd, came the sequel to Châteauneuf's disgrace, the announcement that the Duchess of Chevreuse and certain other ladies of the Court were to be sent to Touraine. Everyone, including Bullen, was busy guessing the reasons behind it. Whatever they were, the incident offered just the sort of material he had been waiting for, a sensational bit of gossip about one of Lady Buckingham's own friends. So, on April 5th, Reymes wrote his letter:

> Since it is by your Grace's comands that I should not ... let pass any thing worth your notis, I have presumed to make my intelligence knoun ... which is no less whispered then greatly admired in seeing the change of the time, by the disgrace of the Duches of Cheveruse and Madame de Monbason,[11] and Madame D'Vallie, with some other ladyes that weare the cheafe and only at Courte, and now commanded from thense, som tow dayes since, by the king. The cause is not as yet knoune, only by som, imagined to be that they are of the partie with Mons. de Chatauneuf, which [a] few dayes will discover. In the meane time, the Queene is very malingcolly & much trubbled that thes, her peculiar and most intimate Ladyes, should be the same unto whome this ill fortunate hathe befallen unto.
>
> Cheva[lier] de Vare[12] whome your Grace hath alredy heard, is of the same party, had yesterday the Gehenne, being the third time, and yet confesses nothing, only saying his life is at the king's commande ... But to relate more than hee is giltie of, hee will rather dyee the most misarablest man in the world.
>
> The king is to parte from St. Germaine tenn dayes hense toward laurain [Lorraine] wheare he will be the best parte of this summer ... Madam St Georges[13] mother deyed 4 dayes since, for greafe yt[that] the Queene of Ingland did not send her a letter ...

The banishment of the Duchess of Chevreuse and her friends did not take place immediately, for, on April 28th, Bullen and Lord Desmond called on her, and a week later promenaded in the garden of the Tuileries with her and her friend, 'Madame de Fruge'. Although Reymes, like most young gentlemen of the day, had been stirred by the exploits of the seductive 'la Chevrette', he was personally more interested in 'Lady de Fruge', with whom he and Desmond had spent several evenings and who, he says, played the lute 'la plus ravissant du mound'. To see her, he went alone one day to the garden of the Tuileries where, for an hour or more, the two strolled up and down conversing. This is the last time that either of the ladies appears in the pages of Bullen's diary, so they probably left for their exile in Touraine early in May.

May was a month of departures. On the 20th, Dungarvan and Cotterell left for Holland, promising to call upon Reymes's uncle, a merchant in Delft, and 'put themselves wholly in his hands'. Bullen gave each of them a letter 'To his deare Unckle Mr. Barnabe Reymes'. In the one presented by Lord Dungarvan, Reymes asks his uncle to bestow his courtesy upon

> the bearor heare of, a noble and sweet lord, one whose merret and goodnes hath so eternally bound me unto him, by his exces of favors and frendly courtises, as my great fortune will never be able to recompence ... I doe most earnestly intreate you ... for my sake, to treat him with as much respect ... as you may. He is sonn to the Earle of Corke ... He has spent some 8 munths heare in Paris and now, his curiositie hath brought him to the low Countryes to pase 2 or 3 munthes more ... I beseach you once more to expres the love (you owe me) unto the good lord whome I so much honor, by shewing him the Remarcabel things of the towne ...

Reymes had promised Dungarvan to write him regularly of events in Paris and of news from England. His letter of June 4th is full of the latest English scandal — the seduction of Eleanor Villiers, one of the Queen's maids of honour and the niece of the Duke of Buckingham, by Henry Jermyn, Queen Henrietta Maria's favourite.

> ... You may be pleased to know ... of a evell misfortune fallen unto Mrs. Villers, maide of honor ... who, latly being found to be with childe, was presently sent to the Tower with Mrs. Beaumont, the mother of the maides, and Mr. Henry Germain, likewise, who is accused by her to be the father of it, and, thearfore, to saulfe [save] all, is desired to marry her.
>
> My lady Duches and the rest of her frends offer 8 thousand

pounds with her. He, answering, if hee thought it weare only his worke he may be brought to it, but as yet he is louth to hazard the feouf [fief] of all the world, confirming that my lord Newport[14] and my lord Filding did as much as he, at the same time, thay holding the dore, one for a nother.

Whearfore, the last tow [two] are to sweere upon the holy communion, that they are free, otherwais they must waite that which will follow. And, if free [of the charge], it is hoped by us, of that family [the Duchess of Buckingham's], he [Jermyn] will be forsed to mary her. In the meane time the tow lords goes into Scotland with his majisty ...

The day after I receved your love letter, I dined with my lord Andover at a Tavern wheare my lord Russell ... dined likewise, being ... the day they parted from Paris ... My lord Desmond ... kisses your hands, not forgetting the good wenches respects also, wheare I find M. Perf allwaies uppon theare hands, in the same posture of admiration. And Mr. Bellas[15] is now a great man in theare good graces and my lord Desmond is, for the most parte, theare likewise. This may serve ... to assewre you, wee Inglish, of what ranke whatsoever, are not unwellcom to faire ladies ...

The titillating exploits of Eleanor Villiers might have passed unnoticed in the Court of Charles II, but in the reputedly model household of Charles I and Henrietta Maria they were viewed with dismay. Eleanor was questioned by the Lord Chamberlain, by Secretary Coke and by the King. Charles insisted that, since there had undoubtedly been a promise of marriage, Jermyn must either marry the lady or be banished from Court. But Eleanor, with refreshing honesty, declared that he never promised her marriage, for she loved him so much she never asked it. Jermyn, after he came out of prison, protested that he could not marry because he had no fortune. So the King, getting no co-operation from either of the interested parties, contented himself with excluding his wife's favourite from Court, though only briefly. Henrietta, who loved Henry Jermyn's good stories, insisted on his reinstatement.[16] What happened to the accommodating Eleanor we are not told.

Reymes's first reference to an Italian journey was in the

autumn of 1632, when he wrote to Lady Elizabeth Feilding of her brother's proposed trip to Rome and of his own plan 'to serve him there'. But by spring Desmond had lost all interest in Italy. Disappointed, Bullen began to explore other possibilities. Finally it was arranged that he and his two friends, Giles Porter and Robin Jacob, should make the trip together. The three young men had planned to start their journey early in June, but the plague in Tuscany and difficulties about getting a courier delayed their departure until mid-September. So, contrary to expectations, they spent the long, hot summer in Paris.

Feeling somehow responsible for Giles's unexpectedly long wait, Reymes undertook to acquaint him with the French city by a series of what might be called conducted tours. If that young man missed anything of importance it was not Bullen's fault. Their first expedition was across the Pont Neuf 'pour voire le jouie de charlatan sur le Pont'. They went everywhere. They visited the churches and convents; saw the fireworks, 'la feu d'artifice', at the Place de Grève, and promenaded in Reymes's favourite spot, the Pré-aux-Clercs, north of the old abbey of Saint-Germain-des-Prés.

After more than two years in Paris, Reymes knew the city well. He had grown used to the huddled narrow streets, the cries of the hawkers, and the ceaseless, pious tumult of the church bells. He was not particularly anxious to leave. Perhaps, however, his regret at leaving was bound up with his growing attachment to his young neighbour, Marie Aumont. He seized every opportunity to be with her, and the opportunities were frequent, for Bullen had persuaded her father to paint his portrait — an excellent excuse for almost daily visits in the Aumont home. Even after the picture was finished, paid for (it cost two pistoles), and packed in a wooden box, ready to send to his mother at Buckhurst, he found pretexts for visiting the Aumonts. One day he brought Marie a 'tartlet', another time he presented her mother with a pair of stockings, and the next day brought a pair to 'sa servant'. Often he and Marie walked together on 'la pont', twice he says they quarrelled, but for the most part he simply writes 'chez Mad: Marie'. Apart from the fact that he wrote to her from Venice and saw her briefly in the spring of 1635, this is all we know of the romance of Bullen and Marie.

THE EDUCATION OF A COURTIER

The first two weeks of September were crowded with last-minute preparations. All the plans for the trip and all financial arrangements were left to Reymes. He spent the whole of one day with his merchant, Mr Draper, and 'un Merchand de Venise', who promised him 'credit pour tout Itale'. And for hours on end, he sat dutifully writing letters. He wrote letters of gratitude to the Duchess and to Peter Golding, the steward at York House, for their 'noble presents', and he wrote to Mrs Mosly, the 'mother' of the maids, in reply to her news of some unhappy changes at York House:

> I greave in ... the ill fortune whear of you thought no place capable to relate it me but Durrum walke ... I must confese the alteration I shall finde in Yorke house, when I returne, makes me thinke my stay heare not tedious — nay, rather, is the cause I shall never retourne with content.

Reymes also wrote notes to aunts, uncles, cousins and to his three sisters, Elizabeth, Mary and young Judith. With the exception of the one to his dear Mary, they all are perfunctory and formal. The letter to her, like those to Patience Adams, is teasing and affectionate:

> ... I would be glad to heare ... as well that you weare well mareyed, as I doe desire to be an unckle. You must not stay to see my sister Besse goe before you, but in such case, every body for him selfe, and god for us all. You cannot want subject to write on, for anything will serve you, your health, how you spend your time ... how many chickens my mother has. If you did imagin how I esteame a letter of the health of my mother and your seives, you would write every day. Whearfore, I pray, spare som of your idell ours and doe not goe to print your words, but rather, in plain Inglish, let me know how all things stands ...

In writing to his mother, Reymes touches again upon her fears that he may be converted to Catholicism. After asking her blessing during his travels he says,

> I shall not faill to doe my duty to you, as one who will ever give you this assewrance, that it is impossible for Pope or

preast, as well as cuntry or fations, to any wayes impoyson me with any other beleafe then that whear in you have ever bred me (which is according to the Church of Ingland) in the which I am holy resolved to dy ...

September of 1633 sees the end not only of Reymes's letters but of his expense accounts as well. So, before following him on his journey into Italy, let us see what this young Englishman did with his money during his years in France. According to his own figures, Reymes's expenses for the twenty-seven months from June 13th, 1631, to September 13th, 1633, add up to £259. 2s. Of this he paid £63 for food and lodging; £3. 14s. for laundry; £4. 11s. 1d. for his peruke and for shaving, trimming, curling and powdering; and £76. 15s. 1d. for clothes. The remaining one hundred and ten-odd pounds had to cover masters' fees, doctors' bills, medicine, clothes for the boy who ran his errands, paper, lute-strings, books, pictures, gifts, trips to the country, and all the nameless items that hid behind the 'spent idelly' column.

Compared with the amounts spent by the majority of English gentlemen who 'studied' in France, Bullen's expenditures were moderate enough. Although to pay so much for clothes may seem out of proportion, it was quite in keeping with the custom of the day, when one of a Cavalier's chief concerns was to be well dressed and well groomed. That he managed to 'goe hansome' on his limited funds was a tribute to Reymes's ingenuity. He was always having his boots and shoes resoled and revamped; his falling bands, those deflated descendants of the ruff, mended, and the crowns and brims of his hats relined. Punctilious as he was about his appearance, Bullen probably seldom went out without hat, cloak and gloves. How he and his companions dressed on their long ride into Italy he does not say. Booted and spurred they were, of course, and they must have worn hats, for when one of the party lost his in the river, it was considered a major catastrophe.

CHAPTER SEVEN

DISCOVERING VENICE

At eleven o'clock on Tuesday morning, September 13th, Bullen and his two friends, Giles and Robin, rode out of Paris. They had joined a group which was going to Lyons under the guidance of a 'messenger', a sort of seventeenth-century courier, who, for a set fee, took care of hiring the horses, of food, lodging, and all other expenses. After Lyons the three would be on their own.

The travellers spent the first night at Milly, '12 Leagues de Paris', and the next at Montargis,

> which belongs to Monsieur 'Gaston' the King's brother. It is a small town, poorly fortified but beautifully situated on the slopes of a mountain and in the midst of a great forest. Around its walls flows a river which joins the Seine at Moret.

On Friday the group reached Nevers, 'un ville tres jollie', which was governed by 'M. de Nevers, Duc de Mantua', and by Sunday they had climbed all the way to Pacaudière, '80 leagues de Paris', whence they made their way along a narrow and difficult trail 'up and down the mountain to Tarare'.

At two o'clock on Tuesday afternoon the party was at the gates of Lyons, where the Swiss guards stopped them, asked their names and destination, and, after some delay, handed out entrance tickets, marked with the day and hour of their arrival. Here at Lyons they met Sir Henry Blount,[1] who was on his way to Venice, and the ubiquitous 'M. la Tabarier', whom Bullen was to run into so often during his travels in Italy. M. Tabarier, who knew his way about, helped Reymes hire horses, including 'un cheval pour nostre bagage', for the next lap of the journey; took him to the 'salle' of a dancing master, and to visit some Jesuits.

On the morning of September 29th, the four — Blount had joined them — left for Chambéry, the capital of Savoy, where, says

Reymes, 'I saw the Chateau ... and the stables where there were 140 carriage horses, the hunting preserve and the grand Salle ... There is a Parliament which meets three times a week.' For the next three days they slowly made their way, over narrow and difficult roads, to the foot of Mt Cenis. Here they entered a pass 'easy enough to ascend on the Savoy side but extremely difficult to descend' — so difficult, in fact, that Reymes came down 'a pied'.

By October 6th the travellers had reached Turin. Almost immediately Blount left for Venice, but the others stayed on until the end of the month. Once the capital of Piedmont, Turin had long been ruled by the Dukes of Savoy. It was an important listening post and a pleasant meeting place for both English and French travellers. Here Bullen made two new friends, Walter Montagu[2] and 'M. le Cont Carnarvon'.[3] With them he visited the Jesuits; attended a comedy given at the Court; climbed the hill to a Capuchin monastery, and afterwards saw 'a charlatan in the plaza ... and watched the Duke as he ate his supper. He [the Duke] was very sad;' and with the help of a merchant, Mr Bartlett, Reymes exchanged '12 pistoles' for '10 Jacabens'[4] and made reservations on the boat which was to carry him and his companions down the Po.

On the last day of October the three Englishmen left Turin in the company of a 'Roman count, named Julio de la Masse and Silvio Antonio ... fort brave Cavaliers'. The river boat used going down stream with the current was a flat craft which the crew guided with long poles. Sometimes it carried two masts with lug-sails which could be used with a favouring wind. The passengers did not sleep on the boat and ate only their noonday meal aboard. The small craft left its various ports between eight and nine each morning, after Bullen and the others had had an opportunity to hear mass, buy the provisions for the day's journey, and, perhaps, do a bit of sightseeing.

For five days they drifted down the river, past towns and villages 'in complete ruin because of the late war', stopping each evening at some small port, and sleeping in a wretched inn near the water.

On Saturday, November 6th, after passing Cremona, 'without entering because it belongs to the King of Spain', the boat pulled into the little town of Borgoforte. Luckily the inn was 'assez bon', for they had to spend three nights there 'because of the sickness [the plague] nearby'. They might not have been able to go on at all had it not been for the Count, journeying with them. He wrote 'to the Cardinal de Magalotte at Ferrare for permission to enter the estate of the Pope', and, thanks to the Count's influence, the boat was allowed to leave for Pontelagoscuro on Tuesday morning.

There the Englishmen left the boat and went with the two 'brave Cavaliers' to their native Ferrara, where Reymes saw

> the beautiful church of the Benedictines and heard the mass at St. Pere ... The Citadell is very strong and built in the shape of a pentagon, and all around the city is a big moat full of water. Once the city belonged to the Duke of Ferrara, a sovereighn prince, but, because he died without heirs, it has belonged to the Pope for almost thirty years.

After bidding farewell to their Italian hosts, Reymes and his friends rode back to the river where, 'at 3 o'clock we took a little Venetian boat ... We lodged at Grispina [Crespina] having gone 25 miles.' Early in the afternoon of the next day, November 9th, they reached Venice.

During their first week in Venice, Bullen and his two friends were together in a reasonably comfortable inn, La Carona. But, on the theory that they would learn Italian more quickly if separated, they decided to live apart. Robin Jacob stayed on at the Carona, Reymes found a room 'pre de St. Marke' and Giles Porter rented quarters near by — the exact location is never mentioned.

For all their good intentions and separate establishments, the three young men spent most of their time together or with some of the other Englishmen who roamed the streets of Venice. But Reymes was determined to learn Italian. So, with the aid of two grammars he had bought in Paris and a French-Italian dictionary, the gift of Robin Jacob, he attempted to study the language on his own. And whenever he got a chance, he practised 'conversation'. He talked with his landlady, with the gentleman who occupied the chamber next to his, with the boy who ran his errands, with the shopkeepers and the gondoliers, and with all the other Venetians he met here and there on his sightseeing tours.

CONSCIENTIOUS CAVALIER

When Bullen first saw the Piazza of San Marco, late in the afternoon of November 9th, it was thronged with people, for it was the favourite hour for a promenade, when the Venetian gentlemen, in their long black gowns and round black caps, strolled up and down aloof from the crowds. The Piazza was Reymes's introduction to Venice, but he soon learned to know other places as well — the busy Merceria, and the Rialto itself, the 'Exchange of Venice', where twice a day the gentlemen and merchants met to discuss their affairs.

As he records each day's happenings, Reymes takes us with him to almost every well-known corner of Venice. On Thursday, November 10th:

> I promenaded in the place St. Marks. I met Mr. Blunt and he dined with us, and after dinner we set forth to call on my lord Desmond, but on the way Mr. Porter and Mr. Jacob, as they were getting into a gondola, fell into the canal (I almost did), so they could not go with us. Mr. Blunt and I went on alone to find M. Desmond sick abed ... then I bade goodby to Mr. Blunt, because he is leaving for Padua.

Bullen never explains how or when Desmond had come to Venice.

On Saturday Reymes and his two friends went

> to give our names to the Senate and afterwards we were in a gondola shaped like a lute, where I played my new lute which I bought for six pieces of eight ... I went to the Rialto where Mr. Yeats [his merchant] took me to see a tailor, a Scotsman, who took my measure ... I bought 8 yards of material at 34 liver a yard to make a suit and a cloak ... Then I went with Mr. Rowlandson who showed me the grand Salle [the famous hall of the Great Council in the Doge's Palace].

Thomas Rowlandson, currently acting as English Resident in Venice, had once served as Sir Isaac Wake's Italian secretary. A Catholic and a poet, he had lived most of his life in Venice and was well versed in Italian affairs. During the next three years he and Reymes were to become fast friends.

On November 18th Bullen again registered his name at the

office in the Ducal Palace. A traveller was not only required to present *un bolletino de sanita*, a certificate of health, upon his arrival, but at stated intervals thereafter was obliged to report his name and address to the proper officials. The threat of the plague was always there.

The next morning, Reymes and Walter Montagu, who had arrived only the day before, were strolling in the Piazzetta, when they saw

> a man executed between the two pillars, the place where they are ordinarily executed. He had his head chopped off and afterwards he was cut into 4 parts for having killed his master. He was also drawn and had his hand chopped off.

The two ancient granite columns, one bearing the Winged Lion of St Mark, and the other, St Theodore on a crocodile, stood at the southern end of the Piazzetta, near the quay and the 'lagune', and were, as Reymes says, the place of public executions.

Two days later, Lord Carnarvon, of whom Bullen had seen so much in Turin, arrived to swell the ranks of the visiting Englishmen. For the next few weeks the six, Carnarvon, Montagu, Desmond, Porter, Jacob, and Reymes, spent most of their time together. They met often at La Striana, an inn and popular rendezvous; Desmond had several parties, and Bullen, with the help of Giles Porter, entertained twice at his lodgings. On November 25th, 'We carried a barrel of wine to my place and I made a colation for my lord Desmond and the rest, of dragé [sugared almonds] and confitures.' And, in spite of the advent of 'two teeth which made me very sick', Reymes, along with the rest, continued his sightseeing. One entry begins, 'Lord Carnarvon sent for me to go with him to the Arsenal, which I found very grand and magnificent,' and others tell of climbing the 'tower of St. Mark' and of visits to the mint and to the 'Sala del Collegio' in the Ducal Palace.

It is significant that, with the possible exception of Robin Jacob, all these men, and, for that matter, the majority of Bullen's other associates in Venice, were either avowed or secret Catholics. It would have been strange if the opinions of those about him, the beauty of the services he attended and the music he heard, had not begun to have their effect.

CONSCIENTIOUS CAVALIER

If any type of Catholicism could have tempted Reymes at this time, it probably would have been that practised by the sophisticated Venetians. Having long since shaken off the control of the Pope, they were at once free to follow the best interests of their state and to enjoy the emotional and aesthetic appeal of their religion, undisturbed by any conflict of loyalties. It was a situation which might well have appealed to a Church of England man.

Whatever their significance, the pages of Reymes's diary are full of references to the 'beautiful churches' whose services he attended.

> We were at the church of Nostre Dame [Santa Maria della Salute], where there was a great service to commemorate the late deliverance from the plague. I saw many processions of many different members of all the different orders ... I was with Mr. Carnarvon and Mr. Montagu at the church of St. Caterina, where I heard wonderful music. The church was beautifully decorated ... I heard two masses.

And so on.

Stirred though he was by the splendour of the Venetian churches, Bullen was even more profoundly moved by the music he heard in these candle-lit edifices. It is to this that he alludes most often, and little wonder, for much of the religious music of seventeenth-century Venice was inspired by great masters. To one of these, Claude Monteverdi, Reymes alludes often.

> After dinner I was with Mr. Porter and Mr. Jacob to hear the music of the Friars ... Signor Claude Monteverdi composed the music ... I was at St. John de Paulau where I heard the beautiful music of Claude Monteverdi.

On two other occasions he must have seen Monteverdi himself, for one Sunday in December he writes, 'I was at St. Johns [SS. Giovanni e Paolo] where I heard Claude Monteverdi and his music,' and another time, 'I was at St. Juliano [Giuliano] where Monteverdi conducted.'

The last days of December were crowded with festivities. It was the season of the fairs, of the carnival, of the plays — the theatres had opened on the 22nd — and of *la guerre de poignée*, the war of fists. The 'gare', as Reymes calls it, was a battle on one of the bridges between young men from either side of the Grand Canal, in which no weapons, only fists, were allowed.

I saw a contest between certain of the common people which is fought now every day. One side is called the Castilean and the other Niccolet. The Castileans won.

On December 26th Bullen made his first visit to St Stefano, both 'in the morning and after dinner'. What interested him was not the old Gothic church but the long, narrow piazza adjoining it. As in Paris at carnival time, he and his friends went in masquerade.

> After dinner we were all at St. Steffino and then we went everywhere and to the house of —— where we danced with the ladies. I played the lute everywhere we went ... I paid six realls for our costumes. We went to the comedy but got there only in time for the end.

The last entry for 1633 reads:

> I was at the Rialto where Mr. Rowlanson asked me to dine with him tomorrow ... I went out again in masquerade and I played before the whole world in la piazza de St. Steffino. I was also at the Comedy.
>
> Finis de l'Anne

Reymes started the new year conventionally enough by attending mass at SS Giovanni e Paolo, but on coming out of the church he caught sight of 'a beautiful lady, the wife of a citizen and the daughter of Signor Foses', and 'followed her in a gondola as far as her house'. After this morning adventure and 'un grand diner' at the home of the Resident, Mr Rowlandson, he 'went in masquerade, dressed as a woman, to St. Steffino', and to 'the home of la Signora Laudivicia, a courtezan', and later to a comedy with Mr Porter.

On only two days during the remaining fortnight in Venice did Bullen fail either to go in masquerade or attend a comedy. Usually he did both. Unfortunately, the bare phrase, 'J'este a la comedie,' is seldom elaborated. Once he says the comedy was 'fort belle', and another time, January 14th, 'We were ... at St. Luca at the new comedy of the company of Prudentia and Horatius.' But that is as far as he goes. This failure to discuss the plays is particularly regrettable, since it was during his years abroad that Reymes was developing that appreciation of the theatre which was to impress Pepys so many years later.

Seventeenth-century Venice boasted various types of plays and of performers, and as many kinds of stages. On the Piazza of St Mark or of St Stefano, the mountebanks, on their temporary platforms, and the charlatans, on their improvised stages blocked out in charcoal on the pavement itself, often interspersed their medical harangues, their jugglers' tricks, and their obscene jests and songs with their brief extemporary plays, peopled by the familiar *commedia dell' arte* figures. Often a mountebank would eschew all but the play itself. Then there were the public theatres, such as San Luca, in which both the wandering troupes of extemporary 'comedians' and the actors of the more formal written drama presented their plays. Consequently, when Reymes speaks of a comedy, it is impossible to know to just what sort of play he is referring.

Since, however, the piazza performances went on all the year, it is fairly certain that the comedies which Bullen first mentions on December 22nd were either the memorized written plays or the popular extemporary comedies. The chances are that they were the latter — the *commedia dell' arte*. Certainly that is true of 'the new comedy' he saw on January 14th, for from 1632 through 1634, Prudentia was the prima donna of the *Affezionati*, one of the most popular of the *commedia dell' arte* companies. Whatever the title of the play, it would in all probability have included, besides Horatius and Prudentia, a comic servant, Trappolino. Possibly, some time during the season, Reymes saw one of the company's favourite plays, *Il Creduto Principe*, which Sir Aston Cokain had seen twice in Venice the winter before, and upon which he based his *Trappolin Supposed a Prince*.[5]

Even before they left Paris, the three friends, Reymes, Porter and Jacob, had looked forward to a year or more of travel in Italy. Since then their ideas had grown more expansive. Now Bullen and Giles (Robin Jacob had decided to stay in Padua) were planning a trip to Greece and Constantinople, via Rome and Naples.

The departure date, January 16th, was close at hand and there were dozens of things to be done. Reymes and Porter went to the Merceria to buy gloves and a new hat for Giles, who had lost his, one gay night; Bullen had a long consultation with his merchant, Mr Yeats, who provided him with 'a letter of credit for Naples and 400 ducats in cash'. And, just the day before they left, there was a dinner at Malamocco, 'aboard a ship belonging to Captain Hid, called le Freman ... Many other Englishmen were there and they gave us a salute of nine guns.' This salute was the grand finale of the Venetian visit, for the next day Giles and Bullen were off for Padua in 'le barque ordinaire'.

CHAPTER EIGHT

BY BOAT, COACH, AND SADDLE

AFTER the celebration on the ship at Malamocco, Bullen and Giles overslept and missed the morning boat for Padua. The 'barque ordinaire' which they took at four in the afternoon was a far less comfortable one. The trip was tedious — a matter of some eleven hours — for at Fusina the boat had to be lifted over a sluice by a crane, then set down in the river and pulled the rest of the way by horses.

When they finally reached Padua at three in the morning, the two young men, chilled and weary from their long hours in the little boat, hired a room at la Stella, an inn near the river, and slept until noon. After dinner they sought out Mr Blount and Mr Jacob, who showed them the city.

> I saw the grand Hall of Justice and the palace ... of the Podesta [the chief magistrate] and I saw a wooden horse made like the one at Troy ... We also saw the schools. There are sixteen ... Mr. Jacob and Mr. Blount slept with us.

On the following afternoon, January 18th, Reymes and Porter left for Vicenza. It was only an eighteen-mile journey but they didn't get there until midnight because 'the baggage horse fell into the ditch and damaged all our things.' In Vicenza,

> We saw the Piazza of St. Mark where there is a beautiful tower, very tall and thin ... and a garden in which there was a labyrinth and a walk bordered with lemon and orange trees ... I saw the Academy, one of the most beautiful theatres for presenting a comedy that I ever saw. I played the lute.

The trip to Verona meant eight hours of hard riding.

> We made thirty miles today, paying a real for each horse. We left Vicenza at three and reached Verona at eleven. I am going to bed for I am very weary.

BY BOAT, COACH, AND SADDLE

Next day they visited 'the Amphitheatre, where there is room for 10,000 men (for viewing their ancient pageants) with seats so arranged that one did not interfere with the other ... ' They received their 'boulatin de sante' and again went to bed early.

By Sunday morning Bullen and Giles were on their way to Mantua by coach. 'We rode along one of the pleasantest roads in the world. On each side there were trees, arched so beautifully that one would think oneself in a garden.' And of their day in Mantua:

> I saw the Louvre and the Gallery where there are twelve pictures, the most beautiful I have ever seen ... I also saw the Duke in his carriage, followed by a splendid retinue of guards — twelve men, with their red helmets and white crosses, on horseback. On each of their helmets was a band embroidered in black ... These were followed by their lackeys and their pages. I took a walk through the town all alone. I found it a beautiful city, but deplorably ruined.

The young men went on, still by coach, to Montichiari, driving through a gorge and up the slopes of a mountain 'where there was a stupendous view'. They stopped at Brescia, where Reymes says

> I saw ... a fort and a chateau at the foot of the mountain, well and advantageously situated and provided with everything necessary. In the fort there are three passages; there are 400 soldiers; there is a mill and nearby a place to make powder — all inside the fort ... I attended mass.

The travellers reached Milan on Friday night, January 27th.

> In the morning we heard mass and I saw l'enfant Cardinal. He is blonde and not very tall ... I saw the Cathedral where the body of St. Carolo is interred, very beautiful and large but not finished ... I saw the church of St. Ambrose where there is a serpent which the heathens of other days adored. I also saw St. Maria delle Grazie where there is the Inquisition ... and St. Paolo and St. Celso where there is a veil of our blessed virgin. At the sight of this I touched my chaplet ... I saw more rich and beautiful churches than I ever saw before in my life.

The next day, Sunday, they were off for Pavia, where they waited a day for the boat that was to carry them down the Po to Piacenza. The trip was no new experience for Giles and Bullen, who had passed this way on their journey down the river from Turin to Ferrara. But even for twenty-year-olds it was a hard trip in the middle of the winter. When they pulled into the port of Piacenza at the cold, dark hour of two in the morning, they were in no mood to walk to the city a mile away, but took a room in 'a very bad hostelry on the river and went to bed'. The next morning, February 1st, they moved to 'un bon hostelrie, la Fortuna' in Piacenza, where they rested and 'saw several churches, attended mass at the Augustines and watched a man dance on a rope'.

By February 6th, the two were in Bologna where they stayed for two days.

> I saw ... the Palace of the Cardinal, Signore a' Crouch who is the legate here. The bishop is Cardinal Colona ... I watched the masqueraders in the Piazza ... I climbed to the monastery, St. Michele en Bosque, on the slope of the mountain, from which I had a view of the whole city which is very large and encircled by a strong wall ... I heard mass at St. Francesco and we arranged for a carose to Rome for 16 ducats for M. Porter and me.

The 'carose' to Rome, to avoid as much mountainous country as possible, followed the road to the south and east, towards the sea. Even so the journey must have been difficult and slow, for 'part of the way,' Bullen says, 'Mr. Porter and I went on foot ahead of the coach.' By Friday the 10th, they were in Rimini, where they had a chance 'to promenade in the Piazza and walk along the shore of the Adriatic'.

In Loreto, Giles and Bullen called on

> Father Robert Corbinson, who showed us *la santa Maison* and the treasure and allowed us to touch the crown and the medals. We attended his mass ... When we left, he followed us to the very edge of the town on foot. We gave him a real to finish the work he had commenced ... the Bishop of Laureto has forty cannon and two hundred priests ... The city is at the foot of a high mountain.

BY BOAT, COACH, AND SADDLE

At Loreto the coach left the shore and followed the road to Macerata and on, south and west, over difficult and dangerous ways. The diary for the next four days is little more than a series of brief jottings, indicating the places where they stopped — Macerata, Tolentino, Spoleto and Castellana — and commenting on the wretched roads and slow pace. Finally, at ten o'clock in the evening of February 19th, the weary travellers reached Rome and found lodging in a 'mauvais hostelrie, la *Montaigne de Brianza*'.

It was good to be in Rome, the city 'of glory and splendour' of which Reymes had heard and read so much. At the moment, however, he and Giles were less interested in Rome's glory and splendour than in the circle of old friends in whose midst they suddenly found themselves. By the 1630s, now that the fear of the Inquisition had dwindled, more and more Englishmen were flocking to Italy's Roman Catholic stronghold. But, though Protestant parents may have had less cause to worry over a son's personal safety, they still had reason to fear his conversion to the old faith.

Had Mary Reymes realized the extent of Bullen's associations not only with Catholics but also with the Jesuits, she might well have regretted her reluctant consent to the Italian journey. As in the days of Tobie Matthew and Reymes's uncle, Sir George Petre, the Jesuits in Italy, and especially in Rome, held a strong fascination for visiting Englishmen. And little wonder, for these clever and dedicated men were ready at every turn to offer help and advice to Protestant as well as Catholic travellers. How easy it was to become indebted to them and lose any lingering trace of prejudice, Bullen was soon to discover.

On Monday, the day after his arrival, Reymes

> called on Mr. Slingsby[1] who took me to the Jesuits where I saw Mr. Fitton,[2] who went with me to Mr. Twisden's.[3] After dinner we were at Mr. Carnarvon's and from there to the Cours where we saw a tournament of Jews.

The 'Cours' to which Bullen refers so frequently was the famous Strada del Corso, a broad street, almost a mile long, running from the Piazza del Popolo to the Piazza de Venezia. It was a popular promenade and carriage road and during Reymes's stay in Rome, at the height of the carnival season, the frequent scene of races, or tournaments, as Bullen usually calls them. The reference to the Jesuits is, of course, to the College or Seminary of English Jesuits.

On the following day 'Mr. Slingsby sent his lackey to conduct' Giles and Bullen to the Jesuits where they were entertained with a comedy presented by the seminarians. 'I saw there at the comedy,' says Reymes, 'Mr. Thin and all the English gentlemen.' Henry Thynne, the old friend whom Bullen had seen in Paris and again in Venice, after several months of study in Padua, had come to Rome late in the autumn of 1633. He was one of the group going to the Levant. The Earl of Carnarvon was to go too, and a Mr Bartlet, and, so they all thought, Walter Montagu.

Ever since their first night in Rome, Porter and Reymes had been trying to find pleasanter and cheaper quarters. Their failure to find a room had reached the ears of the Jesuits, for on the 22nd, 'The father of the Jesuits sent a man here who found a room for us for two guliettes and a half a day [about 1s. 4½d.] not far from our hostelry.' They moved into their new quarters immediately after dinner, and later in the afternoon

> promenaded with Mr. Thin ... in the Cours ... and went to a ball nearby where we danced.

Of the events of Friday the 24th, Reymes writes,

> I was with Mr. Thin at Mr. Slingsby's and then to the College where Mr. Slingsby and I discoursed for two hours together ... After dinner Mr. Porter and Mr. Thin and I called at Mr. Carnarvon's and from there we went to the vineyard of Cardinal Borghese where I saw beautiful statues and pictures and gardens full of fountains ... there were statues made by Cavalier Bernini, very beautiful, ... many handsome and costly statues of the Emperors and many pictures by Bassan and Raphael.

The entry for the next day tells of an all-night race or joust, a private affair for which Lord Carnarvon had procured the invitations.

> We were at a joust which lasted from seven in the evening until two o'clock in the morning, which I enjoyed extremely,

it being very magnificent and costly. The Marquis of Bentavolet won the prize. His team ran against six others, in each of which there were four men who ran, three times, the length of the course. His ran faster than any of them ... There was also a ship in which some men were dancing. Afterwards I saw all the men who had been in the joust playing cards with the ladies in a palace nearby. Here I saw Count de la Mosse who greeted me cordially and gave me a drink. And for the rest of the ceremonies of the joust, I leave them to my memory.

The next day Reymes went to another comedy by 'our Jesuits', after which he was 'in the chamber of the padre Rector', where he heard a 'discussion'. Later he 'was in the *Cours* where the horses run alone'. (This was a race held in the Strada del Corso, in which riderless horses were goaded by sharp spurs hanging down by their sides.)[4]

On February 28th, Shrove Tuesday, Bullen attended a comedy in Italian.

I was with Mr. Thin at a Seminary where I saw a comedy put on by the students of the Roman Jesuits. They had many very rich costumes and the scenery was very costly and beautiful, but their acting was extremely poor.

Two days later Walter Montagu arrived. After talking with him, Reymes went out to purchase 'a chest and maps of Italy'. Now that Montagu had come, the travellers would soon be on their way.

In the afternoon we were at Monte Cavallo where we saw a pleasant garden with many fountains which Clement 8 brought here ... the Pope comes here the eighth of August every year and does not return to St. Peter's until the middle of November.

On Saturday Bullen went to the Capitol where he made out his health certificate, hired the horses for the journey to Naples, and attended a party which the Earl of Carnarvon was giving 'for those of us who are going together to Naples'.

Late on Sunday afternoon, March 5th, Carnarvon, Montagu,

CONSCIENTIOUS CAVALIER

Bartlet, Thynne, Porter and Reymes rode out of Rome and along the old highway to the south. Beyond the dutifully recorded hours of arrival and departure, and the number of miles covered each day, Reymes has little to say about the leisurely five-day journey to Naples. Only Gaeta, sitting high on a promontory and looking down into its own 'deep bay', inspires any but the briefest comment:

> Here is a rock ... which split in two at the death of our Saviour and, in the chatteau, the head of Francisco de Bourbon ... I saw a Spanish garrison and many pretty girls. On the way out Mr. Bartlet cut his face when his horse threw him.

The party reached Naples on the night of March 10th. The next morning Porter, Reymes, and Thynne set out 'pour voire les antiquities autour'. They saw the tomb of Virgil, Cicero's villa, the lakes of Agnano and Lucrinus — all the approved sights. What particularly delighted Bullen was 'le Grotto de Sibilla' at Pozzuoli, where he crawled through a passage into a room 'with mosaic pavement, all defaced and where there was water very hot above and cold below'.

On the following day, Sunday,

> Mr. Baker and many other English merchants came to call upon us. After dinner they came again with a carriage in which I rode with Mr. Montagu and Lord Carnarvon. Then I went with Mr. Montagu to call upon M. la Tabarier.

Tabarier was the ubiquitous Frenchman whom Bullen seems to have encountered at every turn.

It is amazing to see how many friends and acquaintances English travellers met on their tour of Italy. They need never have felt completely isolated, for, in lieu of embassies to direct them to their fellow-countrymen, there were always English merchants, for the most part prosperous and trustworthy men, whose financial advice, knowledge of their foster countries, and wide acquaintance with travelling Englishmen, made them persons to be cultivated. There were also in Naples a number of English priests, some of whom Bullen visited in the company of Walter Montagu, as well as several English noblemen who were residing temporarily in that city. One of these, 'Baron Hadding-ton', was particularly gracious, lending his carriage to Mr Montagu and Lord Carnarvon for the whole of their stay in Naples.

Naples, a Spanish possession, was ruled over by a Viceroy whose Court was the centre of one of the most aristocratic societies in Italy. Apparently M. Tabarier had an entrée into this regal circle, for it was he who escorted his English friends to the palace to call upon the Viceroy. Tabarier was familiar with many aspects of Neapolitan life. On several occasions Reymes, Porter, and Thynne, after visiting a church or a convent, went with him to a 'bordelle' or brothel. One day Reymes writes:

> We were at a monastery, named la Conception, where I saw the Vice Regent and many beautiful ladies. From there we went to a bordelle where there were four garces [strumpets],

and another time:

> We were at a Spanish church and then in a Spanish bordelle where there were two belles garces.

Much of Reymes's twelve-day stay in Naples was spent in the company of Walter Montagu. The entry for March 13th is typical of their days together.

> I went with M. Montagu to the Jesuits and to St. Maria Maggiore where we saw Father Gregory, an Englishman. Afterwards I dined with him in the Castle of St. Elmo on the side of the mountain, and we were in the convent of the Carthusians, near which there is a beautiful view ... and we were at Mont Olivet where there is a large convent ... There is a nun in this convent named Teadore de Lalinas who is amorase avec M. le Conte [Carnarvon]. Mr. Montagu lost his hat. We discoursed.

With Montagu and Carnarvon, Bullen seems to have visited practically every church in Naples.

On March 21st, the six Englishmen left Naples, riding in a 'carose' as far as Vietri, thirty miles away. There they took a small boat which sailed close to the coast as far south as Paola, where it 'veered out' towards Tropea and on to Sicily. That six-day sail, crowded into a small boat and in exceptionally rough seas, must have been rugged. Bullen, as usual, was sea-sick. Probably most of the others were too, for when they stopped, as they did each night, at some small, unsavoury coastal village, none of them seems to have felt much like eating. This lack of appetite may, however, have been the fault of the inns. Despite its name, Belvedere, says Reymes, boasted 'more beggars and the worst hostelry I ever saw in my whole life'. But with each succeeding stop he had to revise that opinion, for the inns grew steadily worse.

In Messina, which they reached on Monday, March 27th, things were better.

> We are lodged in the home of Mr. Garroway, the merchant here. After we had a colation, we rode about the town in his carriage. This is one of the best harbors I ever saw. There are five or six fountains in the town and a bronze statue of King Philip. Near the harbor the city is very beautiful but elsewhere it is sordid. There are 2 or 3 fine churches. And here in the harbor is a ship from London, called the *William and Thomas*, going to Constantinople, which Carnarvon, Bartlet, Thin, Porter and I have decided to take. The name of the captain is Mr. New. The merchant, Mr. Garroway is going with us.

The *William and Thomas* was to sail on April 1st. While they waited, the six men talked together; walked about the town and along the harbour, where they 'saw Scylla and Carybdis', and made their necessary purchases. Reymes bought 'stockings, a bed, sheets and covers and a guitar'.

On the last day of March, just the day before the ship was to sail, Walter Montagu left for Naples and Rome, taking passage on the same wretched little boat that had brought them all down the coast to Sicily. Why he didn't go with the others to the Levant, and whether his decision to return to Italy was a sudden one or not, Bullen does not say. But there must have been some good reason which made him take that arduous trip to Messina, only to turn round four days later and travel back all those long miles alone.

Bullen, on that day in March of 1634, was probably closer to the Roman Catholic faith than he had ever been before. Religion had never been, for him, a mere matter of form. In the spring of 1632, when he was living at the embassy in Paris, he had written to his father, 'beseeching' him to excuse his short letter, 'being not desirous to be troubled with any thing till I have ben at Communyng, which my lord intends to have here on Easter day.' After the death of Sir Isaac Wake, his diary, it is true, seldom refers to Protestant services, and, as the weeks go by, 'I heard mass' appears more and more frequently. But it was not until the months in Venice that Reymes seems to have been even slightly tempted to change his faith. Even of this there is no proof, although his daily attendance at mass during the six weeks' journey to Rome, and his instinctive touch on his chaplet on seeing the veil of the Virgin, would suggest a surrender to the older Church.

Certainly before he reached Rome, Bullen was emotionally receptive to the spell of Roman Catholicism. In Rome, where religion was a much more serious matter than in Venice, he was in daily contact with men who were deeply concerned with the doctrines of the Church. Like others who frequented the Jesuit College, he listened to religious discussions and may even have voiced opinions of his own. When he and Mr Slingsby 'discoursed there for two hours together', they were probably talking about religion. But more than Slingsby or any of the others, it was Walter Montagu who was best able to present the arguments for the Roman Church. And when Reymes, some thirty years later, referred to the 'shock and battery of all opinions beyond the sea', it may well have been the prowess of the brilliant Montagu that he was remembering.

Only ten years older than Reymes, Walter Montagu had behind him a decade of unofficial diplomacy. As early as 1624, when the Duke of Buckingham had sent him to Paris on a mission concerning the French marriage, he had won the good will of Henrietta Maria, of the French Queen and of the powerful Duchess of Chevreuse. Subsequently, as one of Queen Henrietta's favourites, he was sent to Paris approximately once a year. Conversant with the various factions in both the English and French Courts, he developed great skill in ironing out differences among them, and, despite an earlier disagreement with Richelieu, he was, by 1631, one of the few Englishmen able to negotiate with that powerful figure. To Sir Isaac Wake's annoyance, Walter Montagu could see the Cardinal whenever he wished, whereas he, the ambassador, had to confer by proxy.

In 1634 Montagu had not yet openly declared himself a Catholic. Possibly he had not completely made up his mind. But that he was at least on the brink of a decision, deeply concerned with his problem, and devoting much of his time to reading authorities and discussing unresolved points, there can be little doubt. As he wrote to his father, the Earl of Manchester, in the famous letter of 1635, 'On my last journey to Italy I did apply all my leisure to a more justifiable settlement of my beliefs.'[5]

The 'last journey to Italy' must have lasted for more than a year. Bullen first saw Montagu in Turin in early October of 1633, and was with him in Florence late in October of 1634. Apparently Montagu left for France early in the following year, and, some time before his departure for England in July of 1635, went with Thomas Killigrew to Loudun, where he saw an Ursuline nun exorcized of the devil. This supposed miracle is said to have brought about Montagu's conversion. Yet he fails to mention the incident in the letter to his father. In that involved epistle his chief point is the visible continuity of the Catholic Church, an unbroken thread of doctrine to conduct man through the dark passages of the world.

The sincerity of Montagu's struggle to justify his inclinations is evident, and, if one accepts his premises, his reasoning is sound enough. Engaged as he was in rationalizing his beliefs, it is not improbable that he discussed his problems with Reymes on the many days that they were together. The fact that Montagu sent him a copy of the 1635 letter is in itself an indication of Reymes's interest.

CHAPTER NINE

CONSTANTINOPLE AND RETURN

THE *William and Thomas* was ready to leave Messina on Saturday, April 1st, and so were her passengers. Reymes had received from the merchant, Mr Garroway, '200 ducats which are 50 lb sterling' and 'at 6 hours after dinner', he and his five companions went aboard, expecting to sail within the hour. But they had reckoned without the wind, which proved so 'contrary' that they 'had to sit in port all night'. This delay the group, wise in the ways of sailing ships, accepted philosophically enough. Even the next day, when the wind still blew 'always contrary', they settled down good-naturedly to pass the time — sleeping, talking, playing at cards and chess and listening to Bullen trying out his new guitar. After four more days of waiting tempers were on edge. Reymes had an argument with Mr Bartlet over a game of chess, 'so hot, that Mr. B. promised never to play with me again'.

On Thursday, the 6th, in spite of a still 'strong and unfavorable' wind, the ship finally sailed; whereupon the gentlemen all took to their beds. Bullen, never a good sailor, was too sick to raise his head. 'The waves were so high they washed over my cabin which is on the quarter deck ... For two days I neither dined nor supped.' But by Sunday he was strong enough to hear the captain, Mr New, preach two sermons and 'say prayers, as he does everyday'. The next day they sighted a Turkish man-of-war which chased them for two hours. 'Then, we finally did the same to her and she left, finding us too big for her.'

Towards evening of the following day, they met another Turkish boat,

> a small one with 34 persons aboard who were in very bad straits, having lost their barque because of the tempest, and having been at sea 6 days without anything to eat or drink. We gave them some bread and wine, and took their arms and

tied their boat to the stern of our vessel. There was a Fleming with them whom we took on our ship ... Our captain has asked 500 dollars for their passage as far as Zante. They paid 300 now and gave a note for the rest. He gave them all they needed to eat and drink. Four persons in their boat died tonight and 15 before we met them, because of the salt water they had drunk.

On Thursday, April 13th, just a week from the day she had left Messina, the *William and Thomas* 'passed by the island of Cephalonia and by Morea and entered the harbor of Zante.[1] They would not give us pratique because of the Turks and we stayed aboard.' By the next morning, however, Captain New had his pratique, the permit to enter the port, and the party went ashore.

Living in the home of the consul, Mr Hide, the travellers stayed for almost a week in this delightful island, 'the flower of the Levant', as the Venetians called it, and one of their few remaining eastern possessions. On their first day they dined with a group of merchants, Messrs Yeatwood, Whitman, Southern, and Bromwell.

After dinner we went to Mr. Bromwell's garden and on the way we saw the whole village spread out. It is very small and unattractive.

But the garden, with its fruit trees and fine bowling green, Bullen thought delightful, as he did all the countryside and the hills encircling the harbour.

To Bullen the stay in Zante was a special pleasure, for the people of this music-loving island were charmed with his lute. One day he writes, 'I played the lute before all the people'; another time, 'After dinner I played my lute before a gentleman from the Castle, and this morning, before another who came expressly to hear me,' and again 'While I was at table, 7 or 8 gentlemen arrived to listen to me play.'

In turn, Bullen seems to have been equally appreciative of the islanders. He watched with delight the dances by the peasants, and one evening, 'while we were supping in a corner of the island near a fountain, we took their tambourines and trumpets and all tried to play. Then I listened to them play — the best music of that sort I ever heard.'

CONSTANTINOPLE AND RETURN

On the evening of April 19th the Englishmen sailed out of Zante on their way to Crete. Although they were chased by another Turk, they had a good wind and a pleasant voyage, reaching Candia four days later, just at nightfall. Unfortunately, a storm came up before they could land and they 'were forced to spend all night on the sea'. The next morning,

> we waited 6 hours in a little house without getting pratique. But an Italian merchant gave us some dinner and finally we were permitted to go into the town. We walked about the town which is very strong, all surrounded by high stone walls. There are many beautiful antiquities such as the mountain of St. Paul and the labyrinth of Daedulus ... There are also beautiful vases and chests of cyprus. There are several galleys but the harbor is not large. The Island belongs to the Venetians. The English merchant gave us a collation.

After waiting a day for a favourable wind, Captain New headed north, slowly making his way among 'plusioures Ils de la Grece'. Then, on Friday the 28th, the weather suddenly changed, and he 'was forced to enter the port of Milos because of a great tempest. We went into the village where ... the women are dressed in the fashion of the Amazons in the Arcadia of Sir Phillip Sidne. Part of the island is very beautiful.'

On May 1st the winds died down and the *William and Thomas* left the island port. 'With scarcely a breeze blowing', she sailed on 'little by little' among the Cyclades, and finally, after three long days, reached the island of Delos.

> There we went ashore and I saw the place where the oracle of Appolo dwells ... I saw the church of St. George. The island is not very large and so sterile that there are no people in the whole island nor anything of value ... There are many islands around us like Tenos which is Venetian and Mykonos which belongs to the Turks ... We could not stay long because we were being chased by an armed frigate ... The boat seeing we were too big for her, came up to our ship, saying they thought that we, like them, were from Malta. But, by her appearance, we judged her to be a pirate.

On Sunday afternoon, May 7th, Captain New brought his ship

into the port of Smyrna, just a month and a day since her departure from Messina, apparently an excellent record.[2] In this city, then the chief port for the British Turkey Company, the merchants, living in their semi-fortified residences, were invaluable to travelling Europeans.

> The merchants, French and English, advised us against staying at the Consul's house and recommended a French hostelry where we stayed in pension ... However the consul visited us at our lodgings and we were with him in his garden with all the merchants. After dinner we all went together to the old castle on the mountain, where I saw the marble head of the Queen of Smyrna, which Mr. Pette [the Rev. William Petty, Lord Arundel's agent] had tried to buy for 400 dollars in gold. I also saw the tomb of Polycarpus, the first Greek Bishop who was a Christian ... I also saw a chapel ... where St. Paul preached, and an amphitheatre and a cistern to hold the water ... and many beautiful gardens.

Another day Reymes attended vespers at a Greek church, and rode on horseback to Burnabat.

> On the way I saw the most beautiful valley I ever beheld, with a great many trees, their boughs loaded with fruit, all sorts of fruit trees — pomegranates, apricots, almonds, olives — and many woods and springs.

The day before they left, the group had dinner with the consul, Mr Freeman, where again all the merchants had foregathered. After dinner Bullen played billiards and then went to the market where he bought '3 purses for 4 dollars and 3 carpets for 74 dollars', which Captain New agreed to 'carry to England'.

On the following day, Friday, May 12th, the five Englishmen — Mr Garroway was staying in Smyrna — sailed for Constantinople on the *Armata de Skio*, 'paying for it 104 dollars'. At the consul's insistence, they took with them two Janissaries (soldiers in the Turkish infantry), and a 'Druggerman' who acted as guide and interpreter. On Sunday they stopped at Mytilene for dinner and slept on 'a very pretty little island nearby' where they all went swimming. The next day,

CONSTANTINOPLE AND RETURN

having a very good wind we made 100 miles, passing Troy where we went ashore to see the ruins. But we found the large ones were four miles further on. Tenidos is vis-a-vis Troy ... In the evening we reached the Castles which are called Sestos and Abydos ... opposite one another and only a mile apart so that no vessels may pass without their permission ...

But the next day the wind dropped and the *Armatta* made only the thirty miles to Gallipoli. They spent the night there,

bought provisions and saw the city ... one of the first the Turks took in Europe. There are many galleys here — 17 or 18. The city is not well fortified but much like the others ... in Turkey.

During the rest of the week the wind blew only fitfully, and it was Monday, May 22nd, before Reymes and his four companions finally reached Constantinople. There they were met by 'the secretary and Druggerman, two Janissaries and two other servants' sent by the ambassador to conduct them to his residence, the 'Hotel de l'Ambassador', where they were to live during their ten days in Constantinople.

The ambassador, Sir Peter Wych, and his wife did their utmost to make their guests feel at home and to show them the wonders of this strange and beautiful city. On Tuesday, Bullen writes:

We attended a Jewish wedding with the Ambassador and Madame, and the Ambassador of Venice and of Holland, where I witnessed many diverting customs ... We went all around the city and in all the mosques which are extraordinarily beautiful, especially Santa Sophia ... We saw the tombs of the Emperors and the place where the Janissaries live. We visited the Greek Cathedral where I saw the pillar to which our Saviour was bound ... I saw the place where the Emperors were crowned and passed the site of a great fire.

The visitors frequented the markets, where they bought Turkish slippers and 'other curios'; played cards with Madame and the ambassador; called on 'le Cappitain Basha' who was in his galley, 'most beautiful and costly', and went to the Pillar of Pompey in the Black Sea, 'upon which,' says Reymes, 'I put my name ... the place where it stands being very hard to get up on ... ' And the day before they left the five young men were in the 'Grande Seraglio where we saw the Cade [Judge] of Stamboul and from there we visited another palace of the ruler.'

By five o'clock on Thursday afternoon, June 1st, the *Armatta* was on its way to the island of 'Scio', or Chios. The wind was 'favorable' and, apart from a pirate ship which they managed to avoid, and another dispute between Bullen and Mr Bartlet, there were no untoward events. In 'Scio', which they reached on June 6th, Reymes and his friends went to the house of the vice-consul, where

> we walked into the orchard and lay down under the trees ... Many Greeks and Italians came to pay their respects to us and to the Jesuit father who came with us on the boat ... We paid the master of the barque Armatta 77 dollars for our journey back.

Here on 'Scio' the English party was waiting for Mr Garroway to come over from near-by Smyrna, before making the final arrangements for the trip home. Meanwhile they made some excursions round the island. On June 8th,

> We hired some mules and rode across the island where we saw a Greek monastery which had been founded by Constantine. It is built in the same shape as St. Sophia at Constantinople. There I drank the wine of Homer. Then we went to the house of the Jesuits where the doctor, a brother of the secretary of M. l'Ambassador, entertained us. Nearby is a fountain with water colder than any I ever tasted. Thence we went to see the mosaics which are unlike those anywhere else in the world. We rode on through many villages and gardens and all through the valley.

On Sunday they attended services in a Greek church where they heard the 'Patriarch of Constantinople' preach; witnessed a wedding in the church of the Jesuits, and after supper saw a 'dance of the peasants'.

After Mr Garroway's arrival on Monday, there were heated discussions about the return to Italy. A small barque of eighteen oars was to leave for Greece or Morea, as they called it, on

CONSTANTINOPLE AND RETURN

Wednesday, and all but Reymes were eager to take it. After a good deal of talk he too seems to have agreed and began 'to prepare for the voyage.' 'Then,' Bullen says, 'I later decided to stay on the island until the return of the ship, the *General*.' Why he wanted to wait for the large ship going directly to Venice, Reymes does not say. Possibly he didn't like Mr Gosset, the master of the barque, who was 'very drunk' one night, or he may have been worried about money, for the trip had proved more expensive than he had anticipated — in Constantinople he had been obliged to borrow one hundred dollars from Giles Porter.

If money was the stumbling block, a loan of eighty dollars from Mr Bartlet may have turned the tide, although the urging of Lord Carnarvon, whom Bullen regarded with deep affection and admiration, probably had its effect. In any case, at the last minute he changed his mind.

> They have persuaded me to go with them by way of Morea ... At 4 hours after dinner we left by a barque equipped with 18 oars, which cost 55 dollars, and 2 Janissaries who cost 200 dollars.

They had no sooner started than a sudden storm came up, 'so fierce' that the little boat, struggling against 'a dangerous wind', took two days to reach the island of Andros, which lies to the south and west of 'Scio' and due east of Athens. There, in the refuge of a small harbour, she waited until the wind was a 'little more favorable', and 'about evening' of Friday, June 16th, made her way to 'the little island of Negro Pont'. On Saturday, the wind again growing 'contraire', the barque could not 'advance' and was forced to spend all day and night 'along the coast of the island'.

On the rocky coast of Greece, just opposite the narrow little island of Makronisos or Negro Pont, as Reymes calls it, is the port of Lavrion. It lies less than ten miles north of Sounion and some thirty miles south-east of Athens. This must have been 'la ville' which the weary travellers 'reached at 9 o'clock' on Sunday morning, and where they 'hired some mules, paying 1 dollar per mule between here and Athens'. They left the town in mid-afternoon, and for five hours rode in the heat over rough, narrow roads; then, exhausted, 'lay down in the fields and slept 2 or 3 hours and afterwards went on through the rest of the night.'

CONSCIENTIOUS CAVALIER

By Monday morning they were close to Athens but too weary to go any further.

So at 8 o'clock we rested again, lying under the trees with a view of Athens before us, and at 12 we went on again, arriving in the afternoon at the house of a Sultan, a visit which had been arranged by our Janissary. We supped with the Sultan in Turkish fashion and afterwards we slept in a bed a la Turkish ... In the morning we saw the city of Athens and the beautiful ruins ... All around Athens there is a beautiful vale filled with olive trees. After dinner we left for Patras by mule, paying 5 dollars per person. Because of danger along the way, we also took with us 5 soldiers to whom we paid 10 dollars. We slept some 10 miles from Athens on the ground in the countryside, and then, after about 3 hours rest, rode on through the night.

Greece, in the 1630s, was under Turkish rule, as it had been for almost 200 years, and Athens, the site of the Sublime Porte (court of Turkey), was a small community of some 9,000 inhabitants, enclosed within narrow walls. The 'Sultan's house', where Reymes and his friends stayed, may have been that of the country's chief ruler, though it was more likely to have been the home of some minor official, for the term Sultan was used loosely.

'The beautiful ruins' which Bullen saw on that June day in 1634 would, of course, have included the buildings on the Acropolis. The Propylaea still stood intact, and the Parthenon, as yet undamaged by the explosion during a siege by the Venetians in 1687, had been converted into a mosque with a tall minaret.

'The danger along the way' was very real. Bandits were everywhere, and the country hostile to strangers. Even with the Janissaries and the five Turkish soldiers to ease the way and make contacts with the unfriendly villagers, the four-day ride to Patras was difficult and perilous.

To avoid riding during the hottest hours, the Englishmen had readily agreed to the Janissaries' plan — travel by night and early morning, and rest during the middle of the day. Even so, the morning sun beat down mercilessly; the roads grew steadily worse, and twice the soldiers reported bandits near by. But the biggest problem was food and drink. The plague was rife in Greece, and the suspicious country folk would seldom allow the soldiers to come near enough to buy provisions.

On Wednesday the party, 'as usual', stopped before noon to dine and rest.

> But, having nothing to eat or drink, we bought a sheep for three shillings which served us well, for having no water we were obliged to drink the milk.

The next day

> we saw before us the gulf of Lepanto at one end of which lies Corinth, a very beautiful city. Two miles from the sea, it is built on the side of a mountain and is surrounded by many olive trees. The passage between the gulfs is not more than 3 miles and is not very high. We rested here and sent one of the men to get wine and bread. Six miles further on we stopped and lay down in a vineyard, sleeping as always on the ground. The weather grew very bad. It rained and thundered all night. We had nothing to eat or drink.

Of the events of Friday, Bullen writes: 'We rode on in the same fashion and at noon came upon a little fountain where we had sherbet.' The sherbet, to which Reymes refers so often during his Levantine journey, was a sort of lemonade made of lemon juice and sugar boiled together and mixed with water. He continues: 'Afterwards, as we were passing a village, we sent our Janissary to buy a capon and some eggs ... Three miles from here a great many people are sick with the plague.'

On Saturday, after hours of rough riding in the burning summer sun, they reached Patras where they stayed overnight in the house of the consul, Mr Bunnington. Early on Sunday morning they set forth on a hard two-day ride to Gastouni, a village lying to the south and west of Patras. On Monday night they 'boarded a boat' and at eight the next morning, June 27th, were in Zante,

> going immediately to the *Mason de pratica*, where we found Mr. Hide and the merchants. Thanks to their influence we were permitted to go to Mr. Hide's house, having two

guards placed over us ... We were, nevertheless, allowed to eat together and to pass the time agreeably enough.

The 'Mason de pratica' was the office which issued pratiques or permits for entrance to the island. As Reymes says, owing to the influence of the consul, Mr Hide, they escaped detention in the 'Mason' itself, which seems to have served as a lazaretto, and were allowed to live in the house of the consul until the allotted time, officially forty days, had expired. The failure to get pratique did not come as a surprise. Travellers from the east often had difficulty, and, in their case, the news of the plague in the very territory they had just crossed had already reached the authorities.

To escape the long period of quarantine Reymes decided to take passage on a ship about to sail for Venice, reasoning that the days aboard would answer the same purpose as the long stay in Zante.

> I have made up my mind to take the *Scippio* back to Venice and leave the company of Mr. Carnarvon and the others ... Therefore I took up 200 dollars from Mr. Grendling Tindall ... and paid Mr. Thinn the 100 dollars I borrowed from him and Mr. Bartlet the 80 dollars he lent me at Scio. I had a suit made of the dimity I bought at Scio.

So, on Thursday, June 29th, Bullen bade goodbye to all his good friends and sailed out of Zante on the *Scipio*, captained by Mr Pennington. He had a large cabin to himself and settled down for what proved to be a tedious three-week voyage, for with the wind against them for days at a time the ship made slow progress. Reymes spent much of his time reading, usually *The History of the Turks*, a large, illustrated volume with pictures of 'Selimus la 2' and of 'Osman the Turke who governs at present'.[3] Occasionally he played dominoes and 'tricktrack' [backgammon] with the sergeant, and, of course, wrote many letters.

On July 8th the *Scipio* stopped briefly at Corfu; on the 16th she passed the 'isles de Dalmatia', and on July 22nd was in sight of Venice. Then Bullen's troubles began. When he records the events of the day, however, he has little notion of the difficulties ahead.

> At 3 hours after dinner we arrived at Mal[amocco] where there were 2 or 3 pilots who conducted the vessel around the

CONSTANTINOPLE AND RETURN

bar of Malamocco. Mr. Pennington had expected to go on to Venice but was not permitted to do so ... We lay by the village all night.

The following morning, Sunday, Captain Pennington went into Venice 'to get pratique but was told to wait until tomorrow', so the *Scipio* lay outside Malamocco for another day and night.

It wasn't until Monday morning, when he went ashore at the town of Malamocco, that Reymes fully realized the seriousness of the situation. That any ship from the Levant was suspect in those plague-ridden days, Bullen was well aware, but both he and Captain Pennington had thought that the long trip from Zante with no instance of the disease aboard would assure them of a clean bill of health. They were soon to be disabused. But to turn back to Reymes's own account:

> I went ashore ... and to la Sanita where I was told that I would have to go to the lazaretto ... After dinner Mr. Pennington and I went ashore where we were obliged to take the ordinary road, following the official ordered by la Sanita to accompany us. On the way I met Mr. Rowlanson, Mr. Yeats and Sir John Milles who accompanied us as far as the lazaretto. Mr. Yeats brought me provisions — a capon, pigeon and other things. Mr. Rowlanson told me all the latest news. I engaged a room in the lazaretto.

Then Bullen waited. Although he was not allowed to leave the premises, his room seems to have been comfortable enough, and, since he bought most of his own food, purchased and purveyed by the two merchants, Mr Yeats and Mr Peterson, he had plenty to eat. He had ample leisure for reading and writing and for entertaining, for, illogically enough, Reymes, although put in the 'suspected' category, was allowed to have any number of visitors. The almost daily calls of Yeats and Peterson with provisions were in the line of duty, but the visits of others who troubled to come all the way to Malamocco and risk exposure to the dread disease must have been heart-warming. Rowlandson and Sir John Milles called twice the first week, and the Earl of Desmond came often, bringing delicacies, news, and, best of all, a new lute.

On Thursday, July 27th, a guardian was sent over from Venice to watch over Bullen and his friend Captain Pennington, also a guest of the lazaretto. Characteristically, Reymes made friends with the guardian, and whenever his store of provisions permitted, gave a party, or collation, in his room for him and Captain Pennington.

When the merchant, Mr Peterson, called on Sunday, July 30th, Reymes and Captain Pennington hopefully gave him their 'fedes' to take to 'la Sanita' in order to get their pratique. Since the 'fede' or certificate of health was renewed only when its owner was judged to be in good health, the two had every reason to be optimistic.[4] But on Monday night Bullen writes:

> We expected pratique all day, then in the evening Mr. Peterson's boatman came with bread and wine and an order to stay here four or five days longer.

After five days without any word Peterson came again, not with the expected pratique but with a request for new 'fedes'. Armed with these he went back to Venice, and the hopes of the waiting gentlemen soared. Then, two days later, word came that they must stay in the lazaretto another eight days. And so, with delay after delay, the waiting game went on.

Finally, on August 19th, after almost a month of waiting, an official arrived with the long-expected pratique. Why the permit was so long delayed, Reymes doesn't say. Probably he didn't know. In any case his experience was not unique and, though tedious, was not as unpleasant as that endured by the famous Doctor Harvey two summers later.

In August of 1636, Dr William Harvey was stopped at Treviso and summarily ordered into the lazaretto there. Deeming it dangerous 'to goe into such a place ... whear they use to putt infected persons', the spunky doctor chose instead to sleep in the 'open base fields'. But, in spite of his protests, Harvey was forced to share a 'very nasty room' in the lazaretto with three other men. Like Reymes, he was tantalized with promises of speedy release, only to be followed by orders for another stay of '7 or 10 or 20 days'.[5] Because of the arrangement with his merchants, Bullen did not suffer from the bad food that Harvey complained of, and he had a room of his own. But, in spite of all of Rowlandson's efforts, he sat out twenty-eight of his forty-day quarantine — a dull end to the Levantine journey.

CHAPTER TEN

AUTUMN IN FLORENCE

REYMES had received his pratique early on Saturday morning, August 19th. Within an hour he had left the lazaretto and by noon was in his old lodgings, talking with his landlady, Signora Angela. It was good to be back in these familiar quarters, to walk again in the Piazza of St Mark and across the bridge to the Rialto, and to talk with old friends. But this time there was little chance to enjoy life in Venice, for Bullen's two weeks' stay was crowded with preparations for a trip to Florence.

Conferences with the two merchants, Yeats and Peterson, to settle for the expenses at the lazaretto and to arrange for new letters of credit, and a shopping tour for 'fans and other trinkets' for his father plus purchases of his own, took up much of Reymes's time. On Sunday afternoon, with 'Signor Julio Cesero',[1] a friend and 'very good critic', he visited 'the studio of an artist' where he selected three pictures — 'the head of an Emperor, one of two figures, and another of 14 courtesans' — all to go to England via the *Scipio* and Captain Pennington. The obliging captain was to 'carry' these and the other pictures, and numerous books and curios which Bullen had collected, to the elder Reymes in London.

There were many callers, and Bullen was sometimes hard put to to be polite and yet avoid social entanglements. The erstwhile guardian at the lazaretto was an almost daily visitor. Once Reymes took him to dinner, and another day presented him with 'un reall et demy', for the gentleman was apparently in need of funds as well as food. But there was one person whom Bullen had no wish to avoid — the English Resident, Thomas Rowlandson.

At the moment the Resident was full of news about the new ambassador, Basil, Lord Feilding. To Reymes the appointment of Lord Feilding, to whom he had been so attracted in Paris in the winter of 1632, seemed a great stroke of luck. Apparently Rowlandson too was pleased, no doubt confident that his knowledge of

Venetian affairs would make him indispensable to the young ambassador. Meanwhile he was trying to find a house large enough for Feilding and his staff, and making arrangements with the Jews to rent the furniture for the embassy. Just two days before his departure for Florence, Bullen 'was with him ... to look at a residence for M. l'Ambassador near St. John de Paulo'.

Reymes's account of the trip to Florence by way of Bologna is brief. He travelled with a 'messenger' who made all the arrangements and, apart from a day in bed with a migraine headache, he found the journey comfortable and short — only five days all told. By two o'clock on Thursday afternoon, September 7th, he was in Florence, and within an hour had chosen from his list of suitable lodgings a room 'close to the Cathedral'.

Why Reymes was so anxious to go to Florence is never stated, but he was probably influenced by the reputation the city enjoyed for the purity of her language, and as an excellent place to pursue the 'exersises' he had neglected for so many months. There may have been another reason. Walter Montagu was to be in the Tuscan city some time in October, and Bullen, who had been writing letters to him and to Father Fitzherbert in Rome, was no doubt eager to talk with him again.

Armed with a list of the city's most highly regarded masters, Reymes had come to Florence to work. After months of idleness his conscience was bothering him. The very day of his arrival he wrote: 'I now begin to carry out the resolution I made a long time ago — not to waste any more time.' And he was as good as his promise. Day after day the diary records, 'I did all my exercises, I played the lute and guitar ... I went to bed early.'

On Monday morning, September 11th, Signor Pietro Paulo Pistello made the first of his daily visits, and Bullen's study of Italian under a rigorous master began in earnest. A few days later he made arrangements for lessons on the guitar with Signor Donato, in mathematics and design with Dr Couconpanne, and in 'painting and color' with his brother Gismonde. The elder of the brothers, whom Reymes refers to simply as Doctor, not only supervised his daily lessons, but accompanied him on tours of the churches 'to teach me to recognize the hands of the masters'. He soon came to regard the brothers Couconpanne as his friends and spent many hours in their home 'in Via Largia by the Cardinal de Medici's house', where he often 'supped and played the lute'.

As a rule the Englishman abroad lived in a world largely made up of other British travellers, many of whom spent their time moving from place to place in seemingly endless rotation. English embassies and English merchants did little to bring the roving Britishers into contact with the countries they visited; their chief service was to apprise the travellers of each other's whereabouts, a procedure which simply tended to keep them within their own tight little circles. A visitor could, it is true, learn a good deal from his contacts with servants, shopkeepers, landlords, and other caterers to man's physical needs, but to know people of his own class or with his own interests was another matter.

There was, however, one small group of educated foreigners whom the young Englishman could, and often did, learn to know well. These were the 'masters'. Many of them invited their pupils into their homes and introduced them into the circle of their own associates. Bullen had made some of his warmest friends among his masters in Paris, and now, in Florence, he was already supping with Signor Pietro and with his frail guitar-master, Signor Donato, and soon was to find himself completely at home in the Couconpanne household.

There were distractions even in Florence. The better part of one day and night was taken up with changing rooms. Reymes had been dissatisfied with his dark chamber, and the host had promised him one with a view. So, on September 24th, Bullen moved. 'I changed my room for another with a view, but there were so many bugs in the bed that I could not sleep. Finally, at 4 in the morning I was obliged to get up and sleep again in the other room.' Happily, two days later he writes: 'They have rid my room of the bugs.'

Many Englishmen visited Florence, some of them old friends who managed to take up a good deal of Reymes's time. Mr Bartlet, his companion on the Levantine journey, was constantly shuttling back and forth between Rome and Florence, and John Tracy[2] and Mr Pickering had come for an indefinite stay. One evening when Bullen came home he found Mr Pickering and his guitar waiting for him. 'He wanted me to play the lute, so we played the lute and guitar until 1 hour after midnight. Then I conducted him to his lodging, playing the lute all the way.'

For one friend, Giles Porter, whom he hadn't seen since Zante, Reymes gladly neglected all his studies. Giles was on his way home via Genoa and Paris and could stop in Florence for only two days. He moved in with Bullen and the two 'discoursed very late' each night. They visited the Cathedral, 'which pleased me exceedingly', and walked along the banks of the Arno, and when Giles left Bullen rode with him 'in the carriage for Pisa and Livorno, sleeping at Scalia 20 miles from Florence'. They ate their dinner next day at the hostelry of The Three Beautiful Ladies in Pisa, and slept at the Monte d'Aure in Livorno. At noon, Wednesday, October 4th, Giles, carrying with him Bullen's letters, boarded a 'phelouca' (felucca) bound for Genoa. Reymes, 'very sad' at his best friend's departure, left 'by carriage for Pisa. It turned over on the way.'

By Saturday Bullen was back in Florence. 'Signore Donato failed because of the rain ... I was at the Couconpannes but I didn't accomplish anything there because of my unhappy frame of mind ... I did not sup. I played the lute for a long time.'

For the next two weeks Reymes worked steadily. Then, on Friday, October 20th, Walter Montagu arrived for a ten days' visit, staying with the Duke de Guise, whose home was a favourite meeting place for French and English Catholics. Bullen was with Montagu whenever that popular gentleman had a moment to spare. On Saturday he talked with him for an hour; dined with him on Sunday and 'was with him ... in St. Croce where there is a tomb of Michael Angelo'. The following day he went to the comedy with him and 'saw dame Prudentia in the part of the Countess, and talked with him and the Duke of Northumberland'. On Tuesday Reymes again called at the home of the Duke de Guise where he 'discoursed with Mr. Montagu ... and was with him to hear a damoiselle with a very beautiful voice, and at the comedy'.

All Wednesday Montagu was busy with some newly arrived Englishmen, but on Thursday Bullen 'was with him at the house of the Cardinal and ... at the home of the Duke of Northumberland ... where I saw all the English'. The next day Montagu left for Venice, Reymes accompanying him to the outskirts of the city. Although he wrote to him often, this was the last time he was to see Walter Montagu until the summer of 1635 in England.

AUTUMN IN FLORENCE

During his last six weeks in Florence Reymes often 'discoursed' with the Duke of Northumberland. He met and talked with him almost every Sunday and was frequently invited to his beautiful villa. It is not hard to understand the attraction the brilliant and romantic Robert Dudley, the so-called Duke of Northumberland, would have had for a young Englishman of Reymes's background and interests. Undoubtedly Bullen was familiar with the storybook adventures of this supposedly bastard son of the Earl of Leicester who, failing to prove his legitimacy, had left England, his inheritance, his wife, and his numerous daughters, to take up a new life in Florence. That he was accompanied by his beautiful cousin, Elizabeth Southwell, disguised as a page, did not detract from the glamour of the picture.[3]

The most remarkable part of Sir Robert's story was the fact that he made good in his new environment, becoming a sort of self-made duke. His initiative, his skill as a shipbuilder, and his knowledge of science and mathematics soon caught the attention of the Grand Duke, Cosmo II, and by 1620 he had been made Earl of Warwick and Duke of Northumberland in the Holy Roman Empire. Needless to say he had repudiated his earlier faith along with family and possessions, and adopted Roman Catholicism with the usual fervour of the convert. When Reymes knew him the Duke was at the height of his fame and prosperity. He had won the esteem of the then Grand Duke, Ferdinand II, by draining the swamp between Pisa and the sea, and been granted a pension and his palace, Villa Castello, just north of the city.

Sir Robert well illustrates one of the phenomena of the seventeenth century, the combination of swashbuckling cavalier, ardent Catholic, and practical scientist. His home, like that of de Guise, was a rendezvous for visiting Catholics. The same situation seems to have prevailed in Florence in the 1630s as that which Sir Henry Wotton had deplored some twenty-five years earlier when he spoke of a 'certain knot of bastard Catholics ... who with pleasantness of conversation ... do much harm ... of any Englishman that shall go thither'.[4] Apparently both Northumberland and Montagu used their skill and charm in an effort to convert one young Englishman, Bullen Reymes, to the Catholic faith.

CONSCIENTIOUS CAVALIER

In spite of all the visitors, Reymes had managed during the first two months in Florence to go to mass every day, keep up with his studies, write dozens of letters — nine to Rowlandson alone — and practise on his lute, even composing a song to send to one of his friends. It wasn't until the arrival of Michael Mosly and Lord Carnarvon that his resolution began to falter.

Michael, or Michell as he insisted on calling himself while in Italy, was an old friend, a nephew of Mistress Mosly, the 'mother' of the maids at York House, of whom Bullen was so fond. On Thursday, November 16th, 'Mr. Mosly arrived here from Rome and moved in with me ... I talked with him until 8 at night.' From this time on, all through the remaining weeks in Florence and the journey to Venice, the two shared their quarters and their pleasures.

On Sunday Reymes took Michell with him to a convent. 'I was at St. Agatha with Signore Mosly where we witnessed the ceremony of a nun who is entering the order ... I talked in the parlatorio a long time with ma tante who had sent a present of comfits to my room.' Bullen went to the convent again twice that week. Once he 'discoursed for a long time', and another day 'listened to a young woman sing and play the theoboro and guitar and on the spinet'. On Sunday, November 26th, there is an even stranger entry: 'I sent my hat with my sword and mantle and a robe and other things to the convent for their comedy ... Ma tante gave me a Galantina [a capon pie] ... and this evening someone sent me a song from the convent.' Then a few days later comes this surprising statement: 'I was at Signore Gismonde ... he has finally finished my portrait ... I sent it to the convent of St. Agata.'

Whether the picture was a loan or a permanent gift, Reymes never says. Nor does he tell us the name of the comedy or the part of the nun who wore his clothes. Neither, for that matter, does he reveal the identity of 'ma tante'. Save that he wrote to her often during the next year, we hear nothing more of this lady of the Florentine convent.

When, on December 2nd, Bullen heard that Lord Carnarvon had 'arrived from Rome', he hurried, he says, 'as quickly as I possibly could to greet him. We dined together and afterwards we went in some churches ... I supped with him and went to the

Comedy with him ... ' The next five days are full of excursions with Robert Dormer, Earl of Carnarvon, whom Reymes had learned to know so well and to regard so highly on the long journey to Constantinople. They went 'to St. Marco ... to the Jesuits ... to Maria Novella ... for a ride in his carriage and to the Comedy'. And on Thursday 'we all went early to M. le Conte's to bid him good-bye. I played the lute for him before he was up ... He left at 2 in the afternoon in the carriage for Pisa.'

Four days later, on December 11th, Reymes's own Florentine visit was at an end, and he and Michell Mosly were on their way to Venice.

CHAPTER ELEVEN

THE NEW AMBASSADOR

1. *Il Palazzo Giustiniani*

IN his last letter Rowlandson had said that he expected the new ambassador by the first of the year. Anxious to be in Venice well in advance of Feilding, Bullen had fretted over the bad weather which had slowed their journey, but by December 18th he and Mosly were in Venice, in Reymes's old quarters, the house of Signora Angela 'pres San Marco'. Then, eager for the latest news, he had hurried to the home of the Resident only to find that Lord Feilding would be delayed another three or four weeks.

There was much speculation about the new ambassador, both among the Venetians and the English. Basil, Lord Feilding, it was said, was a young man of intelligence and charm as well as a person of quality, the nephew of King Charles's favourite, the late Duke of Buckingham, and the son-in-law of the Lord Treasurer, Richard Weston, the Earl of Portland.

Reymes hoped for a place in the ambassador's household. His friendship with Basil's brother, the Earl of Desmond, with his mother, Lady Denbigh, and with his aunt, the Duchess of Buckingham; and his own pleasant encounter with Lord Feilding in Paris, were all in his favour. But he was worried. He felt that the impression he would make on the new ambassador would be the determining factor. In the anxious interlude all he could do was to wait.

On January 1st Bullen started his 1635 diary — in Italian this time! Quickly and easily he picked up the old, idle pattern of life in Venice. Desmond, Porter, and most of his friends of the year before had gone, but gay Michell Mosly was there, living in the adjoining room and ready to walk with him to the Rialto or in the Piazza of St Mark, or to go in masquerade to St Stefano. And within the week two of Michell's friends, Robert Martin and Ned Warr, arrived and found lodgings near by. With them and a clever, hard-drinking merchant, Mr Sothern, and with two Italian couples, the Ursettas and the Veneras, Michell and Bullen pursued the gaieties of Twelfth Night and the carnival season.

Signor and Signora Ursetta lived on the upper floor of Signora Angela's house. Almost every evening they — and sometimes Signora Angela — supped with Reymes and Mosly, occasionally in Bullen's room, but usually in theirs. And, with their friends, Signor and Signora Venera, they went with him in masquerade to St Stefano, to the comedy, and to the Twelfth-Night celebration. Of Saturday, January 6th, Reymes writes:

> La Signora Venera and I, dressed like the sheperds of Arcadia, went to St. Stefano and, today being Epiphany, we and the others tarried in the gramento [?] below my room. I was the King and la Signora Venera was the Queen.

With Sothern, Mosly, and Ned Warr, Reymes frequented the two taverns popular with the English — the Sturrion and the Trumpet — where they played cards, ate, and 'drank together late and hard', while almost every day he went out with one or another of them in masquerade, or to the comedy.

> I met Mr. Sothern at the Trumpet. He gave me a silver earring and took me to the home of Signora Bettina behind St. Giovanni and Paolo where we dined ... and then I went to the comedy with Mr. Mosly. Mr. Sothern was there with his Damma. It was the comedy of Scappini.[1]

One Monday late in January the group had gathered in Reymes's quarters. 'The Signoras Ursetta and Venera were here ... I gave the verse of Signor Mosly to Signor Warr ... ' The 'Poem by Michell Mosly, Venis the 29th of January 1634/5', though no literary gem, gives something of the flavour of carnival time in Venice.

TO NED WARR

> Last night, as on St. Steffano I stood
> Where wants no people, when the masks are good,
> Thousands of humors there I saw, and all
> Did strive to celebrate the Carnavalle.

> Into the place, immediately did come
> Tow tripping nimphes, after a bellowing drum.
> Nor arms, nor armor had they, nor no scarr,
> But yet I knew them to be maydes of warr.
> Deare frend, 'tis said thou wert the author: some
> Say thou wert he that bangd the rattling drume.
> Had there but been the Trumpett, that same size,
> Would made m'a sworne the invention had been thyne.
> O rare conceyt, no fault there could be founde.
> Itt was the drum did make the plott hold sounde.
> My thought you girles followed with discontent.
> But Bulleyn sayd they volentaries went.
> Ursetta, when she saw with what desire
> Moll, Isabella and the little Squire
> Followed the eccoing noyse, she did dispute
> Orpheus, to beat the drum, had left the lute.
> But Venera, laufte, and veered, and turned her bum
> To see corrantos dansed after a drume.
> Fayth Ned, our ladyes when they maske or mume
> Shall follow better music than a drume.

Reymes didn't spend all his time at the comedies or in masquerade. He was often with the Resident helping him make ready for the ambassador and his official family. For the embassy, Rowlandson had rented one of Venice's famous old palaces, the Palazzo Giustiniani (later the Hotel Europa), built in the curious pointed style of the fifteenth century and situated on the north side of the Grand Canal, not far from the Piazza of St Mark.

Late in January the Resident 'heard some news from Turin' — Feilding had started on his journey down the Po and would be in Venice early in February. As the day of the ambassador's arrival drew closer, Reymes's hopes soared. Rowlandson, who was to meet Feilding and his retinue at Loreo, had asked Bullen to go with him.

On Sunday, February 4th, 'after a collation ... at the Resident's we set out in a piotta to meet the Ambassador. We slept at Chioggia where I went with the Resident to the Palace to hear news of his Excellency.' Next day they continued their slow journey, and on Wednesday, 'after having engaged a horse to

THE NEW AMBASSADOR

draw the boat, we met with his Excellency. Mr. Rowlandson boarded his boat and Winde[bank],[2] Hide, Reeves and Captain Feilding got into ours. We slept at Loreo where I greeted the Ambassador and la Signora Ambasadress.' They stopped at Chioggia, where 'the Podesta gave a great feast and ball in his Palace', and after dinner on Friday left for Venice, 'on the way receiving salutes of guns from all the ships'.

On Sunday Reymes went 'to hear a sermon by Signor Ambassador'. After the sermon Lord Feilding 'and the others left', and Bullen walked home, where he was alone and 'very sad'. Then, happily, a messenger came — 'the Ambassador wished me to return and dine with him.' Reymes, it seems, had made the desired impression, for from that time on he was at the Giustiniani Palace every day. He was not only a member of the ambassador's official family but was soon to be Feilding's most constant companion.

Of all the gentlemen of the household, the two whom Reymes found most congenial were Captain Richard Feilding, the ambassador's 'cousin', and Benjamin Weston, Anne Feilding's youngest brother. (George Feilding, the Earl of Desmond, was in England, possibly called home by his wife's threat to divorce him.)

Reymes's own situation was better than he had hoped; the Resident was not so fortunate. In August, Rowlandson, 'because his experience was considered necessary to assist the young Ambassador', had been named chief secretary of the Embassy. For some reason, however, Lord Feilding seemed reluctant to accept this assistance, and when he left England carried with him 'power to dispose of Rowlandson as he thinks best'.[3] But the Resident's efforts in preparing the embassy evidently mollified the new ambassador, for when he wrote to the Lord Treasurer of his safe arrival, he said:

> ... Mr. Rowlandson is very punctual in the discharge of his duty to the King and his obligation to your lordship, wherby I receive great advantages. I find in him so much worth and merit that I shall not use the letter of revocation till I receive further orders. He has taken great pains in making provision for my house, making ready my gondola and furnishing the rooms for receiving visits. As the furniture is hired of the

Jews, who exact near a hundred pound a month for it, I have made bold to take up moneys to buy it outright ... '4

For a time at least, Rowlandson was secure.

The regimen of the ambassador's household in Venice differed as markedly from that of Wake's embassy in Paris as gay young Basil Feilding differed from the studious Sir Isaac. Lord Feilding did, it is true, conduct services each Sunday (one wonders if his Catholic wife attended), but there is no reference to the morning and evening prayers which had been a part of the daily routine in Wake's household. Even on the ambassador's first Sunday in Venice, Reymes tells us, 'We all went in masquerade to St Stefano with his Excellency and Madam.'

And other February entries read:

(Tuesday 12) ... After dinner I went in masquerade with the Ambassador to St. Stefano. I was dressed as a damsel. Madam, Weston and Feilding were also there ...

(Thursday 14) I dined with his Excellency and ... we went in masquerade to St. Mark's where we saw the ceremony which is held there every day. The French Ambassador joined us. I went to the comedy with the Ambassador ... and then went with him to the festival and returned again to his house.

(Sunday 18) I heard a sermon by his Excellency ... I went with him in spasa on the Grand Canal, then with him and Madam to the Comedy ...

(Tuesday 20) ... I dined with the Ambassador then we went in mask to St. Stefano. I was dressed in the Ambassador's clothes. I danced in the piazza. Later I went to the fair with his Excellency and Madam where I played the lute before all the ladies. After supper his Excellency and I came alone to the ball ... and then to the regular festival where we were entertained for more than five hours ...

The gay days of 'mumming and masking' slipped by, with Reymes almost constantly at the young ambassador's side.

Except for one slight cloud the skies seemed clear. For several weeks Reymes had been disturbed by the increasingly hostile

THE NEW AMBASSADOR

attitude of the merchant, Mr Yeats. On three separate occasions he had written of 'Mr Yeats' strained and rude behavior', and on February 17th, when he called to ask about his quarterly payment, 'Mr Yeats was very rude, saying he would give no more money without a respondent.' The trouble all stemmed from the old problem, Reymes senior's delay in sending the quarterly allowance. Yeats had been in the habit of advancing the money and Bullen had come to expect the accommodation as a matter of course. He had long regarded Yeats as a personal friend and, characteristically, believed that the merchant returned his trust and affection. Thursday, February 22nd, was the day of rude awakening. Of its unhappy events Reymes writes:

> ... After dinner I went to the Rialto and to the House of Yeats and Peterson, where I signed my name to 3 letters of credit drawn on my father in London for 417 ducats and 21 grosee to be paid in 30 day after the first sight. I also signed my name to a bond, binding me to give all my possessions for the payment of the money in question. In turn they gave me a reciprocal bond promising to return ... my bond, when I paid them. But when I left their office, there stood a soldier who seized me and took me to the prison in the Rialto in a gondola. This was at one o'clock. I wrote Captain Feilding asking him to help me. He came quickly to the prison, then went to Yeats' place ... Next he went to the Ambassador who sent me 100 pieces of 9 lira each which, with the money I had in my room and the 32 scudi Mr. Gatwood [another merchant] sent me, amounted to 200 pieces of eight. After paying the guard in the presence of Captain Feilding ... I was released from prison ... When we left the prison it was 6 o'clock. I went immediately to the ambassador who demonstrated the greatest testimony of his regard for me and promised to stand by me to the end of this business ... [5]

And so the world which had looked so bright came crashing down on Bullen's head. To make matters worse, the police went to his lodging and sequestered all his possessions — bed, clothes, everything — leaving two receipts, one for his landlady and one for him. Meanwhile, Reymes shared Captain Feilding's room in the embassy, where he discussed his troubles with him, with Mr Rowlandson and with the ambassador, who again promised to help him 'in every possible way'.

Everyone, the gentlemen at the embassy and Reymes's other friends in Venice, aghast at Yeats's high-handed actions, were ready with sympathy and indignation. What Bullen needed was money. The jaunty Mr Sothern, the merchant with whom he had spent so many idle hours, readily agreed to a loan of '100 livres', but 'instead of the money sent a letter saying he would not be able to get here'. That was on Sunday. The next day Reymes and Mosly went to 'the Rialto and to the Piazza looking for Mr. Sothern, but he was nowhere about'. Then by chance they ran into him at the Trumpet. Again he promised to send some money — '200 pieces of eight' this time — and again he failed. 'He was not anywhere.'

Tuesday morning was spent in conference with Signor Joseppi, the lawyer whom Rowlandson had engaged to help his friend.

> I talked with my solicitor about my business then I went to the prison to visit my comrades there ... I stay always in the house of the Ambassador and sleep with Captain Feilding.

Although he dined and supped with 'his Excellency' and in the evenings 'played on the lute before Madam', Reymes spent most of the week closeted with his solicitor. For a few days in the following week, however, engrossed in the affairs of the ambassador, Bullen pushed his troubles into the background.

Monday, March 5th, marked the beginning of Lord Feilding's official reception by the Venetian authorities, ceremonies in which Reymes himself was an active participant. As was the custom with new ambassadors, Feilding was rowed across the lagoons to the monastery on the island of St Spirito, followed by the members of his household and by any Englishmen who chanced to be in Venice. There he was met by some sixty senators dressed in their scarlet robes, and conducted back to the embassy. Bullen, writing of that day's events, says:

> I dined with his Excellency and after dinner went with him in his gondola to St. Spirito where all the Senators had come in their gondolas to meet the Ambassador. He was accompanied by all the English. The Senators gave their hands to

those of us who were opposite them and conducted his Excellency to his gondola, we being always on their right hand ... The one who conducted his Excellency ... was the Illustrious Angelo Contarini; and the one who conducted me was the Illustrious Signor Nicoleto Erise, a relative of the Doge ...

At 5, [on Tuesday] all the Senate came again to the Ambassador's house and conducted him to the College, where he had his first audience. We went in a gondola by the mole of Latin time [the breakwater at the lower end of the Piazetta in front of the Doge's Palace] ... I was accompanied by the same one who accompanied me yesterday. He promised me any favor he could possibly do for me.

Lord Feilding, followed by his retainers, entered the Doge's Palace and climbed the stairs to the famous Sala del Collegio where, after bowing and kissing the Doge's hand, he made his speech.

He spoke in French in a very low voice, stressing the wisdom of the Venetian State, so widely admired. Then he presented the King's letter and received the Doge's sympathy for the hardship of his journey.[6]

On the following day, March 7th, 'Il Signor Ambassador went to the College again ... where we all saluted the Doge.' He presented all his gentlemen and made a speech saying that, for the time being, he had decided to keep Mr Rowlandson. 'So,' as Reymes put it, 'Il Signor Resident is still the Resident.'

Three days later the ceremonies were over, and Bullen was once more engulfed in his own affairs. His solicitor, having received no reply to repeated letters to Yeats and Peterson, had decided on a bold course of action.

I went with Signor Joseppi to the Justice of the Criminal Court where, on the recommendation of Signor Rowlandson and his Excellency, I gave an order to have Yeats and Peterson put in prison. This was done. Peterson was arrested in the Rialto and Yeats in his house. They were taken to St Mark's prison where they were held until 12 that night, when they were released, a respondent having signed a note for 6000 ducats. Signor Weston and Captain Feilding and other Englishmen were at the Rialto to see the arrest ...

This harsh treatment proved effective. Two days later the chastened merchants appeared before the ambassador 'with great penitence to ask his pardon for what they had done, saying they were content to let him conclude the business without going again before the justice ... ' They came again on the following day and

> The Ambassador told them to give me the money and also pay for the expenses I had incurred in prison. This they promised and speedily brought me 1329 lbs. It was 37 lb less than I had paid but, not wishing to dispute the matter, I agreed. My solicitor ... counted the money and gave them an order to bring back my bed ... Peterson also promised to send an order to lift the sequestration of my clothes ... The Ambassador promised to write my father ... I sent a flask of wine to my comrades in prison where I went again to visit.

So Reymes was vindicated. In many ways he was in a better situation than before. The embarrassment, inconvenience, and worry he had endured were more than made up for by the sympathy and help of his loyal friends, from his landlady Signora Angela to the ambassador himself. And, to offset the loss of his supposed friends, the wily Yeats and Peterson, and the undependable Mr Sothern, Bullen had made a new friend, and a good one, his solicitor Signor Joseppi.

Secure in the affection and esteem of both Rowlandson and Lord Feilding, Reymes had reason to be confident, to believe that he soon might rise to a position of real importance in the household of the ambassador, who was already beginning to depend upon him in more serious matters than expeditions to St Stefano. But again Fate stepped in and upset Bullen's hopes.

Feilding's young wife Anne, who had never recovered from the rigours of the winter journey to Italy, had been half-sick ever since she reached Venice. On March 16th Reymes says,

> Madam has become very ill ... There was a consultation of doctors ... I went with the Ambassador to visit the Resident of Mantua ... Madam was much worse when we got

IL PALAZZO GIUSTINIANI
from a photograph taken about 1900

home. The doctors ordered her bled. The Ambassador sent for the French doctor.

And on March 20th,

> His Excellency came to me at a very early hour to ask me to play the lute for Madam who was much worse. In the midst of my playing the doctors from Treviso arrived and stayed close by her. I went to the Rialto with Captain Feilding. When we returned she was dead. His Excellency is very melancholy and full of sorrow.

The next day Anne Feilding's body was carried to the church of SS Giovanni e Paolo, accompanied by priests with torches and by all the English in Venice.

> ... at five o'clock Madam was taken to the church in a gondola. On arriving she was borne by Coronal Duglas, Captain Feilding, and Rowlandson and me and Parker and Reaves. His Excellency is still very sad and full of deep unhappiness.

That evening, after supper, Captain Feilding asked Reymes if he would be willing to carry the news of Lady Feilding's death to England. Bullen writes, 'I said yes.' It was hard to leave Venice just when his prospects seemed so bright; on the other hand, Bullen had been away from home for four years and was glad of the opportunity to see his family and friends. Then again, to be sent on so important a mission to the King himself was a signal mark of favour and one of the important steps up the ladder of diplomacy. Another, and perhaps determining factor was Reymes's confident belief that he was soon to return to Venice. In any case the die was cast. He was to leave on March 26th.

Every day Bullen climbed the stairs to the little room at the top of the embassy where Basil Feilding lay in his bed, weeping for his young wife, the windows closed and the heavy curtains drawn to keep out the light. The day before he left Reymes says, 'I talked with the Ambassador in his room for two hours about my trip ... He was very sad.' Beyond this and one unfinished sentence — 'I went to the Trumpet and from there went with Knoles' — Bullen has nothing more to say. The rest of the diary is blank.

A curtain descends, and for over a year we know but little of Bullen Reymes and his activities.

II. *English Interlude*

'A gentleman of the Ambassador Feilding who arrived here this week, brings word of the death of the Ambassadress. They are very sorry for this at Court.' So reads the dispatch sent by the Venetian ambassador to the Doge on April 10/20, 1635. When Bullen Reymes, the gentleman in question, went to the Court of King Charles with his unhappy news, he learned that another messenger of ill tidings was on his way to Venice with a report of the death of Anne Feilding's father, Richard Weston, the Earl of Portland and England's Lord Treasurer.

Bullen heard other news. Only a few days before his return, the Duchess of Buckingham had married Randall Macdonnell, the Viscount Dunluce and future Earl of Antrim, and had moved to Wallingford House. London was shaking its collective head at the spectacle of a middle-aged widow and a boy groom. Actually the Duchess was just thirty-two and her new husband was no beardless boy, but a dashing Irishman, only six years her junior. Had she confided in the King she might have won his consent, but Kate, so the story goes, married first and asked permission afterwards. Charles was angry, telling her that he no longer wished to see her at Court, and the Duchess, it was rumoured, was soon to leave for Ireland.

Both Reymes and his father must have recognized the blow Kate's marriage had dealt their own plans and hopes. Bullen could no longer count upon her gifts or her influence at Court; his father's situation was more serious — without the Duchess there would be no place for him in London.

Mary Reymes's letters to her son had been few, brief, and unsatisfactory, but in that bleak summer of 1635, it was Mary who came to Bullen's rescue. Shrewdly alive to young Reymes's needs, she had persuaded her nephew, William Coker, to make over to Bullen the estate of West Chelborough in Dorset, property he had long held in trust for her. It was the income from this estate, a virtual gift from his mother, that was to tide Reymes over for that year, and for many years to come.

THE NEW AMBASSADOR

When he left Venice in March, Reymes had fully expected to return within a few months, but a situation had arisen which was to keep him in London for over a year: recognizing in Bullen a young man of integrity and dependability, Lady Denbigh had decided that Desmond should accompany him to Italy. Lord Desmond's domestic life was in a tangle. The only details about this unhappy affair are in a letter to Basil Feilding:

> Your sister, my lady Desmond, is now suing a divorse of your brother, accused of that I have heard fewe Fildings guiltie of, insufficiency to please a resonable woman. They are in the High Commission Court.[7]

Reymes's departure, depending, as it did, on Desmond's affairs, was constantly postponed.

By the time he was ready to leave, early in May of 1636, Bullen's fortunes had improved considerably. The Duchess, once more enjoying the King's favour, had decided to stay on in London, where the elder Reymes continued to serve her; a portion of the rents from the West Chelborough property was to be sent along with the quarterly allowance, and Lady Denbigh, in recognition of Reymes's duties as Lord Desmond's guardian, had agreed to pay part of his expenses.

CHAPTER TWELVE

COURTESANS AND BANDITS

Early on Thursday morning, May 5th, 1636, Reymes and Desmond left London on the first lap of their Venetian journey. And once more Bullen began to keep a diary. Although it is written in English, the pages are so soaked with heavy blots that many of the entries are unintelligible. The unusually legible first page reads:

> A iournale of my voyage with the Right ho:nble, the Earle of Desmond beginning the 5th of May 1636 when wee both set out together and continewed as followeth, my lord taking with him onely one man, and my selfe,
> Wee departed from London about 5 of the clock, in a coch which cost 18s, and wee overtooke the messenger at Brumbly [Bromley], 7 miles from London, where he stayd for us. Here we tooke horse and went out the rest of that post, which was to Chipsted 10 miles from Brumbly. Thenc to Flimwell 22 miles, where we dyned, thence to Rye 20 miles, where we came about 8 of the clock. We lay at the Mermaide. This night wee shewed our Licence to the offisers. I gave the messenger 18 lb to defray us to Paris ...

Next morning they set sail by '9 of the clocke' and 'at 7 at night came to Dieppe being in all ten houres in the passage. By the waye we were very sicke.' Soon after they landed Reymes met 'Thinn, Pickering and other Inglish gentlemen' who told him that Mr Rowlandson 'was in toune also bound for Ingland'. Surprised and disturbed by this news, Bullen called early next morning at the King's Head, the inn where Rowlandson was staying, only to find that the ship for England had already sailed. So, with his curiosity unsatisfied, he rode on with Desmond and the messenger. By three o'clock on Monday afternoon, May 9/19, they were in Paris.

COURTESANS AND BANDITS

The journey from London to Paris was over the same route that Reymes had taken five years before when, as a boy of seventeen, he had set forth on his first foreign adventure. This time he was all of twenty-two and a seasoned traveller. And this time he had his hands full, for it was he who made all the arrangements, paid the bills, supervised Desmond's expenditure, and wrote regularly to Lady Denbigh, briefing her on the progress of her feckless son.

On May 30th, after almost a fortnight in Paris, Reymes, Desmond and Bastian, 'my Lords man', left for Lyons, travelling by coach over the same roads that Bullen had taken in September of 1633. But from Lyons the route was new. They went by boat down the Rhône to Avignon, where they 'took horse for Axe' (Aix-en-Provence) and Marseilles, whose harbour 'is deep ennuf to beare a ship of 1000 tuns'. Then they 'took horse' again, this time for Nice, and thence by boat to Genoa, where Julio Gentileschi showed them the 'churches and palaces and a fine closet of pictures'.

In spite of rough weather and bad roads and Bastian, who was too ill to travel one day, the three reached Florence on June 28th, and two days later were in Bologna. Here, says Reymes,

> as I was walking through the Piazza I saw a man with a pitcher [picture] in his hand. His name was John Felipe Landa. I went to his house where I bought 3 of him. My lord bought 3 more. In our Inn was loged one Allen Townsen, an Inglish marchant, who is making a dixonare ...

By Thursday evening, July 3rd, the travellers were in Venice, 'most welcomely received by my lords brother. We both lodge at his house. I lie with Capt. Feilding.' So once more Reymes was living in the beautiful palace on the water's edge, an assured and welcome member of the ambassador's 'family'. It was almost as if he had never been away.

The pages of the diary reveal the familiar pattern:

> I went with his Excellency and saw som picturs ... and to the French Ambassador ... where I playd the lute ... My Lord Embassador gave me a lute which cost 3 pistoles. After supper I went with my Lord Embass: in fresco as I was wont ... We had fine musique on the Canall grande ... I playd chess with my Lord Embas: thence to the Course

wheare we saw a match at rowing, the which they call a Regatto ... With Capt. F. and others to St. Marks and to the Trumpet wheare I and all did exceede ... went home with Capt. F. at 4 houres ... Not being well I lay a bed till diner and after diner I did not stir abrode ... I made a vow to Sav[iour] the which I beseach him I may keepe.

Although life in Venice was, as the diary suggests, much as Reymes had known it in 1634, there were some differences. For one thing, Bullen, who had never done any serious studying in Venice, was determined this time to make the most of his opportunities. He had been back only two days before he started Spanish with 'Moyse Garson, a Jew', and a week later was taking lessons on the violin. And there were changes at the embassy. Two new members had been added, Mr Middleton, the chaplain, and Mr Basford, once a member of Wake's household in Paris. On the other hand, Feilding's brother-in-law, Benjamin Weston, and Thomas Rowlandson had gone back to England.

Bullen missed Rowlandson at every turn. He wanted to know why his friend had left. Feilding was unwilling to discuss the matter, but eventually Reymes heard enough from various members of the household to piece together the picture whose background he knew so well. In March of 1635, aware of recent differences between the two men, he had been surprised and gratified to hear Feilding praise the Resident before the College and to see Rowlandson presented with a valuable chain. Six months later the ambassador had changed again, declaring that he could no longer repose any confidence in the Resident and was eager to discharge him. Subsequent to this, however, there seems to have been a reconciliation, and Rowlandson stayed on until the spring of 1636. Something of all this Reymes may have heard while he was in England, but that day in Dieppe he did not know that, at Feilding's request, the King had ordered the Resident's return to England, nor that Rowlandson was soon officially to terminate his position in Venice.

Rowlandson's absence troubled Bullen for other than purely personal reasons. The loss of his stabilizing influence was increasingly apparent as Feilding, carried away by an exaggerated sense of his own importance, grew more and more

COURTESANS AND BANDITS

arrogant and difficult to deal with. Reymes himself seems to have had little trouble with the colourful and usually charming ambassador, but he could not be blind to the resentment that was building up against Feilding in Venice. Possibly he saw other changes in his friend. In March of 1635 he had left the ambassador sorrowing dramatically, but none the less sincerely, for his young wife's death. Now, a year later, he found Basil happily consoling himself with Felecine and certain other accomplished courtesans, and more engrossed than ever in the lighter side of Venetian life. Not that Bullen objected to this type of entertainment. He was no prude, and shows no aversion to his role as Feilding's favourite playmate. He probably upheld 'the unyoked humour' of his friend's 'idleness' partly because it was his job and partly because he enjoyed it.

At least one of Bullen's many lists suggests a degree of cooperation. Eleven names are written under their proper heading which is spelled out in large letters across the top of the page:

THE NAMES OF THE MOST FAMOSE HORES IN VENIS

First	la Honda Perina	Bouconere [?]
et	Juliet Xave	la Bianca
	la Gregetta	Beneta Filtrina
	Lucretia Mantuana	Filiterita qui canta
	la Cernese	Laudivica
	La Sansona	la ——

Here the lists breaks off. Had Reymes continued he might well have added three other names: la Felecine, la Paulina, and la Janette. These were the three whom Lord Feilding and Bullen visited most frequently. Possibly Reymes should have substituted the word 'courtesan' for 'hore'. Certainly the ladies upon whom he and Feilding called were in a different category from the common strumpets and the good-natured wenches who served the gentlemen at the Trumpet and who, apparently, satisfied Lord Desmond's tastes.

As Coryat wrote in 1611, 'The name of a Cortezan of Venice is famoused over all Christendom.' The name, he says, is derived from the word *cortesia* because 'these kind of women are said to receive courtesies from their favorites.' Their toleration in Venice, according to Coryat, is due in part to the belief that, by assuaging the appetites of the men, they serve as a protection to Venetian wives — a belief which he discounts. The main reason they are allowed, he thinks, is the revenues they pay to the Senate, which are large enough to maintain a dozen galleys. Some live in veritable palaces, wearing gowns of damask and bedecked with 'chains of gold and orient pearls'. In warning his reader against the courtesan's seductive charms, Coryat says:

> She will endeavor to enchaunt thee partly with her melodious notes that she warbles out upon her lute, which shee fingers with as laudable a stroake as many men that are excellent professors ... of Musicke, and partly with that heart-tempting harmony of voice. Also thou wilt finde a Venetian Cortezan ... a good Rhetorician, and a most elegant discourser.[1]

Reymes's accounts, though lacking the colour of Coryat, do bear out some of that author's statements. On his arrival in Venice early in July, Bullen had found the ambassador enamoured of la Felicine, and soon was accompanying Basil to the lady's house. His comments on the visits are brief — 'I played on the lute before my Lord and Felicine' and 'After supper we went to Felicinas to heare her sing' — but they do suggest the same attainment in music as described by Coryat.

But before the summer was over, Feilding had transferred his affections. Now Reymes was his regular companion on visits to one Paulina. This was pleasanter, for Paulina had a friend, la Janette, who lived with her in a large house, attended by a retinue of servants. Paulina was unusually accomplished. She played the virginal and lute, sang, and could compose. 'I went after supper with my lord Embassador to la signora Paulina's house, where wee playd the lute ... we stayd till day.' Twice Bullen 'made a saraband' for Paulina, and once she sent him a 'coranto'. Sometimes 'la signora Paulina playd on the Verginoles', but more often she sang, or she and Reymes played together on the lute. He has nothing to say about her conversational powers.

Reymes's position was an anomalous one. He was at once Lord Desmond's business manager and guardian, and the confidant and ever-available comrade of Lord Feilding. How demanding this latter office was, is indicated by Desmond's criticism. 'My Lord Desmond gave me an item for going abrode with any other but my Lord Embass:' A few days later, however, when Bullen talked the matter over with Feilding, 'My Lord Embassador tooke notice of what had passed between Lord Desmond and me and told me what he thot.' What Basil thought was that Reymes was to spend his free time as he wished.

Venice was full of friends with whom Bullen could have spent his 'free time', but those whom he saw most frequently were Dr Cademan, Mr Burrowes, and Captain Richard Feilding. Reymes had a warm spot in his heart for his room-mate, the good-natured and generous Captain who had been the first to come to his aid that day, more than a year before, when he had waited, angry and frightened, in the unsavoury Venetian prison. With him Bullen went to St Stefano, to the plays of the mountebanks in the Piazza of St Mark, and to the various taverns, La Striana, the Green Embers, and their favourite, the Trumpet, where often they 'fell in a vayne of drinking'.

With Dr Cademan, in whose home he had often been entertained in Paris, Reymes often 'did discourse' on surgery, and saw to it that both he and his wife were frequently invited to the embassy. With Mr Burrowes he went to the churches 'to heare the musique'; visited the 'paynters closets' to examine and sometimes to buy their pictures, and haunted the book stalls, where one day he purchased '6 Italian and Spanish books'.

Reymes was reading books as well as buying them. Three or four times a week he writes, 'I red Inglish,' or 'I red Italian and Spanish.' But he mentions only one author — Shakespeare. The entry for August 9th reads: 'I red in my Chasbers booke;' for the next day: 'I red in Shakespeares playes:' and for August 22nd: 'After diner to St. Georges with Mr. Burrowes wher we red in Shakpers booke.' On this and several other afternoons, the two were rowed across the lagoon to the island of 'S. Giorgio Maggiore', where, probably, in the cloister garden of the old Benedictine monastery, they 'red in Shakpers booke'. They must have read aloud, but what plays he and Burrowes chose, Bullen does not stop to say. We wonder if he brought his Shakespeare Folio with him from England or managed to purchase it there in Venice.

Most of Reymes's time, however, was spent with the Earl of

Desmond and Lord Feilding. Every day or so, he played chess with one or the other; on warm summer days he went with them 'in fresco' on the Grand Canal, or 'to St. Marks to heare a mountebank'; he gave His Excellency lessons on the guitar and accompanied him on all his formal calls to the various foreign embassies. Reymes and the young ambassador had much in common: their interest in music, painting and the theatre, and their boundless enjoyment of life. They spent hours together looking at statues, pictures and medals, for Feilding, a connoisseur of sorts, was appreciative of Bullen's taste and knowledge. Basil, when he was not crossed, had much of his famous uncle's charm and affability, so it is little wonder that Bullen, to whom he seldom showed his less attractive side, was devoted to him.

It would be a mistake to conclude that all of Feilding's days were 'playing holidays'. Intelligent and well educated, he was quick to grasp the significance of the many problems which confronted an ambassador, from international affairs to the difficulties regarding merchants' rights. He had developed under Rowlandson's tutelage, and might have gone far had he learned to keep his temper and temper his pride. Whatever reservations Bullen may have begun to feel about some of Feilding's actions, he was gratified to find that the ambassador was beginning to depend upon him in an increasing number of ways. He regularly took Reymes with him to the College and 'discoursed on matters' with him at night, either in his own or Bullen's chamber; he consulted him about his correspondence, and turned over to him, among other things, the 'business of Mr. Henry Hider', a merchant who was having some difficulty about currants.

All seemed to be going well when, on November 3rd, 'My Lord received a bandite into his house.' The idea that an ambassador's house was a sanctuary, where no one could be touched by the Venetian officials, had resulted in a good many abuses and much hard feeling. Apparently Reymes indicated that it was a mistake to harbour such a person, to which opinion Feilding, always insistent upon his rights as an ambassador, took exception. Bullen, told to say nothing about the man's presence, seems to have acquiesced — 'Here came a man to me about a bandit but I did nothing in it ... ' This incident was as close to a misunderstanding with the ambassador as anything Bullen records. He

COURTESANS AND BANDITS

continued to be disturbed by it, and, a few days later, when Feilding was ill with chills and fever, he not only played to him on his lute but 'went to Gilbarts where I bought a statew and gave it to my Lord Emb: It cost me 7 pieces of 8.' The next day 'My Lord Embassador gave me a silver dublet.'

The two were better friends than ever. Feilding went with Bullen to the painters' 'closets' and helped him select the three pictures, whose subjects and the names of the artists who painted them appear in one of Reymes's lists:

> Augustin Carate, Bolognese, made my Olde Man which cost me 10 p. of 8; Dose made my Venus and Cupid which cost me 5 p. of 8; Dionetia Casavia made my St. Katarine which cost me ———.

Then, late autumn brought the opening of the theatrical season. On November 21st, Bullen writes in large letters, 'THE PLAYERS CAME TO TOUN TODAY,' and every entry for the next ten days — until December 1st when Reymes became ill — records a visit to the 'comedie' in the company of the ambassador. Sometimes they went 'to the play at St. Luca's house', and sometimes to St Giovanni e Paolo, for Feilding had a *palco* [box] at both theatres.

Reymes, whose 'indisposition turned to an agew', was ill for more than a month. He missed the Twelfth-Night party at the embassy and gave up both his Spanish and his 'fiddel' masters, but beyond this we know little, for he neglected his diary.

In February there was an occurrence which shook the embassy. It was the affair of the bandits — two of them this time. These disreputable characters, Antonio della Nave and Francesco de' Boni, had found sanctuary in the same little house in which Feilding had harboured a bandit in November. The house, rented by Lord Feilding for the use of his servants, was on the Grand Canal, just across a wide public way from the Giustiniani Palace. The men, who, as it turned out, were seasoned criminals guilty of high treason, had won the credulous ambassador's sympathy. Della Nave said all he had done was to pay a Jew for using his influence with a judge, and de' Boni insisted that all he had done was to eat flesh in Lent.[2]

To the ambassador's dismay the bandits' hiding-place was

discovered. Shortly before daybreak on February 11th, the *sbirri* [Venetian police] broke into the little house to arrest the men. Della Nave, dagger in hand, leaped from the balcony into the water, was fired on by the officers, wounded in the arm, and quickly captured. The other bandit, Francesco de' Boni, was found hiding either in, or under, his bed.

All the shouting, shooting and splashing awakened the people in the embassy across the street. Feilding, furious at what he considered an insult to his house, himself, and his King, hurried to the Collegio in high dudgeon. He told the Senators that unless some apology was made and the men released, he would be unable to continue as ambassador. He went again next day, speaking with even greater passion, and angrily refusing to listen to the Senate's explanation — that there was nothing to indicate that the house was part of the embassy and that the men were guilty of treason, a crime not covered by any immunity or privilege.

The seriousness of the prisoners' crime was evidently a surprise to Feilding. But he had gone too far with his angry protests — or so he foolishly thought — to back down now. He again insisted that the prisoners be released and the *sbirri* punished. The ambassador was probably angered by his gullibility in believing the culprits' tall tales, but he also was blinded by a childishly exaggerated notion of his importance. Moreover, he was in the process of writing the King his own version of the affair, and was in no mood to spoil his story.

The account Basil sent to England had the desired effect. The wrath of his mother and his brother-in-law, the Marquis of Hamilton, fanned this tempest in a teapot into something like an international incident. The energetic Lady Denbigh, who had been trying to get the post of Gentleman of the King's Bedchamber for her son, saw in this affront a good excuse to get him back to England, reasoning that with him there on the spot, his chances for a royal appointment would be better.[3]

Meanwhile, Feilding continued to demand punishment for the *sbirri*, and finally the Venetian Senate wearily agreed to have two of the officers arrested. If found guilty they were to receive punishment. The 'if' was a nice way out for the Venetian authorities, but Feilding's face was saved. The ambassador had his way, but he forfeited the good will of Venice, lost the respect of the French, and was being severely criticized at home. Even some of his friends had written urging him to 'abandon his indefensible attitude'.[4]

Reymes was in the midst of all this altercation, accompanying the ambassador, as was 'his wont', to the *Collegio*, and listening to his angry harangues. He too must have regretted his 'indefensible attitude'. That he voiced his disapproval is doubtful. The remembrance of the November episode was too vivid for him to have made another futile protest. He could not, however, have failed to see the writing on the wall, and this further revelation of Lord Feilding's shortcomings may have softened the blow which the 'affair of the bandits' was to deal him.

As it turned out, the chip-on-the-shoulder sense of importance which Feilding displayed on this occasion was but an earnest of his future conduct. It was a forecast of his later treatment of King Charles, when Basil, piqued because he did not get all the favours he had expected, and forgetful of what Charles had done for him, was to desert his King; fight for Parliament; waver uncertainly back and forth between the two sides and, at length, after the Restoration, come limping back to the Royalists. Truly his was a tragic figure, one endowed with great gifts but corrupted by his own peculiar brand of foolish pride.

Of these future events, Reymes, of course, had no knowledge. All he knew was that he must leave Venice — his career in diplomacy at an end. When Lady Denbigh had seized upon the quarrel over the bandits as a pretext for her son's return, she had also made up her mind that Desmond as well as Feilding should come back to England. The ambassador put off his return as long as he could. Desmond, financially dependent upon his mother, had no choice but to obey. Probably he was glad to go — Reymes never makes that clear. In any case, Bullen, as her son's guardian and, apparently, dependent on Lady Denbigh's bounty, was obliged to accompany 'my Lord Desmond' on his homeward journey.

Whatever his feelings may have been, Reymes indicates no resentment when, on March 5th, 1637, he set down the first — and last — entry in 'The Journal of my Voyage from Venice'.

We came to Padua in a Piotta. My Lord Embass:, Sir John Smith, Windebank, Knowles and Mr. Litten came to Fusina to bring us on our way. Mr. Couet came with us, and Cap. Feilding and Linze and Coronell Duglas is to come with us as far as Brescia. Wee lay at the toune but sent one before to keep the dore open.

Here, as far as the journal goes, the 'dore' closes. On this March day in 1637, Bullen wrote the last lines in the diaries he had started more than five years before.

CHAPTER THIRTEEN

FIGHTING FOR THE KING

Reymes and the Earl of Desmond followed the familiar route to Paris by way of Turin and Lyons. As usual Bullen took over the correspondence. On March 17th he wrote to Lord Feilding from Turin, describing the hospitality of 'the Ducke and Madame', their gift of 'frute, fowle, wine and such like things', and listing the persons who had called to pay their respects. And, writing again on May 5th, shortly after their arrival in Paris, he reports a dinner with 'my Lord Scudemore', the Ambassador in Ordinary, where they were 'most courteously received', but is obviously annoyed by Lord Leicester,[1] the Ambassador Extraordinary, from whom, he says, 'my lord rec'd so littell respect, and such cold entertaynment ... as he is resolved to goe there no more ... '

According to the May letter,[2] Reymes and Desmond daily expected 'to go straight for England', but for some reason their plans changed. When, on July 21st, Bullen wrote again, the mercurial Desmond was chafing to get back to Venice. Possibly the change was due to Lord Feilding himself who, in spite of his mother's entreaties, had decided against going home, and wrote urging Desmond and Reymes to come back to Venice. His 'invitation to the sweete frescoes and musike on the greate Canale' had set Desmond 'on fire to be there', but Lady Denbigh frowned upon the idea, and by September of 1637, the gentlemen were back in London.

This time Reymes was in England for good, and the problems he met were immediate and disturbing. As usual his father's finances were in a sorry state, and his mother, still at Old Buckhurst, was struggling to provide dowries for her daughters. Yet, in spite of this, Mary offered to help her son. But Bullen refused the offer, urging his mother to use all of the Chelborough rent and 'whatever else she had' for his sisters. He intended, he said, 'to stand on his oun two leggs'. Perhaps it was because of this dramatic gesture that by the end of the following year all three of the girls were married.[3]

'To stand on his oun two leggs' was easier to say than to do. The way of an impecunious young gentleman was hard. The only professions open to a man of Reymes's station and training were the Court and the Army. Since, at the moment, there was no opportunity at Court, Reymes chose a military career.

England's long years of peace were almost at an end. In the early spring of 1638 news came of Scotland's National Covenant, a manifesto defying Charles's attempts to change that country's manner of worship, accompanied by a threat to expel all who refused to sign. To deal with the Covenanters, Charles chose as his Commissioner the Marquis of Hamilton, instructing him to tell the recalcitrant Scots that he himself was ready to come with a 'power' to enforce obedience. By the following spring England and Scotland were at war. If Reymes fought in the First Scots War — there is no evidence that he did — he could have seen but little action, for the conflict was brief and, for the English, disastrous. By June 19th, 1639, the war was over.

Charles was going steadily ahead with his preparations for a Second Scots War when, on August 16th, 1640, word came that Newcastle was threatened by a Scottish invasion. Four days later the Scots crossed the Tweed, meeting the English at Newcastle upon Tyne, where they defeated them ignominiously and overwhelmingly. Whether Reymes, who was serving as sixth Captain of Foot under Sir James Hamilton, saw any action, we do not know. In any case, the war with Scotland and the first brief chapter in Reymes's military career had come to an end.

Both Mary Reymes and her husband and, for that matter, Bullen himself, were well aware that neither military service nor a career at Court would do away with financial worries. In the seventeenth century there was only one sure and approved remedy for a gentleman in need — a provident marriage. For careful parents to arrange marriages for their children was the accepted procedure, and sons, as well as daughters, usually accepted their suggestions. Parents seldom searched far afield. As one squire put it, 'I never look farther than a rabbit can hop.'

The little village of Mapowder in central Dorset, some twelve miles north of Dorchester, would have been a rather long hop from Mary Reymes's native Devon, but it had been close to her affections ever since she could remember. She had stayed there often with her sister Thomasine, who had married Robert Coker when Mary was only six. Even after Thomasine's death she had continued her visits. The principal object of her affection was her nephew William, but she adopted as her own all the Coker clan, even her brother-in-law's new wife, Amy Molford Coker. Bullen, as a child, had visited the many-acred estate of the Cokers and had early developed a healthy respect for his great aunt, his 'deare Aunt Eme Coker', as he called her. Writing from France of his many obligations to her, he assured his aunt that 'only the earnestnes of my studyes, and diligence in my exersises heare in Paris hath forced me to live all this time with out presenting my duty to you — with whom my tyes are so infinite.' The 'tyes' were to be more 'infinite' than he had realized.

Amy Coker was a remarkable woman. When her daughter Anne died in 1633, and Anne's husband, Thomas Gerrard, the following year, Amy took their five orphan daughters into her home to rear as her own. When the little Gerrard girls were brought to Mapowder late in December of 1634, Elizabeth, the eldest, was only twelve. It was Elizabeth whom Mary had long hoped her son might marry. Besides belonging to a family close to Mary's heart, Elizabeth possessed the worldly goods Bullen so sorely needed. She and her three sisters — Amy Gerrard had died in 1637 — were co-heirs of their father's extensive properties, the manor of Trent (then in Somerset), and the estates of Waddon, Broadway, and Nottingham in Dorset.

Of the young couple's reactions to Mary's plans there is no record. Possibly Bullen was influenced by worldly motives as well as by filial obedience. Still, there is no proof of this. In any event, some time in 1640, Elizabeth and Bullen were married in the twelfth-century stone church in the village of Mapowder. Not more than 400 yards across the fields from the church stood Coker Hall, with its sixteen chimneys and its wide gateway, flanked by two stone pillars, atop each the head of a blackamoor. This large, but already crowded, manor house was to be Bullen's and Elizabeth's home for the next eight years.

Probably Reymes spent much of the plague-ridden summer of

1641 in Mapowder. But he would have been back in London by early autumn, for he had been appointed Gentleman of the King's Privy Chamber — possibly Elizabeth's dowry had eased the way — and was slated to serve the third quarter which ran from October 1st to the end of December. There were forty-eight 'Gentlemen of the Privy Chamber in Ordinary' who, as King Charles put it, 'shall be divided to wayt by their Quarters: and such of them as shall not accordingly wayte ... shall loose theire place.'[4] At one time the gentlemen had been paid, but they no longer received a salary, 'being content to serve for the Honour of the Place' and 'by Marks of the King's Favour as Opportunity offers'. Their duties were varied and privileges great, although Charles seems to have set limits to the freedom of their movement about the Court. To quote the King again:

> The Gentlemen that wayt in Quarter shall attend, six of them, when wee eate in our Privy Chamber for the carrying in of our meate to the board & ... four of them by turne shall lodg every night within our Privy Chamber ... No Privy Chamber men ... shall presume to come in Bootes ... nor leane upon the Table nor sitt when the salt is on the board.

Beyond lodging and diet for three months each year, the position offered no material recompense. But daily contact with the King, as well as constant association with important persons of the Court, were enviable advantages. In ordinary times the opportunities for a personable young man of Bullen's intelligence, training, and ambition would have been impressive indeed. These, however, were not ordinary times. In the first place, the King was in Scotland during much of the third quarter, and an atmosphere of gloom prevailed in the anxious and financially straitened Court. The plague persisted, and the second session of Parliament, which had opened on October 20th, promised continuing opposition to the King.

On Guy Fawkes Day, November 5th, John Pym launched his attack, declaring that Parliament should have the right to choose the King's servants. This was followed by the House's acceptance of the 'Remonstrance', a humiliating record of all of Charles's misdeeds, and, on December 7th, by the first reading of the Militia Bill. The most formidable weapon in Pym's arsenal, this Bill sought to transfer the command of the militia and trained bands from the King to Parliament. No wonder the air was electric with discord and fear.

On the first day of January, 1642, an ugly rumour reached the ear of the King: Parliament was about to impeach his Queen. Neither the Remonstrance nor the Militia Bill could have spurred Charles to such speedy action as did this threat to his beloved Henrietta. On Monday, January 3rd, Pym and his associates were accused of high treason, and on Tuesday afternoon the King himself marched to the House to arrest the five recalcitrant members. But the secret had leaked out, and even as Charles was approaching Westminster, the so-called traitors were being rowed down stream to London. All his birds had flown.

King Charles's bold plan had ended in humiliating defeat. By his defiance of Parliamentary privilege and his futile show of force he had alienated the entire House and lost any lingering good will in London. Six days later, his confidence gone, and fearful for the safety of his Queen, Charles hurried away in the dark of a January night with Henrietta Maria and three of their children, turning his back on Whitehall and Westminster, places he would not see again until another dark January, eight years away, when he, the King, was to be condemned as a traitor to his country.

The conflict between King and Parliament was rapidly changing from a political debate to war, recognizable, if undeclared. Weeks before August 22nd, 1642, when the King raised the Royal Standard at Nottingham, men had started to take sides. Neighbours, friends, relatives were often in opposing camps. Reymes saw rifts among his friends and in his own family. William Russell, the Earl of Bedford, a Parliament man, was at odds with his sister Ann and her husband, the Royalist George Digby. And there was conflict in the Denbigh family. The Earl of Denbigh was to die fighting for Charles, but his son, Basil, Lord Feilding, in spite of his mother's grief and protests, deserted the King and became a leader in the Parliamentary forces.

Even the tranquillity of little Mapowder was broken by political quarrels. The majority of the Cokers were for the King. Bullen's cousin, William Coker, was one of the commissioners appointed to levy contributions for the King's forces, and served as Colonel under Lord Hopton, but his eldest son, Robert, was Lieutenant-Colonel in the Parliamentary forces. Another son, Henry, served Charles for a time, but later went over to the Roundheads.

Although religious differences played their part, the Civil War was not primarily a religious war. Nor was it, strictly speaking, a class war. Too many of the gentry and nobility fought on the side of Parliament to justify that label. In its essence it was a conflict of principles. Some, it is true, blindly followed the opinions of others, and some were moved by personal ambition, but a surprising number of persons honestly tried to find and follow the 'right' course. There was a probing of consciences amongst Cavaliers as well as Puritans.

The first important battle of the war was fought at Edgehill on October 23rd, 1642.[5] This was the conflict in which the cavalry charge of the King's nephew, the dashing Prince Rupert, brought such dismay to the Parliamentary leader, Lord Essex. In one sense Edgehill was a victory for the King. He had thrown off his pursuers and had a clear track to London. Had he marched straight on, Charles might, some say, have won the war in its first year. But he lingered at Oxford.

Here, in this ancient seat of learning, where Charles held his Court, allegiance was divided. The University was solidly behind the King, but the town was pro-Parliament. The town's loyalty was, however, tempered by the nice profit it was making from the visiting Cavaliers, crowded into dingy quarters and paying exorbitant prices for their food and lodging.

As Gentleman of the Privy Chamber, Reymes had been serving in the exiled Court almost continually from the late fall of 1642 until the following spring. In April, less than a month before he left Oxford, he witnessed an unpleasant spectacle: Colonel Richard Feilding was tried and threatened with death and disgrace for his part in the surrender of Reading. This was the generous, outspoken Captain Feilding who had shared his room with Bullen at the embassy in Venice, and who had been the first to come to his aid when he was thrown summarily into the prison behind the Rialto.

Lord Essex, on April 16th, had advanced from Windsor to lay siege to Reading. Sir Arthur Aston, in command of the Royalist garrison there, not wishing to risk his reputation on so poorly defended a place, was 'conveniently struck dumb'[6] by a falling tile, and the responsibility fell on the shoulders of Colonel Feilding. Realizing the futility of defending the town, Feilding was concerned only with saving the garrison, and on April 27th surrendered on favourable terms — the honours of war and safe passage of the soldiers to Oxford.

There was sharp criticism of Feilding, some suspecting that since his kinsman, Basil, Lord Feilding, was fighting for Parliament, the Colonel had been bribed — as much as £16,000, it was whispered. Feilding was brought before a court martial and condemned to death, the King approving the sentence. But when he mounted the scaffold there was such an angry protest that Charles relented, and the prisoner was allowed to descend. Then, the voices of his enemies prevailing, the King about-faced and the poor man once more climbed the steps to the scaffold. At this crucial moment Feilding was saved by the pleadings of the young Prince of Wales, and climbed down for the second and last time. It was Rupert who, sympathizing with Colonel Feilding's dilemma, had urged Prince Charles to intervene.[7] Reymes could not have failed to side with his old friend's supporters. Perhaps his voice helped to turn the tide.

On May 15th, 1643, Reymes left Oxford, marching into the west with Prince Maurice and the Marquis of Hertford. Apparently 'they did little on the march but raise men and arms'[8] until June 4th, when they met Sir Ralph Hopton and his Cornish Cavaliers at Chard, the 'lace town' in west Somerset. Hopton's forces, combined with those of Maurice and Hertford, added up to around 7,000 men. The Royalists had managed to occupy Taunton, Bridgwater, Wells and Dunster Castle with little difficulty, but Waller, in command of the Parliamentary forces in the west, had taken Bristol and Gloucester and was now concentrating his army in the vicinity of Bath. The inevitable struggle between the two forces reached its climax on July 13th at the Battle of Roundway Down, a clear and sweeping victory for the King.

At about this time the elderly Marquis of Hertford retired to Oxford to act as one of the King's councillors, and Prince Maurice assumed command of the Western Army. Shortly after the fall of Bristol to the Royalists on July 24th, Lord Carnarvon, the Lieutenant-General of Horse in the west, advanced towards

Dorchester with Horse and Dragoons, Maurice following a little later with the slow-moving Foot. When, on August 4th, Carnarvon summoned Dorchester to surrender, that city, although well fortified and Puritan in its sympathies, was won over by Carnarvon's promises of good treatment, and gave up without firing a shot. Unfortunately, Maurice, inexperienced in English ways, gave his men permission to plunder. Whereupon Carnarvon, angry at the wrong done those to whom he had given his word, threw up his command and rode to Gloucester to lay his case before the King who, characteristically, did nothing about it. This was the last time Bullen ever saw the good friend he had learned to know so well on the Levantine journey, for Robert Dormer, Earl of Carnarvon, was killed that same year at the first battle of Newbury.

Reymes had been with the Western Army ever since he left Oxford in the middle of May, but with what rank we do not know. Possibly he had been serving as a volunteer while awaiting a suitable appointment. When, however, he returned to Dorchester with Maurice, the Prince, on 'this 10th day of August 1643', commissioned him 'Captayne of a Company of 100 Foote'.

In Dorset only Poole, Wareham, and Lyme Regis were still faithful to Parliament. When Maurice realized that Poole could not be reduced without a long siege, he decided first to complete the conquest of Devon. So Reymes marched west again with Prince Maurice and the Western Army. They moved first against Exeter, and when its governor, the Earl of Stamford, refused to surrender, they blocked all entrances to the city. Finally, on September 4th, the garrison, deprived of all hopes of relief, surrendered on 'Articles of agreement made in the Cittie of Exon ... the 5 of Sep: 1643'. The 'Articles' seem eminently fair. Whether they were carried out to the letter is another matter. The chances are, however, that Sir John Berkeley, the new governor, did his best to live up to their spirit during the Royalists' three-year occupation of the city — this despite such visitors as the difficult George Goring. But one account, 'The Tyranny of the Cavaliers', gives a grim picture:

> They which are called Prince Rupert & ... Maurice his Cavaliers are ... addicted to such cruelties, that they shew

themselves like Tigers ... The rude Souldiers would not forbeare ... to draw their Rapiers upon the Citizens ... but especially when they are in their Cups they swagger, roare ... and domineere ... To break shops and houses they count as nothing, taking away Boots, Stockings, Hats ... Sir John Berkeley is ... of such vile disposition that he favours their wicked designes ... and that perfidious Chudley who ... betrayed us ... at Stratton for which piece of Service he was made a Commander amongst the Cavaliers ... [9]

That 'perfidious Chudley' was to become, for a short time, an important person in the life of Bullen Reymes, who on September 5th, the very day the 'Articles' were signed, was made Lieutenant-Colonel in Chudleigh's regiment. Whether his rapid advancement was due to some special service he had rendered or merely to the exigencies of the time, Reymes does not say. Although his commission, signed by Maurice, refers 'to yr Courage, deligence, dexterity in Martiall affaires', these were words commonly used in military commissions.

The actual evacuation of the Roundheads took place on September 7th. On the 19th Maurice and his men left for Dartmouth. The Cavaliers sent '500 Dragoneers to Salcombe to stop the passage of any provision coming thither, also they seized all their Boats, Barks and Horse, but men of Dartmouth behaved ... so bravely that they found a piece of hot service there.' So reads the same *Thomason Tract* which described the Cavaliers' occupation of Exeter.

The service was hot but the weather was cold and wet, and before Dartmouth finally surrendered on October 6th, the Cavaliers had suffered many casualties. Some of the men succumbed to the 'raging fever' which played havoc with the soldiers forced to sleep on the cold, damp ground; and some died on the battlefield, among them Colonel James Chudleigh. The death of this fiery and able young officer meant advancement for Reymes, next in command. Just when he succeeded to Chudleigh's post is not clear, for his commission as Colonel has not been preserved. It must, however, have been before October 17th, for on that date Reymes, writing to one William Guy, signs himself 'Colonell'.

CONSCIENTIOUS CAVALIER

Prince Maurice seems to have suffered from the 'raging fever' or 'new disease', as Dr Harvey described it. Possibly that was why he stayed on at Dartmouth for more than a month after its surrender.[10] Most of the Cavaliers had left for Plymouth, the next point of attack, much earlier. In fact, a few had been stationed in the environs of that city since the middle of September. Bullen kept a letter which his friend Colonel John Digby, on September 29th, 1643, sent 'To the seduced Marriners and Souldiers in Plymouth', in which, after assuring them that the reports of cruelty and wicked aims of the Cavaliers are false, he writes:

> We have thought fitt to ... assure you that such as shall quitt that rebellious toune of Plymouth and come unto us ... shall have free liberty to depart to their homes, or if they have a mind to serve in the just cause we fight for, shall be entertained and duly paid six shillings p. weeke as our Souldiers are.

This attempt at recruiting not only proved unsuccessful, but on October 8th, Digby's guard was routed by Colonel Wardlaw, the Commander at Plymouth, and his supplies and fifty soldiers seized.

The people of Plymouth had built a wall extending from the Castle as far east and south as Sutton Pool; they had a fort on the Hoe, the elevated esplanade overlooking the Sound, and bulwarks on Drake's Island to the south; and north of the town they had constructed a low, earthen rampart and ditch which connected a series of earthen redoubts. In addition there were a number of detached 'works' and, of course, they had the sea which formed an almost complete natural moat. Yet, in spite of their strong defences, the townspeople had become increasingly apprehensive, as more and more Royalist troops began to pour in.

Maurice had five regiments of Horse and nine of Foot stationed at a variety of places, most of them within a radius of five miles of Plymouth. On November 16th Antony Kempson, Maurice's secretary, wrote to 'Coll. Reimes' that

> all Foote ... are to bee all in Armes ... That the Randevous for the five old Cornish regiments ... with those that are att Saltram House shall be held by nyne of the clock tomorrow

FIGHTING FOR THE KING

morning on this side Newbridge and that the Randevous for the rest of the Foote shall be held ... at Mount Stamford.

Probably other officers received comparable orders. The city was more or less hemmed in, and when on November 18th the Royalists offered terms of surrender, the townsfolk were ready to accept. But Colonel Wardlaw refused the offer and the Royalists made no attack.

The next four weeks were comparatively quiet, the only action on the part of the Cavaliers being an assault upon a small redoubt near Lipson Mill and south of Compton Hill.[11] Colonel Reymes may have taken part in this engagement, for on December 12th he received from Joseph Wagstaff, the Sergeant Major-General of Foot, the following letter:

> You are to be with your Regiment tomorrow morning an hour before day on Compton Hill ... Sr., heare is allso two hundred dragoons of Collonell Digby's Regiment. When you have done with them you may send them to there quarters ... '[12]

Apparently the engagement at Lipson Mill met with little success, and when, on December 20th, almost a hundred of their men were lost in an attempt to surprise Maudlyn Fort, the Cavaliers, disheartened by the disease in camp — the wet weather 'breeding such a rot' that the soldiers lay in the trenches, sick and maimed and dying — decided to abandon the attack. On Christmas Day, the very day Maurice had boasted that Plymouth would be taken, the siege was raised.[13]

Maurice, leaving a garrison under Colonel Digby at Plymton, marched to Tavistock, some twelve miles north of Plymouth, where he took up quarters for the rest of the winter. There, on December 27th, Reymes received from Thomas Bassett, Major-General in the Brigade command, the following order for review of troops:

> Sr, You are required upon receipt hereof to give comaund to e'vy Capt of your Regiment to drawe his whole Company into Armes. And you your selfe in your oune p'son to view all the Armes in your Regimt and to take especiall care that

the unfixt Armes be fixt with all possible speede, and that noe Muskett want a scouring stick and that every Soldier have allwayes in garrison, 12 bullets att his bandeleers, fitted to the boare of his peece. And that hee never charge his peece when hee hath leasure without putting a Tampking after the Powder and another after the bullett, and that heere you give me a speedy account ...

The orders from Bassett indicate the detailed knowledge of, and responsibility for, the equipment of his troops expected of the Colonel of a regiment. As a matter of routine responsibility, Reymes would have done his best to equip his men — many of whom he had himself conscripted — with their regulation coat, breeches, stockings and cap; he would have been familiar with their armour and weapons, and would have understood the difficulties his musketeers encountered with their matchlocks, useless in the rain and inaccurate at best, and with their so-called 'Twelve Apostles', the far-from-adequate twelve cartridges hanging from their broad belts or 'Bandoleers'.

Colonel Reymes did not stay continually at Tavistock during the winter months of 1644. With the exception of occasional trips to Mapowder, he was with Sir John Berkeley in Exeter. In early spring, however, he rejoined Prince Maurice and marched east with him to Lyme Regis, the small Dorset port which had been in the hands of Parliament since early in 1642.

Lyme Regis, 'a praty market-toun set in the rootes of an high rokky hill doun to a hard shore',[14] lay on the Dorset coast just east of the Devon border. Lyme was small but strategic and, like Plymouth and all coastal towns, could depend for supplies and occasional military aid upon the Roundheads who, having seized the major portion of the navy, were in command of the sea. Hence the Cavaliers' attack must be by land. This looked easy enough, for the town was not well fortified, boasting little more than a few forts on the land side and five guns which guarded the 'Cobb', the roadstead which served as a harbour. In fact, so small and defenceless did the little sea-side village seem, that the Royalists are said to have declared it would be 'but breakfast work ... that they would not dine 'till they had taken it.'[15]

But little Lyme was to prove as stubborn as tough old Plymouth.

FIGHTING FOR THE KING

At the start the Royalists seem to have had everything their own way. Early on Saturday morning, April 20th, Maurice marched 'with a full body before the towne' and that night took possession of a number of near-by houses.[16] The next day, Easter Sunday, Colonel Reymes commanded a successful attack on Stidecombe House, some three miles from Lyme, where a garrison of Roundheads was quartered. These small initial successes were followed by weeks of fruitless attacks in which many Cavaliers were slain or wounded. Among the most seriously wounded was Reymes's own Lieutenant-Colonel, William Phillips.[17]

By June the attack had degenerated into little more than a blockade, which the town, under the able leadership of Colonel Robert Blake and fortified by supplies brought by sea, withstood with a minimum of discomfort. So when Prince Maurice heard that the Parliamentary commander, Lord Essex, was on his way to relieve Lyme, he gave up the siege and, at two o'clock in the morning of June 15th, 1644, withdrew his forces, burning, as he went, a number of country homes, including Stidecombe House which Reymes had taken two months before.

The loss of the two ports, Plymouth and Lyme Regis, was a serious blow to the Royalist cause. Maurice has been criticized for his failure to take the 'little vile fishing village' of Lyme, but his stubborn siege of that small town did accomplish one thing — it drew Essex away from Waller and the pursuit of the King.[18]

Reymes, marching back to Devonshire with the 'Great Western Army', had been in Exeter for some time before the King arrived on July 26th to review Maurice's troops. Whether he stayed on in that city or accompanied Prince Maurice into Cornwall, taking part in the King's spectacular success at Lostwithiel on September 2nd, we do not know. Since, however, he makes no reference to the Lostwithiel campaign, the chances are that, with the exception of the siege of Taunton the following spring, he was in Exeter continually until its fall in 1644.

Exeter and the Devon countryside were no strangers to Bullen. His own visits and the stories his mother had told him of her old home and her Petre relatives were part of his earliest memories. There were still Petres living in Exeter, and his grandfather's home, where Bullen had been born, still stood in its spacious grounds in the parish of St Thomas, across the river Exe. At the moment the city was crowded with soldiers, and, like Oxford, was a refuge for exiled courtiers and even for members of the royal family.

Reymes had been on his way to Lyme Regis when, on April 17th, 1644, the Queen, pregnant and ill, bade farewell to the husband she was never to see again, and set out for Exeter. There she was welcomed by the garrison and loyal citizens and conducted to Bedford House where, on June 16th, she gave birth to a daughter, Henrietta. The baby was christened in the Cathedral, Bullen's friend, Sir John Berkeley, acting as one of the sponsors. A few weeks later, fearing that she might fall into the hands of the Roundheads, the Queen, leaving her baby in Exeter with Lady Dalkeith, went to Falmouth and, on July 14th, barely two weeks before the King and the Prince of Wales arrived in Exeter, sailed for France on a Dutch man-of-war.

In spite of the brilliant victory at Lostwithiel there was growing discouragement amongst the Cavaliers. In the summer of 1644 they had lost the north of England at the battle of Marston Moor, and by the following spring the discontent had spread. Prince Maurice had rejoined the Oxford army and, in the west, the courageous but quarrelsome and dissolute George Goring was in command. On March 11th he laid siege to Taunton, which was defended by the same Robert Blake who had held out so doggedly at Lyme Regis the year before. After a two-month siege, when Goring, aided by Hopton and Berkeley — under whom Reymes was serving — had finally reduced the exhausted garrison to the point of surrender, General Fairfax came to Blake's relief and the Royalists were forced to withdraw.

The loss of Taunton on May 11th, though a serious blow, was but a prelude to the series of disasters which crowded the remaining months of 1645. On June 14th the King's main army was totally defeated at Naseby by Parliament's 'New Model Army', and on July 10th Sir Thomas Fairfax overcame Goring at Langport in Somerset. Before the end of the month he had taken Bridgwater and Bath, and on September 10th had defeated Prince Rupert at Bristol. By the end of December he was at Crediton, barely eight miles from Exeter. Little wonder that the garrison there was filled with foreboding.

With 1646 the outlook for the King's forces was still darker.

FIGHTING FOR THE KING

After relieving Plymouth and storming Dartmouth, Fairfax marched against Hopton at Torrington and, with the surrender on March 14th of that doughty soldier, all hope for Exeter faded. On March 31st Fairfax 'summoned' Sir John Berkeley, the Governor of Exeter. Berkeley, in want of provisions, and with no hope of succour, agreed to a truce of six days, and surrendered on 'Articles' on April 8th.

The twenty-four Articles of Surrender are very fair, perhaps even more liberal than those of 1643. The garrison was at liberty to go home or to the nearest garrison of the King; the citizens were not to be plundered, could choose their own magistrates, and enjoy all the privileges they had had before the war, and, most important of all, no oath or covenant, protestation or subscription was to be imposed on any person within the walls. Nobody, except those exempted by Parliament from pardon and composition, was to be

> questioned or accountable for any Act past by them done ... relating unto the unhappy differences betwixt his Majesty and Parliament, they submitting themselves to reasonable and moderate composition for their Estates, which the General, Sir Th. Fairfax, shall really endeavour with the Parliament, that it shall not exceed two years value of any mans reall Estate ...

When the Cavaliers marched out of Exeter on April 13th, 1646, Reymes's military career was at an end, and so, for that matter, was the great Civil War. It dragged on, it is true, for a few more months, but Parliament, with such men as Fairfax and Cromwell in command, was too powerful for the waning forces of the King, a fact which most Royalists were wise enough to recognize. The country was too exhausted, too war-weary to continue the struggle. Peace was in the air. What Englishmen, Roundhead and Cavalier alike, wanted and expected was a reconciliation between King and Parliament.

CHAPTER FOURTEEN

PAYING THE ROYALIST PENALTY

1. *Restrictions and Fines*

ON that April day in 1646 when Colonel Reymes rode out of Exeter with his 'two servants and horses and necessaryes' he carried in his pocket a precious paper, endorsed 'My pas to London From Exeter by Lord Fairfax'. Henceforth passes were to be some of the most important items in his life. Until the Restoration, fourteen years away, plagued by fines and prohibited from travelling more than five miles from home, he was to live under virtual house-arrest.

Like so many of those about him, Reymes must long since have realized the inevitability of the Royalist defeat. And, like others, with little notion of the long years of waiting that lay ahead, he probably believed that some sort of agreement between King and Parliament was close at hand. At the moment, however, his concern was with his own immediate problems — the welfare of his family and the journey he must make to London 'to compound with Parliament' for his estate, which the pass from Fairfax 'suffered' him to make 'quietly and peaceably without any interruption or Molestation'.

As early as March 27th, 1643, Parliament had issued a sequestration ordinance, naming all who aided the King delinquents, and ordering their property to be sequestered by the commissioners of the county in which it was located. A later ordinance had mitigated this sentence and, by 1646, a delinquent who wished to free his estate from sequestration was allowed to present himself before the Committee for Compounding at Goldsmiths' Hall in London. There he was obliged to take the Negative Oath, by which he agreed to declare the full value of his estate and promise never to take up arms against Parliament. Although members of Parliament who had sided with the King might lose

PAYING THE ROYALIST PENALTY

half their estates, ordinary Royalists often had to pay no more than one-sixth. In Dorset, however, one-fifth was demanded.

Now that the war in the west was over, tensions in Mapowder had relaxed. Any animosity which may have existed between the dedicated Royalist, William Coker, and his son Robert, a Lieutenant-Colonel in the Parliamentary forces, seems to have disappeared. Robert Coker, now a member of the Dorset Committee for Compounding, was doing his best to lighten the fines of his father and his cousin Bullen.

During his stay in Mapowder, Reymes apparently worked on his petition for compounding as zealously as he had once struggled over his letters to the Duchess of Buckingham. He made several drafts, but the one he finally decided on and presented at Goldsmiths' Hall in London on June 27th was brief and to the point:

Humb. sheweth
That yr Pet. being a sworne Servant to his Maty: was by him Commanded into the West, where he bore armes in his servis, and was at Exeter at the late rendring thereof to Sir T. F.

One of the discarded drafts is longer and more informative:

Humbly Sheweth
That yr petitioner being a sworne servant to his Maty in the place of gent. of his prive chamber 'did according to his duty wayte' [erased] and being 'commanded' [erased] warned to wayte on him at Oxford, did so, till his Maty commande him into the West with the Marqs of Hertford, where according to his former proffession of a souldier he toke up armes, and there continued till within this year and halfe, at which time yor petitioner reformed himselfe and ever since remayned quietly in Exeter, but in all this time was never violent in the prosecuting the person of any man, or did ever take the goods of any man directly or indirectly to the vallew of a farding. May it therefore please yor honours to admit him to compound ...

Meanwhile the Dorset Committee had written to Goldsmiths' Hall on Reymes's behalf:

Right Noble
At the request of Coll: Reymes, we doe humbly certify that

the sayd Coll: Reymes was by us sequestered for taking up armes against the Parlement ... yet ... he hath not committed any violent act against us ... nor borne armes since the sedge of Taunton ... and hath ben always reddy to protect well affected persons from the violence and rappen of the souldiers when that partie did prevaile, and likewise he hath payd the 20th ... part of his estate, and therefore in regards of his estate come by his wife, who hath a great Charge, we humbly recommend him to yr loships favor ... A perticuler of his estate wee send here inclosed.

The 'perticuler' states that Reymes is 'seized of an estate in the right of his wife' for the fourth part of Broadway and Waddon in Dorset of the yearly value of £40, and of Trent in Somerset of £20.

It is interesting to note here that a draft of the Dorset Committee letter says that Reymes had taken the 'negative oath'. No doubt this was omitted in the final letter because Reymes had surrendered under the 'Articles' at Exeter which had stipulated that 'no oath ... be imposed on any person within the walls'. Probably it was this fact, plus Robert Coker's influence, which kept the fine down to £100.[1]

But in those lean years £100 were hard to come by. Caught in his old dilemma — lack of money — Bullen wrote to his mother, asking if there was any property of his late uncle, Sir George Petre, on which he might borrow. Mary Reymes replied indignantly and at length. In three closely written but badly torn pages, she explains the ten-year legal battle over Sir George's estate. The executor, cousin John Petre of Exeter, had laid claim to the part of the property which should have gone to George's brother Robert, his sister Mary and his nephew, William Coker. Finally, due to Mary's persistence, the lawyers had decided that John could keep half the estate, the rest going to Mary Reymes and William Coker. Mary writes:

> Soe now all is ended to our grate cost and trobel ... and any suspition yt [that] my loving Motherly intentions are not ... for ye good of B. R. is to me a Mistery but ...

The rest of the sheet is torn off, and the next page, the best-preserved of all, begins:

PAYING THE ROYALIST PENALTY

Queeres to be considered: whether if you had benn a single man you had ever binn jealous of ye carefull love of yr Mother. And wts [what's] become of yt [that] consayt [conceit] you had and profes'd to me at ye return from yr travels, yt of wt soe ever [that of whatsoever] I had, you desired, nor looked for ye least mite, nor anything, for you would stand on yr owne leggs, but desired ye matches of yr Sisters. See whether I omitted any ye least occation on all turns to show my Love and diligence for yr good & profitt ... And now shew me when & wher I gave you ye least cause of this yr jealousy. Did I not take ye deed [?] from my nephew Coker in Chelborough & made it conferd on you, for ye grace then & for ye profitt since? I must live on my oune ye wch [the which] you would have yr owne presently. Tell me ... how I have merited this ... having in all things ... complyed to yr desires to my oune great folly ... Soe you see ... sonn yt neither of yr uncles dy'd [died] possessed of one [ac]er of land, ye younger never had any, and ye Elder sold all ...

It is all there in this fragmentary letter — the energy, the shrewdness, the quick anger, the honest concern for her son, the suspicion and the never-failing self-pity — all part and parcel of this exasperating spitfire of a little woman, whom Bullen, in spite of his affection and understanding, must often have longed to shake.

On April 27th, 1646, the day Reymes was in London presenting his petition at Goldsmiths' Hall, King Charles, disguised as a servant, his beard and hair cut short, rode out of Oxford and on to the north and his futile parleys with the Scots. By the end of June, Rupert, Maurice, and all the other Royalists had left Oxford. On July 30th peace was proclaimed and the First Civil War was officially at an end. But, even as the country was rejoicing in the prospect of a return to normal living, the stage was being set for the three-cornered quarrel between the Presbyterian-dominated Parliament, the Army, and the King, a quarrel which was to develop into the unpopular Second Civil War and its tragic aftermath.

In 1647, the custody of the King became a matter of prime importance. When the Scots finally realized that Charles had no intention of satisfying their demands, they lost all interest in taking him to Scotland, and when Parliament, on February 3rd, daid the £100,000 still due to them, they performed their part of the bargain by turning the captive King over to the English soldiers at Newcastle. That same day Charles was taken to Holmby [Holdenby House] in Northamptonshire, where he was to stay for four months in the custody of the Commissioners of Parliament.

The contest for the King now lay between Parliament and the Army. Distrustful of Cromwell's promise that the Army, if paid, would disband, and afraid that it planned to get possession of the monarch's person, Parliament decided to forestall such a coup by taking Charles to a safer place. The Army, to prevent just such a manoeuvre, sent Cornet Joyce of Major-General Whalley's regiment to Holdenby House. And Joyce, on June 3rd, either on orders from Cromwell, or on his own initiative, took Charles to the King's own hunting-lodge in Newmarket.

The Presbyterian-dominated Parliament, with no force other than the London Militia, realizing that they could not uphold their authority against the Army, felt that the only course was to restore the King to some limited authority. Hence developed their tentative alliance with certain of the Royalists. They needed to know where the King stood. How far had he been won over by the Army? Had he left Holmby of his own volition, or had he been seized against his will?

It is at this juncture that Bullen Reymes stepped into the picture. About the middle of June he went to Newmarket to visit the King. Just how this journey came about we do not know, but on Thursday, June 17th, 1647, Reymes gave to the Committee of the Militia of London and to the House of Peers an account of his talk with Charles. Possibly Robert Coker had suggested to Parliament that his cousin, who had served as a Gentleman of the Privy Chamber, would be a good person to discover the answers to their questions. As a member of the Dorset Committee, Coker would have been able to secure the necessary pass.

According to his report, Reymes was greeted at Newmarket by one of the Commissioners, Major-General Richard Browne, who procured for him an audience with the King. While they were waiting in the 'prescence Room', Browne regaled Reymes with an account of an altercation between Charles and Major Whalley, 'whom the King had that day struck for being so presumptuous as to listen while his Majesty was in conference with one whom they suspected to be come from London.' Browne, one of the Parliamentary Commissioners who had come from Holdenby at the King's insistence, was naturally hostile to Whalley and the other Army officers, and told Reymes 'that it did highly concerne both the Parliament and the City to be careful of their safeties', adding that he was 'an ear witness daily to their threats ... and how much they are inrag'd with hatred to Parliament'. Reymes adds: 'This he desired me to deliver, and so led me into the Privie Chamber.'

When the King came out of his bedchamber, Major-General Browne entreated him

> to confirme the Relations he [the King] had given me [Browne] of his Majestie's unwillingness to come from Holdenby, and how much against his will he stayed here: In answer to which his Majesty, clapping his hand to his breast, said, 'Upon my life I came against my will ... But (said hee) rather than be carried by neck and heeles I went along: Nor am I so in love with their proceedings that I should continue here, for I find myself an Absolute Prisoner. As concerning my refusall of returning to Holdenby ... all the reason I had was, that I chose golden fetters, and a lightsome roome before a darke Dungeon, for I conceave this to be the better ayre ... '
>
> Then appealing to the Commissioners, he [the King] said, 'Have I not told the Generall himselfe ... that I admired by what Authority he durst thus resist him and his Parliament: ... Yet for my part (proceeded his Majesty) I know not what they [Parliament] do, or intend ... for they have not sent legally to me since my coming: therefore tell all those whom you think fit Communicants ... that I desire nothing more passionately, then to be with my Parliament.'

Reymes then 'assum'd the boldness' to tell the King that he thought him 'politically absent when his affections, though not his Person, was alienated' from Parliament. To this Charles agreed. And when Reymes said it would be of great comfort to Parliament to hear 'that his Majesties ... inclinations toward them was so great', the King bade him assure them of this.

On June 17th, the same day that Reymes presented his account, it was 'Ordered by the Lords Assembled in Parliament That this Narration be forthwith printed and published'.[2] The tale of a King held an unwilling captive by the Army was exactly what Parliament wanted to believe, a fact of which Charles was undoubtedly aware. While holding out hopes of reconciliation to both, he apparently enjoyed nothing better than widening the rift between the two opponents. That Reymes was completely unaware of what the King was doing, seems improbable.

The Army, anxious to circulate the story that Charles, sympathetic to them, had left Holdenby of his own free will, was disturbed enough by the Parliament-sanctioned pamphlet to sponsor a reply by Cornet Joyce. So, on July 14th, Cornet George Joyce wrote 'A Vindication of his Majesty and the Army'.[3] Buried in a mass of religious exhortations, it is a not-too-convincing attempt to prove Reymes a liar and a knave. Joyce vehemently denies that the King struck Colonel Whalley 'for his presumptious listning'. 'The King,' he says, 'denyes that hee struck him', though he 'did thrust him from him, but not strike him ... ' He attempts to disprove the belief that the King was taken from Holdenby 'against his will', citing a remark of Charles to the effect that 'we had answered his desire', and that 'hee would goe with us whether the Commissioners would, yea or no, and accordingly did.' Then, in his loquacious fashion, Joyce tries to vindicate the Army's seizure of the King as an act in accordance with the laws 'of Nature and of Nations', and accuses Parliament of making all men 'dance after their pipes, kisse their hands, and resigne up their birthrights ... to their tyrannical wills.'

After this brief flurry in the miniature battle of pamphlets, there is no evidence that Reymes ever again attempted to act as mediator between King and Parliament. In fact he may, like his friend, Sir John Berkeley, have come to believe that Charles's best chance lay in a reconciliation with the Army.

Sir John Berkeley, who ever since the fall of Exeter had been in France in attendance upon Queen Henrietta Maria, returned to England in July of 1647. According to his *Memoirs*,[4] he had conferences with Cromwell and Ireton and with the King, doing

PAYING THE ROYALIST PENALTY

his futile best to persuade Charles to accept the Army's proposals. Later, the King, confined at Hampton Court, and frightened by the alleged threats of the Levellers (the radical faction of the Army), made up his mind to escape. He sent to Berkeley, asking his aid, and on 'the excessively dark and stormy night' of November 10th, in the company of William Legge, Sir John Ashburnham and Berkeley, made his way to the Isle of Wight, where he was to find a year's uneasy refuge in Castle Carisbroke.

As they were riding south, Berkeley, increasingly dubious of the island's Governor, Robert Hammond (one-time Colonel in the Parliamentary forces), proposed 'going farther West, where,' he says, 'I was sure I had some friends who would favor our escape.'[5] But the King refused, and walked into another prison.

Later, when Cromwell decided to abandon negotiations with the King and to accede to the Levellers' demand for his punishment, Berkeley made up his mind to go back to France. Unable to get a passport, he sought (for himself this time) the aid of a friend in the west — Colonel Reymes, who had served under him at Exeter. Some time in 1648 Reymes, with the aid of two old friends, Captain William Ellesdon and his brother John, Receiver of Customs at Lyme Regis, engineered Sir John Berkeley's escape from that secluded little port on the Dorset coast.

Meanwhile, Mapowder was having its share of weddings and christenings. In 1646, Anne Gerrard married Reymes's friend, Colonel Francis Wyndham, and Tabitha Reymes, the eldest of Bullen's and Elizabeth's five children, was born. The next two years saw the marriages of the younger Gerrard sisters, Etheldread and Frances,[6] and the birth (in 1647) of Bullen Reymes the third. Death, too, came to Coker Hall. On July 7th, 1648, Elizabeth's grandmother, Amy Molford Coker, closed her eyes and died. The manor house went to William Coker, but 'the goods and chattels thereof' were put up for sale. All the buyers were members of the Coker clan. Elizabeth and Bullen bought '1 Black Mare' for £2; 1 old Drag for 6s., and various household items, including '1 striped carpet' for 6d. and '2 Buttry baskets' for 1s.[7] Shortly after the sale, with their two children, the nurse, Hester Clinch, and their newly purchased items, they moved from Mapowder to their new home, the manor house at Trent.

During his years at Mapowder Reymes had encountered little

difficulty with the sequestrators, perhaps because Robert Coker was a member of the Dorset Committee. But he had been in Trent less than three months when the 'Sequestrators of Somerset' — Trent was then in Somerset — seized upon his estate 'to the value of £100'. He managed, it is true, to have the unjust sequestration removed, but not without considerable trouble (two trips to Taunton) and expense. Among other items, 'A perticuler of my Expences in redeming my selfe from my second sequestration Oct. 6, 1648,' lists 10s. paid 'To James the Sequestrator', and 17s. 6d. for 'Quartering 7 Souldiers & 7 Sequestrators 1 night'.

There are no passes — nothing — to indicate that Reymes was away from Trent during the last two months of 1648. But as that year wore to a close he must have been increasingly concerned for the King's safety. Isolated though he was, he could not have failed to hear of the ordinance passed by the Commons on January 1st, 1649, bringing Charles Stuart to trial. With that ordinance, the alarm which had gripped all of King Charles's friends turned to despair, and then to pity and admiration for the man who endured so patiently the accusations of his judges, and who, without a trace of fear, clung so obstinately to his convictions. His death on the scaffold, that January day, helped to wipe from men's memories, as nothing else could have done, the King's never-ending duplicity.

In 1650, probably in March, another son, William, was born to Elizabeth and Bullen.[8] Mary Reymes's letter of congratulation, dated March 30th, is friendly and chatty:

> By yr brother Steevens [Paul Stevens, Judith's husband] ... I received yr good & happy news of yr wifes safe deliverance ... unto home [whom] I send, as unto yee all, my love, blissing & prayers, not forgetting ... my cosen Mary Weekes, for help & making my little nephew a sweete William, ye name of his 3 greate Grandfathers, and also his only Uncle ... Yr bro: Steevens also shewed me yr 2 letters ... concerning Mr. Drakes busines, by wch I finde you both carefull & industrious, ye wch [the which] qualities I love above any other wor[l]dly thing, save consideration, wch being added thereto, makes a man fully compleat for all things above & under ye sunn ...

PAYING THE ROYALIST PENALTY

I will expect yt [that] att yr coming you bring me some Chelburrow rent, for I am very bare of mony, & yet love not to lett debts run out of my memory ... knowing of old yt short reckninges make long frends ... Yr sister [Judith] desires to be excused ... for not writing ... for indeed she is not well, but allways full of paynes & aches & tooth ach, but in her bulke sound ... & fatt, so we begins to feare her paynes to be som simtume of a windy & ruring gute. She desires her love ... be presented to you both ... she doth not forgett her deare Nephews & neece ... Heare is scarce roome to retourne you all our tha[n]kes for ye tobackea tongs you sent us. Wherefore take som now & som another time.

The Somerset Committee had not been the Colonel's only source of harassment. As early as May of 1647, the Committee of Lords and Commons for the Advance of Money had assessed Reymes at £100. Letters of protest and trips to London, where he patiently explained that he had already paid the £100 to the Committee for Compounding at Goldsmiths' Hall, made no impression. It was not until April of 1650 that another journey to London finally brought results — an order from the Committee of Lords and Commons 'that the Assemt upon B.R. ... for his 20th parte be and is hereby discharged, it appearing by Certificate from Goldsmiths that he Compounded there upon the Articles of Exeter and is comprised in the same.'

The pass for the April journey to London was unusually generous, for it permitted Reymes, after the conclusion of his business there, to go to Hartfield in Sussex 'to see his Mother ... and to returne againe unto Trente aforesaid by ... the first of July.' Perhaps he didn't get back to Trent by July 1st, or perhaps there was some more serious fault which antagonized the cantankerous Somerset officials. Whatever the reasons, Reymes was arrested and imprisoned in Taunton Castle. He was committed sometime after August 15th (we do not know the exact date), and his release was 'Dated at Tanton Castell ... the 16th of October, 1650'.

Apart from some difficulties about horses, there are no records of any other untoward events in 1650. Actually, the horse trouble started in May of 1649, when Reymes received this odd letter from one of his neighbours:

Mr. Rimes

I doe expet yor horse tomory to be sent to my Randivouz by this barer and you shall resieve any favor from me that may be condusinge for ye peace of this poore Commonwealth.

Your Sarvent

WILLI PITMAN

In his reply Reymes assured 'Willi' that he had already given one horse — all he had — to the militia, 'in Cap. Barkers trope', adding, 'if possibly you can redeame him thence, I confess I had rather he were under yor Conduct as my loving frend and neighbour than any other.'

In the following summer there was another dispute over a horse, or half a horse. In some very badly damaged letters there are fragments of an acid quarrel between the Colonel and the always difficult Somerset officials as to whether the Gerrard estate in Trent was responsible for a half or a whole horse. In a letter written in October, shortly after his release from prison, the problem was still unsolved, and so it remains, for there are no more letters.

In 1651, little Robert, Elizabeth's and Bullen's fourth child, was born. It was also in this year, on July 25th, that the final partition deed of the Gerrard estate was made and signed. The deed gave to 'Bullen Reymes of Trent' and his wife the estate of West Waddon in Dorset; and to Francis and Anne Wyndham the property at Trent. The rest of the Gerrard estate was divided between the other two sisters and their husbands.

Bullen and Elizabeth stayed on at Trent at least until the Wyndhams moved in, some time in September. Since the manor house at Waddon was still occupied by the tenants, Alfred Patey and his family, and in need of repairs, it is possible that Elizabeth and the children continued to live with the Wyndhams until the following January, Reymes contenting himself with brief visits. Perhaps they were there when the fugitive King arrived at Trent on September 17th, 1651.

II. *A Royal Fugitive*

The crowning of Prince Charles at Scone on January 1st, 1651, as King of Scotland, and the first news of the summer campaign, when the young King and his Scottish army marched across the border into England, brought to the Royalists renewed hope. But, although they fought bravely, Charles and the Scots were no match for Cromwell. Many Royalists died on the battlefield; some were captured and some, including Lord Wilmot and Charles himself, escaped.

The saga of the new King dressed in old cloth breeches and leathern doublet; his long ride to southern England and his eventual arrival in France — all this is a familiar page in England's history. The part of the story of particular interest to Reymes and his family was Charles's nineteen-day visit to the manor house in Trent.

After days of hiding in wet woods, in the famous oak tree and in the home of Colonel Lane in Staffordshire, Charles, disguised as Jane Lane's servant, had ridden into Somerset, where he decided to seek refuge with Francis Wyndham. Lord Wilmot, who had been with the King almost constantly since their escape from Worcester on September 3rd, rode on ahead to break the news. He reached the manor just at dusk on September 16th with the tidings that Charles would be there 'about ten of the clock next morning'.

Before ten the house was in readiness, and Frank and Anne Wyndham were strolling in a field near by, when they saw two horses coming up a narrow lane, the swarthy young King on one, with a woman riding pillion behind him, and a strange man on the other. The woman was Jane Lane, and the strange man her cousin, who had accompanied her all the way from Staffordshire.

Shortly after Jane and her cousin left — they stayed at Trent only overnight — Wyndham set out for Melbury, some ten miles south of Trent, to ask the assistance of Colonel Giles Strangways in arranging the King's escape. That gentleman, although he sent Charles £100, was unable to help, saying he knew no mariner he could trust at Weymouth and was a stranger at both Lyme and Poole. It is possible that, after his futile visit to Melbury, Wyndham rode on to Waddon to ask his brother-in-law's advice. And, since Strangways knew no one at Lyme, it may well have been Reymes who suggested that he get in touch with his old friend Captain William Ellesdon at Lyme Regis. This conjecture is supported by the fact that it was not until he had returned to

Trent and reported Strangway's inability to help them, that Francis Wyndham mentioned Captain Ellesdon. It was Ellesdon, he said, who 'by means of Colonel Bullen Reymes ... had conveyed over into France Sir John Berkeley ... in time of danger.'[9]

The following day Wyndham, with the help of Captain Ellesdon, made what seemed to be a foolproof arrangement with one Limbry to convey certain Royalist gentlemen to France on Monday night, September 22nd. All was going well, until an incident occurred at the manor on Sunday morning which might well have proved disastrous. 'A Tailor of the Parish informed the Colonel, that the Zealots' were sure that 'Persons of Quality were hid in his House, and that they intended to search and seise them.'[10] Wyndham assured the man that he had no private visitors, but only his kinsman, who was so public a guest that he would probably accompany him to prayers that day. Lord Wilmot, the alleged kinsman, was something of a problem. Unlike Charles, he refused to stay in his room, but wandered openly about the house, stubbornly refusing to use any disguise.

Wyndham did take Wilmot to church with him, a bold move which seems to have stilled suspicions. The 'Zealots' apparently believed that he was Wyndham's real kinsman, Bullen Reymes, whom Wilmot so strongly resembled. The fact that the two entered and left by a private door, leading into a small chapel on the south side of the church, may have facilitated the deception, for this chapel, which had been occupied by the Gerrard family for generations, was separated from the main body of the congregation by a low archway.

On Monday the King, still dressed as a servant, left Trent for Charmouth. This time Mrs Julian Coningsby, a cousin of Francis Wyndham, rode behind him. Colonel Wyndham acted as guide, while Wilmot and a servant, Henry Peters, followed at a discreet distance. Peters had already engaged rooms at Charmouth Inn, regaling the hostess with a romantic tale of a young man (Wilmot) who was eloping with a lady from Devon (Julian Coningsby), attended by their servant (King Charles). They wished, he said, to wait undisturbed at the inn until some time in the night when they might safely continue their journey.

At first everything went as planned, the group settling down at Charmouth Inn to await word from Captain Limbry. But no word came. Finally, at the approach of dawn, fearful of discovery, the little group disconsolately set out on the road to Dorchester. Only later did they learn that Captain Limbry's wife had been responsible for the failure of the carefully conceived plan. It seems that the Captain, going home to get his sea-chest, was locked in his room by Mrs Limbry, to whom he had earlier revealed something of his intended voyage. 'Thus,' to quote Anne Wyndham 'a Design ... carried on with industry and prudence ... by one mans single whisper (the bane of action) proved abortive.'[11]

Meanwhile, the King and his party, finding the main road crowded with soldiers, had turned left on 'Lee Lane'. Towards evening they came to the village of Broadwindsor, where they decided to spend the night. Colonel Wyndham, recognizing the host of the small inn where they stopped, asked to be shown the most private rooms,

> because his brother-in-law Colonel Reymes (whom the Lord Willmot personated) had been a long time imprisoned as well as himself. That they had lately obtained their Paroles, and to be seen together so far from their homes, might create new jealousies.[12]

The good host accordingly took them up to the 'highest chambers' where, says Captain Ellesdon (in a letter to Lord Clarendon),

> the hostess ... came immediately to welcome Colonel Reymes whom she said she knew very well at Exeter when she lived with Mrs. Coventry, and how she caressed Lord Wilmot instead of him, I leave your lordship to be better informed from his Majesty himself that to this day hath not forgot it.[13]

The 'Privateness' of the highest chambers proved a great blessing, for later in the evening there was a great hubbub, a constable and about forty soldiers milling noisily through all the quarters below. Even so the soldiers might have discovered the royal guests on the top floor, 'being,' says Ellesdon, 'proudly inquisitive into the names, qualities ... and business of strangers,'[14] had they not been occupied with difficulties of their own. Shortly after they arrived, a woman in their company falling into labour in the kitchen, precipitated such a controversy as to who should provide for the mother and child — the soldiers or the parish — that they forgot to search the house.

Early the next morning the King and his companions slipped out of the inn and rode back to Trent. There Charles stayed until October 6th, when he went to Salisbury and found asylum in the house of a widow, one Mrs Hyde, who lived near by. Finally another plan for the King's escape was perfected, and on October 15th he and Wilmot sailed on a cargo ship from the small harbour at Shoreham-by-Sea for France.

III. *The Squire at Waddon*

Elizabeth's and Bullen's new home, the grey stone manor house at Waddon, a wooded hill-side at its back, and rolling pastures sloping down to the sea in front, is one of the loveliest spots in southern Dorset. About a mile east of the little village of Portesham, or 'Possum', Waddon is some eight miles from Dorchester, and little more than seven from Weymouth. Abbotsbury lies to its east and south, and the ridge of the Blackdown Hills to the north.

Tradition has it that as early as 1024, King Canute granted to thane Orc and his wife Tolla lands in Portesham that included West Waddon, a gift which they in turn made over to the monastery at Abbotsbury. Apparently the Abbey held the overlordship of West Waddon down to the dissolution of the monasteries, when a John 'Gerarde' acquired the property. It was either John or his son William who built the sixteenth-century dwelling to which Reymes fell heir. But the long, low, stone building lying to its east and south, which Bullen calls the 'Ould House', belongs to a much earlier period.

In 1621, Elizabeth's widowed grandmother, Mary Gerrard, leased part of Waddon to one William Patey, reserving certain rooms for herself and her son Thomas (Elizabeth's father) and 'ground near and about the dwelling house ... for the making of a Court, orchard or garden ... ' In January of 1652, Reymes drew up an agreement with his tenant, Alfred Patey, which, like the lease signed by Patey's father and Elizabeth's grandmother, stipulated that a part of the house be reserved for the owner's use. Bullen seems to have kept the same rooms that Mary Gerrard had

WADDON ABOUT 1700 AND (BELOW) THE WEST SIDE TODAY

reserved in 1621 — the parlour and the rooms behind and above it, as well as the old cellar, with its heavy arches and the trough on the floor for the beer and ale which dropped from the spigots of the big tuns stored there; and 'the kitchen ... with the chamber over, and 2 littell buttrys thereby, I making a partition in the entry to parte both familleys.'

With the exception of the 'new' wing at the front, built around 1700, Waddon today is very like the house Bullen and Elizabeth knew in 1652. On its west side is a pleasant terrace (the old bowling green), with stone steps leading down to the lawn and to a charming formal garden, enclosed by a box hedge which is said to follow the pattern of its seventeenth-century ancestor. The east courtyard looks out, as it did three hundred years ago, on the meadows sloping down to the sea. Even the stone seats at the back of the paved court may well be the same 'groomery seats' where the grooms waited while their masters visited, back in the days of Elizabeth and Bullen.

In spite of its tranquil setting, Waddon was to bring its share of sorrow. Not long after the Reymeses had moved into their new home, probably in the summer of 1652, their two little sons, William and Robert, died. It may have been that same year that Mary, their youngest child, was born, an event clouded by the fact that the baby girl was afflicted with some sort of physical handicap.[15] It was also in 1652 that Bullen's father died 'of Apoplexy' and that his mother decided to make her home at Waddon.

In 1653, unable to repay the £100 he had borrowed for his sequestration fine, Reymes was forced to mortgage part of the estate. Within a few years, however, as Waddon, under his capable management, began to pay better dividends, he was able to 'pay off the mortgage' and begin making improvements. He rebuilt part of the office range — the buttery, larder and brew-house — and started making plans for a new west wing, though he probably did not start building it until 1660. This wing, which extended from the west side of the house almost as far as the garden, must have given to Waddon great symmetry and charm. Unfortunately it was long since destroyed (probably by fire). Today, only its silhouette on the west wall remains.[16]

Reymes did not spend all his time building up his estate and playing the role of country squire, for he was often away from home. Letters and the surviving permits of the late 1650s refer to numerous trips, most of them to London. The Colonel has left no record of what he was doing on these visits nor of his opinion of the Protectorate, but, in January of 1655, he signed his bond of allegiance 'unto his Highness Oliver Ld. Protector of the Commonwealth of England'. And he agreed that 'if he shall repair to the Cittie of London ... he shall within twenty fower howers ... give his true name ... streete and houses where he ... shall lodge ... ' However burdensome they may have been, the numerous 'Certificates' among Reymes's papers attest his compliance with the onerous regulations.

More disturbing than the 'Certificates' was the tax on all Royalists, called the 'decimation' because levied on ten per cent of their real property. The Royalists, who had already been forced to pay so much, resented this additional burden; but almost as distasteful as the fine itself was the manner in which it was collected. England was divided into military districts, a Major-General over each, whose duty it was to collect the new tax, maintain order, and 'stimulate virtue and destroy vice'!

In connection with this tax, Reymes, on December 19th, 1655, was ordered to 'attend at the Red Lyon in Blandford' [some twenty-five miles from Waddon] with an account of his real and personal estate and the names of his 'chaplyns and meniall servants' and of 'such Ministers & Schoolmasters by whom his children, or orphans under his tuition were being taught'. The Colonel's crisp reply, written in the third person, reads:

> By the courtesy of Ingland Hee holdeth during his life the proffitts of some lands called West Waddon in the parish of Portescham ... to the yearley vallew of 140 li of which lands 2/3 parts is mortgaged for the payment of his debts which are at least 1500 li. Personal estate, he hath none other than 2 or 3 old and blind horses and 2 oxen, with some smale household stuf to his naked walls ... Orphants, Chaplins or Surjourners he hath none. His sonn about 7 years of age, is at skoole wth on[e] Mr. Clinch at Chilton ...

But the officials apparently unmoved by the size of Reymes's debts and the pitiful condition of his livestock — all of which they

PAYING THE ROYALIST PENALTY

no doubt took with a large grain of salt — fined him £14. 13s. 4d.

On September 3rd Oliver Cromwell died, and the confusion which his personality had held in check descended upon his son Richard, who, caught between the quarrels of Army and Parliament, gave up his high post and retired to the private life he preferred. Unfortunately this act only added to England's difficulties, for the Rump Parliament, recalled at Richard's retirement, was as muddled and contentious as ever. Completely incapable of coping with a new Royalist uprising in August of 1659, they were forced to turn to the Army for help.

As for the Royalists, although their August revolt had been put down with no difficulty, public opinion was clearly shifting in their favour. By early January of 1660, General Monk had left Scotland, and by the time he and his army reached London on February 3rd the wave of feeling for Charles was too strong to be ignored.

Even before the dawn of 1660, Reymes must have believed that the return of the King was only a matter of time. It was undoubtedly that belief which sent him so often to London in 1659 and 1660. But while he was in London, preparing for the changes ahead, his mother, old and sick, was fretting at his long absences. Soon after March 29th, 1660, when she made the final revision of her will, Mary Reymes died, and was buried in the church at West Chelborough. She left the bulk of her estate to Bullen and 'gives back' his bonds for £200 which, she says:

> I have in my hands together with three hundred pounds of mony wch he hath in his hands ... wch Bonds he shall have in the Barr Trunke Marked with B. R.

CHAPTER FIFTEEN

THE NEW WORLD OF THE RESTORATION

1. *Member of Parliament*

IN spite of the high hopes of the Royalists, events moved slowly in the early months of 1660. Although General Monk, with the 'City' behind him, was in virtual control, he walked cautiously — one step at a time — lagging considerably behind public opinion, which grew daily more impatient for the King's return. But when, on March 17th, the unpopular Long Parliament at last dissolved itself, the tempo quickened. Monk sent a message across the sea to Charles, and on April 25th the new, or Convention, Parliament convened to effect what amounted to a bloodless revolution.

On the first day of May the members listened to the famous 'Declaration' which Charles had signed at Breda almost a month before. Following the combined advice of General Monk and Edward Hyde, the future Earl of Clarendon, the King made two important promises: free and general pardon to all, except those exempted by Parliament, and, to assuage religious animosity, 'a liberty to tender consciences'. As a result of these conciliatory promises, the Commons sent Charles a gift of £50,000 and, on May 8th, both Houses proclaimed him King of England.

Whether Reymes was at Dover on May 25th when Charles stepped ashore, or whether he saw the bonfires which lighted the streets and heard the shouts of the crowds who greeted the King at London four days later, we do not know. But the chances are that he would not have missed these long-hoped-for events.

In that famous May of 1660, Reymes was in his forty-seventh year. What with fighting for King Charles I and paying the penalty for his loyalty, he had given to the cause of monarchy more than twenty years of his life. What changes in his outlook and character these years had wrought is an interesting speculation. When he emerged from his semi-seclusion in rural Dorset Reymes undoubtedly considered himself as staunch a Royalist as ever. Yet it is possible that during those long years he had assimilated more of the changing attitude towards Parliament's role in government than he realized. Despite the fact that the House of Commons, in which he was to serve for the remaining twelve years of his life, was, at times, almost belligerently pro-Royalist, it was, none the less, developing the machinery for a constitutional government. In this process Reymes was an active participant.

That Bullen felt for Charles II the same degree of reverend devotion as he had given his father, is doubtful. His allegiance to Charles I had been part of the unquestioning loyalty of an idealistic young man. He was more sceptical now. What he had experienced in the heightened tempo of the war years, and in the frustrating restraint of the Interregnum, had sharpened the difference between the eager, earnest young Bullen, so impressed by rank and so anxious to fulfil his role of gentleman and courtier, and the middle-aged Colonel who, having seen his way of life crumble, had been forced to adjust himself to a new order. He was less patient with inefficiency and hypocrisy, more outspoken, than he had been as a young man. Yet, in spite of the changes, Colonel Reymes and young Bullen were essentially the same. The mature Reymes was still interested in the world about him; he was still sociable and friendly, and he was still driven by as sharp a sense of duty as he had ever been.

Although the earthy, black-browed young Charles (he was just thirty at the Restoration) was scarcely the stuff of which martyrs are made, there was much about the new King that Reymes must have liked — his urbanity, his quick intelligence, and his easy, friendly manner. Even the licence of his Court, which caused so much head-shaking, seems to have disturbed Reymes but little, familiar as he was with the ways of France and Italy. Rather it was the idleness and extravagance of the royal household which exasperated the Colonel, for his own standards of conduct countenanced no neglect of duty. He was sincere in his service to England, a service he was to render with the full degree of his ability and strength for the remaining years of his life. That he incidentally managed to achieve a degree of prosperity and prestige does not wipe out the very real contribution that Reymes made to the England of the Restoration.

Whether or not he was in London when Charles arrived on May 29th, Reymes was there by late June, serving as a member of the Convention Parliament, having won his seat for Weymouth at a by-election.[1] The combined borough of Weymouth and Melcombe Regis was familiar territory for the Colonel. Early in 1660, possibly with a view to entering politics, he had borrowed money from his mother to purchase an old Dominican Priory in Melcombe Regis. This 'Fryery', as Bullen calls it, included a number of 'tenements' which housed, in addition to ten 'Almes Foulk', a dozen tenants 'that are fitt to paye rent'. One of the buildings, the house of '7 roomes and 3 chimneys', Reymes took over as his own residence during his frequent visits.

The Convention Parliament was dissolved on December 29th, 1660, and the new King's second Parliament met the following May, Reymes sitting for Melcombe Regis.[2] That he took his duties in the new Parliament seriously there can be no question. With the same enthusiasm and attention to detail that he had once begun his travel diaries, Colonel Reymes, on May 8th, 1661, started his Parliamentary Journal.[3]

> In the morning about 7 of the clock, the Duke of Ormond being Lo: Stuard,[4] came into the Court of Request ... [there was] a long table with a Carpet, and a chare placed against the middle of the table in which my Lo: satt, with 2 Bibles, Inck & paper and pens on the table ...
>
> My Lo: being seated, the Clarke of the Croune read a Command from his Ma:tie that none ... should sett ... till they had taken the oaths of Supremacy and Alegance. Then the Clarke ... called over Alfabetically all the names of such as were returned county by County ... and so to the Parlement where the members ... went into the house and tooke there places where they satt, till the Usher of the Black rodd came down and comanded there attendance of his Matie in the house of Peers ...
>
> His Ma:ties speech being ended [Charles stressed the importance of the Act of Indemnity and announced his

THE NEW WORLD OF THE RESTORATION

approaching marriage to the Portuguese Princess, Catherine of Braganza], he comanded the Commons to chuse there Speaker ... then the Commons returning to there house, Sir Charles Berkeley[5] ... Recommended Sir Edward Turner ... The house agreeing, he ... conducted him to the chare where, ere he sat, he [Turner] made a speech very modestly refusing the imployment ... but the house receaving no deniall he sat doun ...

Reymes continued to report each day's proceedings, giving, with some deletions and a few additions, substantially the same account as that found in the *Commons' Journal*. On Friday, May 17th, the diary reports an order ominous to Dissenters and Republicans:

Ordered that the Covenants be burned by the hand of the hangman ... it was a long debate and ... the house was devided, the ayes were 228, the no's 103. Then the mayne question was putt, and caried it clearly that it be burnt.

Not only had the Commons ordered the Solemn League and Covenant to be burned, but had obliged themselves to take the Sacrament according to the Church of England. On Saturday, May 25th, the House 'did not sit, in order to Preparation to the Sacrament the next day at St Margarets,' where on Sunday, 'Doctor Gunning refused the bread to Mr. Prinn because he did not, would not kneele. Biscower took it standing.'

The entry for June 6th is short and poignant. 'My wife being very sick I went into the country.' This brief statement is the only reference to Reymes's journey to Waddon, his hours by his wife's bedside, and her death and burial 'in the aisle of Portisham Church'. How long Bullen stayed at Waddon after Elizabeth's death we do not know. There were many things to attend to, for Tabitha, the eldest of the three Reymes children, not yet fifteen, was too young to assume responsibility. Fortunately, the capable and devoted Hester Clinch, who had been with the family ever since Mapowder days, and had looked after Elizabeth in all her 'sicknesses and lyings in', would stay on and manage the household.

After his wife's death, Reymes became more absorbed than

ever in his public duties. When Parliament, after an adjournment of almost three months, convened on November 20th, 1661, he was in his place once more, setting down each day's happenings. On opening day the 'Black rodd' again 'came doun and Commanded us up to the King where we found him sitting on the Throun with his Croune on, & his Robes, and all the Peers & Bishops with thre robes also, so as in my judgment I never saw so Majestic a sight in all my life.'

The entry for November 25th describes the conduct of the regicides when they knelt at the bar of the House. When 'word was brought that the Prisoners were at the dore ... the Bill for executing the traytors was read the second time and they were called in, one by one, and first, Owen Row who kneeled on both knees at the barr, and Pleaded the Proclamation.'[6] Then each of the others knelt — 'Augustin Garland, a lawyer and he who spitt on his Matie at his tryall ... '; 'Robert Titchborne' who 'spake very well and long but [like the others] in the end relyed on the Proclamation'; 'George Fletwood' who 'seemed som what penitent'; 'Will: Henningham [Havingham]' who 'pleaded he did not signe nor seele': 'Gilbert Millington, an old man & a lawyer', and 'John Downs' who 'made a long speech, pleaded his dissent in Court & that he did not signe till after'. Of the other culprits, Reymes simply states that four pleaded the 'Proclamation', two were in prison, two had escaped, and one was dead.

A subject of great interest to Reymes was discussed on December 19th. The House was informed 'that the King had sent to the Lords to acquaint them of a bewsiness to hard for him to remedy and ... desired them to acquaint us with it that both together might find out som timely prevention.' It seems that 'many ill affected persons' had met and decided 'to enlist the aid' of some seven 'heads or Partys', including disbanded soldiers, Anabaptists, Presbyterians, Independents, Commonwealth men and Rumpers, who were

> to meete & consulte from time to time how to advance there interests ... There 3rd meeting was at greate St Martins ... Here they thought it convenient to there purpose to indeavor that such choyce of Parlement men ... be made as might favor there designes, and ... did nominate those very 4 men

that were afterwards chosen for the Citty of London. And they did also propose that the excise be taken away, that there might be no standing Army ... that Conformity might not be pressed, that Gods ministers might not be silenced ... they met in September last and ordered that the disbanded Souldiers ... be invited to the toune.

Despite the fact that the 'whole Plott' had been discovered and most of the conspirators apprehended, Parliament continued to be apprehensive. The space Reymes devotes to the story is symptomatic of the fear of the government's overthrow by political and religious dissenters which gripped the majority of the Cavalier Parliament. In fact, on December 20th, the very day after the revelation of the seven-headed plot, the House passed a Bill levelled against corporations, the political strongholds of the Presbyterians. This Bill, which Reymes calls a Bill 'for regulating corporations', was the first important attack on Nonconformity, for it ordered all members of corporations to renounce the Covenant and receive the Sacrament of the Church of England.

Although this session of Parliament was not prorogued until May 19th, 1662, Reymes's last entry was for February 4th. That same day 'Admiralty bewsiness' took him to Weymouth and kept him there for the rest of the week. It also put an end to the diary.

ii. *Vice-Admiral and Merchant*

Some time during the autumn of 1661, Reymes had been appointed Vice-Admiral of Dorset, serving under the Duke of York, Lord High Admiral. One of the earliest of the many documents relating to the 'Admiralty bewsiness' is a letter dated Weymouth, December 21st, 'Concerning the Job'. It seems that one John Topson, late master of the *Good Job*, had been taken ill at sea and had died shortly after his ship was piloted into port by a mariner of Weymouth. (The Admiralty expense account lists '£3-04-10 to Phisic, doctor and funeral of sd master and £5-04-10 to Henry Symonds for piloting in ye vessel.') Apparently the ship was considered a derelict. According to the accounts of Reymes's two clerks, the expenses of the commissioners who appraised the ship, and of the Notary Public and witnesses who had assembled at Weymouth to settle the matter, amounted to £19. 12s. 8d. Apart from his share of these expenses, there is no record of anything received by Reymes.

It was not until the start of the Second Dutch War that the more remunerative aspect of Reymes's duties as Vice-Admiral, his share of the Lord Admiral's Tenths of Prize Ships, was to develop into anything of importance. Meanwhile he had other irons in the fire. One was a partnership with his old friends, the Pleys of Weymouth, for the sale of hemp, cordage, and sailcloth to the Navy.

Captain George Pley had fought on the side of Parliament and, for several years before the Restoration, had supplied the Navy with sailcloth manufactured under his supervision in cottages in and near Weymouth. Shortly after 1660, his son, George Pley the younger, his wife Constance, and his friend Bullen Reymes joined him in this venture. Under the able leadership of Constance, the driving force of the joint enterprise, the business expanded to include the manufacture of hemp and cordage and the importation of canvas and other 'stufs' from France. In the twelve years from June 1660 until August 1672, there are almost a hundred letters written by the four partners to Samuel Pepys, Thomas Middleton, Sir William Coventry, Sir John Mennes and to the Navy Commissioners as a body. Constance wrote most of the letters — fourteen to Pepys alone. Apparently he wrote as many to her, although only one of his replies has survived.[7]

The majority of Mrs Pley's letters are pleas for payment of goods already delivered. In dramatic terms she paints a dire picture of the despair of herself, her partners, and her workmen. She writes to Pepys that she 'can apprehend nothing but an approaching ruin' and must end her days in sorrow 'for bringing in Colonel Reymes to suffer with her'. She beseeches 'speedy reimbursement' and remarks, in passing, that one might as well 'press money' from a stone as from Mr Fenn [paymaster of the Navy].[8]

Constance Pley's letters, mingled strands of threats and gratitude, reveal not only a flair for colourful language, but a sure grasp of the financial problems involved and an awareness of opportunities ahead. With her combined vigour and tact, she usually got results. At least she seems to have won over Mr Pepys.

She used various approaches. One letter apologizes for 'following a person of his quality and business so frequently with importunities'; another refers to 'his goodness which has never failed her'.[9]

The Colonel was more forthright in his language and consequently less successful with the Navy Commissioners. When he reminded them of the large sums still owing to him and his partners — at least £20,000 — and bluntly asked what Parliament's gift was for, if it was not to buy cordage and sailcloth, the Commissioners were visibly annoyed. Writing of this to his friend Pepys, to whom he could always speak frankly, Reymes says that he has had the ill fortune to present the necessities of himself and his partners in a style displeasing to the Board, and is resolved to starve rather than trouble them jointly any more on the subject. Instead he has decided to leave all solicitations for money to Mrs Pley, whose 'oil will be better than my vinegar'.[10]

Apparently Pepys had asked Mrs Pley why she had deserted the conventional life of a housewife and entered the world of business, for in one of her letters to him she explains her reasons. Several of her children had died years before and, in more recent times, her daughter, 'within the space of four months was married and buried'. Business, she says, is her 'sole delight in this world ... It is a charity to be kept full of employment.'[11]

In the seventeenth century, for a woman of Constance Pley's station in life to venture into a business fraught with difficulties which would have given pause to a seasoned man of affairs, was a most unusual occurrence. But Constance was an unusual woman. Bullen's association with her was one of the most rewarding experiences of his life. At a time when needy friends and relatives were constantly turning to the Colonel for advice and money, Mrs Pley was one of the few persons — certainly the only woman — upon whom he could depend for sound counsel and even financial aid. Whether there was any romantic attachment between the two is not clear. That there was understanding and affection there can be no question.

Just as years before Bullen had adopted 'little Anne' Smedley as his sister, and depended on her to intercede for him with the Duchess of Buckingham, so now he calls Constance his 'sister' and, marvelling at her daring, her intelligence and tact, discusses with her all the complicated aspects of their business. He is unstinting in his appreciation. But for his woman partner, he tells the Navy Commissioners, he would 'have been aground long since'. And later, during the Dutch War, when Constance had come to his aid with a much-needed loan, he wrote to Captain Cocke,[12] urging payment:

> Pray be punctual with her, she being as famous a she merchant as you have met with in England, one who turnes and winds 30,000 lb a yeare, and that even with ... Sir G. Carteret[13] ... She is also my friend.

Perhaps Reymes was first attracted to Mrs Pley by the very qualities he had admired in his mother — her intelligent grasp of business matters, her industry and drive. Whatever were the reasons, Constance remained Bullen's friend until the day of his death. In his will he writes:

> I give to my sister Constance Pley (my very intimate dear friend and one whom I greatly value and doe acknowledge to have been highly obliged by and as having received many obligations from her ever since I knew her) my great Dyamond Ring already in her possession, desireing her to accept of it in Testimony of my thankfulness and constant ouning her as such to my very last.

Although his friendship with Mrs Pley may have been purely Platonic, Bullen probably had his quota of affairs with the ladies. His latest behest to his son — to destroy all letters from women — suggests as much. Unfortunately for the curiosity of later generations, Bullen the third carried out his dutiful deletion almost to the letter. Only three little notes, endorsed 'about the Widdow', give any hint of Reymes's late romances. One, signed A.B.C., says that 'the lady we drank a health to at this place [Dorchester]' has been here with her mother for three weeks and may 'continew some time longer'. The writer adds that no one knows 'of my writing this', but they all hope 'to see you heare next weeke'.

There seems to be no sequel to this invitation, but the lady in question may have been the widow, Mrs Elizabeth Rodney of Pilton, to whom Reymes wrote the other two notes. In the first, dated at Trent, October 20th, 1663, he refers to having waited on

THE NEW WORLD OF THE RESTORATION

her in the stage-coach from London to Salisbury, 'in which progress I receaved so much delight, in your sweete and pleasant conversation, and so great an obligation in the leave you gave me to wayt on you next time I came into the Country as ... to acquit my selfe of that promise.' But Mrs Rodney was not at home, for a letter written the following April reads:

> Providence having brought me once again so neere to your ladship as Trent, and remembering my former misfortune of not finding you at home when I was last in the Country, am still by the same impulses and obligations desirous to kis yor fayre hands at Pilton. To which purpos thes lines are to beg the favor of your leave to wayt on you ...

And this is the last we hear of the widow of Pilton!

III. *Commons, City, and Court*

The first session of the Cavalier Parliament, which was prorogued on May 19th, 1662, had lasted practically a year. It was not only the longest, but, in many ways, the most important session of Charles II's reign. The King may have come into his own again, but Parliament was dominated by its Church of England squires rather than by the easy-going tolerance of Charles.

The Act of Uniformity, passed in March of 1662, dispossessing, as it did, all clergymen who refused to subscribe to the Anglican Book of Common Prayer, had disregarded the promise of religious toleration made at Breda. By the end of the year nearly 2,000 of the clergy had lost their posts.[14] Probably the motive behind the Commons' enthusiasm for the Act of Uniformity was not so much religious bigotry as political revenge. And political revenge could be most easily secured by supporting the religious claims of the High Church party.

During the next two years, 1663 and 1664, Parliament sat for little more than eight months all told. Again the Colonel was in regular attendance, serving on increasingly important committees and gradually building up a reputation for financial acumen.

Reymes's membership on important committees reflects his ability, but it also suggests both that the government regarded him as a supporter, and that he was working out his apprenticeship towards something more important. He was essentially a courtier or place man, that is to say, a man holding office under the Crown. In other words, Reymes was not a party man but a Civil Servant, one who would have been likely to support any government that did not fly to extremes or run completely counter to his principles.

Although he had been disturbed by the political plots fomented by the Dissenters, the Colonel did not subscribe to the vindictiveness of many of the Anglican squires in the House. In this respect his personal view went hand in hand with government policy. It was largely among such men as Reymes and his two friends, Thomas Clifford and William Coventry, that Charles found sympathy for his attempts to temper the severity of the Act of Uniformity and the Conventicle Act of 1664.[15] It was also among such men as these that the opposition to Clarendon was growing.

Edward Hyde, Earl of Clarendon and Lord Chancellor of England, who had served the King so faithfully during his years of exile, and advised him so expertly when he first assumed the Crown, was growing old and obstinate. The Court circle was weary of his lectures, and so, for that matter, was Charles; both Catholics and Dissenters blamed him for the continuing acts of intolerance, and the up-and-coming young leaders of the country deplored not only the harshness of the 'Clarendon Code' (for which they held Hyde in part responsible), but the Chancellor's growing ineptitude in financial matters.

With the more tolerant attitude towards religion, and with the increasing emphasis on ability and efficiency which characterized the new leaders of England, Reymes was in complete sympathy. With four of these leaders, Bennet, Cooper, Clifford and Coventry, he was to be closely associated during the remainder of his life. For the ability of all four he had admiration: for Coventry and Clifford a deep affection.

Although he was often at Weymouth, and with his children at Waddon, Reymes spent most of his time during these busy years at his lodgings in Gardiner's Lane, Westminster. London was full of friends, of pleasure, and of opportunity. Now that the harsh, weary years of the Interregnum were over, the organs were heard again in the churches, there was riding in the ring at Hyde Park,

THE NEW WORLD OF THE RESTORATION

and, best of all, the theatres were open. In addition to the Cockpit at Whitehall, London could boast five playhouses. Old plays were revived — some eleven by Shakespeare, several by Ben Jonson and many by Beaumont and Fletcher. And there were new plays by Dryden, Davenant, Tuke, and a dozen others. Reymes may not have seen all the plays mentioned by Pepys (there are more than a hundred), but he saw a goodly number, some of them more than once. The only plays he mentions by name, however, are Jonson's *Alchemist*, and *The Little French Lawyer* by Fletcher. For other information we must turn to Mr Pepys who, on January 24th, 1667/68, writes:

> to the King's play house ... and there saw the best part of 'The Mayden Queene' [by Dryden], which, the more I see, the more I love, and think one of the best plays I ever saw, and is certainly the best acted ... sat by Colonell Reames who understands and loves a play as well as I, and I love him for it.

London had changed since the days of Charles I. Many of Bullen's old friends were gone. The Earl of Denbigh, Giles Porter, and Lord Carnarvon had been killed early in the war, and Lady Denbigh had gone to France where, until her death, she continued to serve Queen Henrietta Maria. Her son, Basil, Lord Feilding, had finally returned to the side of the Royalists, and after the Restoration had been made Baron St Liz, but he played little part in the Court of the new King, and there is nothing to indicate that Reymes ever saw him or his restless brother, the Earl of Desmond.

Katherine, Duchess of Buckingham, had died at Limerick in 1649. Of the once powerful Villiers family only her son George, the second Duke of Buckingham, remained in the limelight. He had fought with Charles at Worcester and gained that monarch's gratitude; and he had married General Fairfax's daughter and regained York House. Reymes had known George Villiers well in the old days, and he still saw him often, for the second Duke was a Gentleman of the Bedchamber, a member of the King's Council, and one of the most prominent of the men intriguing against Clarendon. But apparently he neither asked any favours of, nor felt any admiration or affection for this brilliant young rake whose chief attendant he might well have been, had the elder Reymes's plans for his son materialized and the old way of life held.

Reymes had, however, many friends at Whitehall. He was often with Sir Charles Cotterell, the 'cosin Cottrel' of Paris days, now the Master of Ceremonies; he was acquainted with all thirteen of the 'bedchamber men', those gentlemen who, 'each one in his turn' waited 'one Week in the King's Bed-Chamber, there to lie by the King on a Pallet-Bed all night',[16] while among the twelve Grooms of the Bedchamber, who had the privilege of dressing and undressing the King, he counted three old friends, William Legge, John Ashburnham, and Thomas Killigrew.

Whitehall itself was familiar territory. Bullen had known it well during the reign of Charles I, when he had served as Gentleman of the Privy Chamber. But by the 1660s this curious community of gardens, tennis courts, and buildings of sundry shapes and sizes, was familiar territory for many Londoners. In the casual days of Charles II, anyone who wished to pay the price could attend a performance at the Cockpit, while all sorts of people strolled at their ease up and down the 'Stone Gallery', that long passage at the north end of the Privy Garden which led from Holbein Gate to the King's Withdrawing Room. It was the centre of news and gossip, where almost anyone might be seen — newsmongers, politicians, gentlemen and ladies of the Court, and sometimes even the tall King himself, striding hurriedly along.

There was little real privacy anywhere in Whitehall. The King and Queen dined in the great Banqueting Hall, sitting under Rubens's corpulent cherubs, and stared at by the visitors in the gallery; noisy crowds watched the King play tennis, while everyone knew that Lady Castlemaine lived in the apartment over Holbein Gate.

The decorum which had characterized the Court of Charles I had vanished into thin air. Although Reymes had chafed under the restraints of the Puritan regime and welcomed the return of a freer way of life, when Charles II turned his back on all manner of restraint he refused to follow. He was one of many hardworking public servants who, like Sir William Coventry and Samuel Pepys, were distressed by the wanton waste of time and money in the household of the King and in the government of England. He and Pepys often walked together discussing the

THE NEW WORLD OF THE RESTORATION

sorry state of affairs. Of one of their conversations Pepys says:

> I walked into the Court ... and there met Colonell Reames, and he and I walked together a great while complaining of the ill-management of things, whereof he is as full as I am. We ran over many persons and things, and see nothing done like men like to do well while the King minds his pleasure so much. We did bemoan it that nobody would or had authority enough with the King to tell him how all things go to rack and will be lost.[17]

Concerned though he was about the King's neglect of duty, Reymes probably enjoyed Charles's ready wit and his free and easy manner. The two had a good many things in common — their memories of Saint-Germain and life in Paris, courage, resourcefulness, a dislike of hypocrisy and a generally tolerant attitude. As far as religion went, however, theirs were tolerances with a difference. Reymes's tolerance grew out of an honest endeavour at once to remain faithful to the belief of his childhood and to understand the views of others — perhaps even to reconcile the differences among Anglicans, Catholics and a few of the more moderate Dissenters. Charles's tolerance, on the other hand, seems to have stemmed from his lazy indifference to vexing theological problems, though part of this attitude may have been simulated to hide his preference for the Catholic faith. According to Lord Halifax, the *'genteel part'* of that faith, along with its 'exercise of *Indulgence* to *Sinners*', probably recommended it to the King who, 'when he came into *England* ... was as certainly a *Roman Catholick* as he was a Man of Pleasure.'[18]

Whatever the reasons, Colonel Reymes won the King's approval and confidence. Either late in 1663 or early in 1664, he was once again a Gentleman of the Privy Chamber, selected to 'wait' in the Midsummer Quarter, April 1st–June 30th, in the place of Sir John Boys. As it turned out he was able to serve only a little more than two of those three months.[19] Early in June of 1664 came a signal honour. The King called Reymes to him and announced his appointment as special emissary to Tangier.

CHAPTER SIXTEEN

MISSION TO TANGIER

To Charles, Tangier was 'the brightest star in his crown'. Part of the dowry of his Queen, the little Portuguese Princess, Catherine of Braganza, this new Atlantic outpost, on the very tip of North Africa and just across the narrow straits from Gibraltar, was to be a watch-tower against Spain and a key to world trade and colonial expansion. Tangier and all its possibilities stirred the imagination and roused the energy of King Charles as few things had ever done.

Because she brought with her Tangier, Bombay, and two million cruzadoes; because she was a Catholic and had large and beautiful dark eyes, and because she couldn't be as 'dull and Foggy' as the German Princesses who had been urged upon him, the King, on May 21st, 1661, had married shy young Catherine from Portugal. The new Queen forthwith fell in love with her tall husband and he, in his curious way, grew mildly fond of her.

But neither the hopes of the marriage nor the King's dreams of Tangier were to be fulfilled. Catherine seems to have been the only woman with whom Charles slept who bore him no children. And by 1684, the engineers had hacked and blasted the walls, the forts, and the costly new breakwater at Tangier into a desolation of rubble. What was left was abandoned to the Moors. King Charles had struggled with every resource at his command to hold this African stronghold, but he was working against heavy odds — lack of money; the stupidity, indifference, and dishonesty of many of the officials, both in England and Tangier; and the power and cunning of the hostile Moors.[1]

The first Governor of Tangier, Henry Mordaunt, Earl of Peterborough, proving no match for Gayland [Ghailan], the Moorish leader, was replaced in 1663 by a seasoned Scottish soldier, Andrew Rutherford, Earl of Teviot. Pepys, a member of the Tangier Committee, had little respect for Teviot, whom he considered 'a cunning fellow' and one 'who designs to have the profit of victualing the garrison himself'. Nor, for that matter, did he think much of the intelligence of most of the members of the committee:

> At the Committee for Tangier all the afternoon, where a sad consideration to see things of so great weight managed in so confused a manner ... the Duke of York and Mr. [William] Coventry, for aught I see, being the only two that do anything like men; Prince Rupert do nothing but swear and laugh a little, with an oath or two, and that's all he do.[2]

As it turned out, Teviot had barely a year to prove himself, for, on May 3rd, 1664, he and a large contingent of soldiers were ambushed and slain by the Moors. It was this disaster plus rumours of mismanagement which caused Charles to send Colonel Reymes to Tangier.

On June 9th, 'Coll Bullen Rheimes, Gent of Our Privy Chamber in ordinary going to Tangier,' received from 'Charles R' his 'Instruccons'. He was to inspect both 'ye Civil' and 'military part' of 'oure Citty'; 'view ye progress made in ye building of ye mould [mole or breakwater]' and 'ye works and fortifications without ye Toune'; examine all of Teviot's papers and 'informe' himself 'of ye disposicion of Gayland ... toward a further peace or Truce'.[3]

Reymes was to leave on June 12th in the company of Colonel John Fitzgerald, Lieutenant-Governor of Tangier. Fitzgerald, who had been on leave, was now to assume control of the city 'till we [the King] dispose of the government otherwise'.[4] The Deputy-Governor was an Irishman, forthright, able and likeable. In the good graces of the Duke of York and Lord Fitzharding, he had been considered for the post of Governor instead of Teviot, but, according to Pepys, the King and Council had decided against it lest the Irish have 'the whole command there'. Now, once again, his chances looked promising. He and Reymes, who were to be together almost constantly for the next three months, became fast friends, each doing his best to further the other's interests.

Of these three months we know a good deal, for Bullen kept a 'Journal of my Tanger Voyage (from my first taking ship at Portsmouth ... ' The ship he took was the *Swallow*, a frigate carrying forty-two guns and commanded by Captain Hodges. Although Reymes went aboard 'about 3 of the clock', the ship did not sail until seven that evening, for the wind shifted and 'came about just in our teeth'. It was to be almost a month before the *Swallow* sailed into the harbour at Tangier. Early in the voyage they met two ships coming from Virginia, 'loaden with tobaca for Rotterdam ... from whom wee had 3 men, tobaca and ... a flying squirrel'; on June 29th there was 'a good shoure of raine' — a good thing, for their water had begun 'to smelle' — and on July 5th they 'descried a lusty ship of 400 tuns ahead', which was thought to be a 'Turkish man of war' but turned out to be a 'Duchy Marchand bound for Lisbon ... We made her strike [lower her flag, a courtesy demanded of the Dutch in English waters], and sent a bord her and feched 4 Inglishmen from her (seamen).' They sighted Tangier on July 9th, but 'could not wether Cape Spratt' until the next morning, Sunday.

No sooner had he landed than Reymes was hard at work. He visited the buildings where victuals were stored; inspected the bake house 'which had 2 ovens that would bake 800 wayte of meale at a Batch ... each loafe waying $3\frac{1}{2}$ lbs and 2 of them is each souldiers proportions a weeke.' He straightened out the tangled muster rolls so that the soldiers might at last be paid; met with the Commissioners; attended a court martial, and rode 'to the out sentinels and to Fort Charles and Cambridge fort'. He learned to appreciate the formidable cunning of the Moorish leader, Gayland, and not once, but many times, visited and measured the mole, the famous stone breakwater, so necessary in that wind-swept harbour. He talked to the workmen and to Sir Hugh Cholmley, the engineer in charge, and realized, as did all too few of the officials in England, the difficulties encountered in constructing the first great jetty ever built in deep tidal water.

As a special agent of the King, Reymes was in a unique position; he was deferred to and consulted about every major problem that arose. Among other matters he was asked to deal with the 'factious and seditious' Mr Wilson and Mr Davis. Mr J. Wilson, merchant in Tangier, had been imprisoned by Sir Tobias Bridges (in charge before Fitzgerald's arrival) for reviling the late Earl of Teviot. Actually Wilson had done little more than blame Teviot for his rash action and accuse him of running the government in the 'French fashion, making all trades farme their employment of him'. A good many agreed with Mr Wilson. Fitzgerald had had many sharp differences of opinion with Teviot and Reymes told Pepys:

> how it is clear that, if my Lord Tiviott had lived, he would have quite undone Tangier, or designed himself to be the master of it. He did put the King upon most great, chargeable, and unnecessary works there, and took the course industriously to deter all other merchants but himself to deal there, and to make both King and all others pay what he pleased for all that was brought thither.[4]

In view of all this it is not surprising that Colonel Reymes, who seemed to know how to handle the testy Sir Tobias, persuaded him to release Wilson and settle for a milder sentence — temporary house-arrest.

John Davis presented more difficulties. In the first place he was a political prisoner, and political prisoners, sent periodically from the Tower of London, were a source of never-ending difficulty in Tangier. Moreover, Davis was no common criminal, but a Member of Parliament, a victualler to the Navy, and surveyor to the Duke of York. He was also boldly vocal in his criticism of the *status quo*. For uttering 'passionate bold truths' he had been put in the Tower and later deported to Tangier, to the dismay of Teviot, who wrote to Henry Bennet, Secretary of State, beseeching that

> I may be rid of him ... for this is the unfittest place imaginable for a person of his sort. He hath liberty of toun & Castell. What he doth and sayth I am not Conscious to ... [5]

In order to discover what Davis did say and do, Teviot had asked a Mr Frederick Becker to observe him. Becker made this report:

> I have found that he is a person of dangerous principles, on all occasions venting ... his seditious opinions ... saying that men were but fooles to say the King accountable to none but God ... Kings were but men as other men, and the king one man & the people of England nineteen hundred thousand,

and of the number, eighteen hundred and ninety nine thousand were of his opinion. He hath showed letters wherin have been contained great scandals against the King ... about my Lady Castlemaine and Mrs. Steu[art] ... and hath declared his resolution never to stoope to the king ... 6

Like Teviot, Bridges had been unable to handle the troublesome Mr Davis and had turned to Reymes and Fitzgerald for help. The patience and understanding these two showed this outspoken gentleman speaks well for the tolerance of seventeenth-century England. They dined with him and reasoned with him, and finally persuaded him to agree to his wife's plea that he seek asylum in Spain. At last, on July 18th, Mr Davis was won over and signed his 'Consent to bee sett ashore in Spaine'. And, after one last, rebellious flourish, 'great Complaints ... concerning monys for his voyage', John Davis, early in August, meekly departed for Spain.

Two weeks later, on August 16th, Reymes himself left Tangier. 'The Governor and all the officials brought me to my boat and gave me eleven guns. We sett sayle about midnight.' Next day they 'came to an anchor in Calez [Cadiz]'. Here Reymes stayed in the house of the Consul, Martin Wescombe, who showed him the town and took him 'to a playe'. Early on Sunday morning, August 21st, he was again aboard the *Swallow* waiting to sail. 'Severall still came a board with the mony. The lyon came also a bord ... We set sayle about 2 o clock.'

Were it not for a letter written that same day by the Consul to Henry Bennet, the 'lyon' who 'came also a bord' would continue to puzzle posterity. This letter from Wescombe which Reymes carried to Bennet, along with a 'white round box', reads:

> These are only to accompany a lyon in a cage with collar & chayne ... sent by the Governor to yr honor. The lyon was sent hither 8 March since by Gueland [Gayland] and presented to the Governor of this place. And hee sent it [to] the Conde de Mollina. Its a very tame beast, even as a lamb, [I] having kept him heare in my house since Aprille last. I now send him by the Swallow frigyit ... Ye ... Capt. [Capt. Hodges] hathe my dirrections conserning the dyet of ye creature. There is a white round box sealed upp, which

Coll. Bullen Rheames hath done mee the favor to undertake to deliver yr honor ... in which is a collar for sd [said] lyon with ye Conde de Mollina's coat of arms & motto ... Coll. Rheames canne and will aquent yor Honor of all affayres in these ryn [regions] & Africa.[7]

The docile lion which had been passed so deftly from Governor to Count, to long-suffering Consul, to Secretary of State, apparently found not even a temporary residence with Sir Henry Bennet. The chances are that the 'tame beast', probably bereft of its unique collar, became a permanent guest in the menagerie at the Tower of London, already famous for its collection of lions.

On Thursday, August 25th, Reymes went ashore at Lisbon where he was entertained by the Consul. On Friday afternoon he saw 'the Catchia dell torro [bullfight]'; on Saturday 'went after dinner to see the Queen Mother ... but she having seene no man since her retirement sent me her answer by a gent: named Francheses de Gonsalves', and by Tuesday, laden with gifts — 'Melons and Grapes ... baskets of frute, bread and 6 loaves of sugar' — was once more aboard the *Swallow*. But the winds were contrary and it was Friday before they, 'God be praysed got to sea'. Fortunately the winds 'continued favorable' and nine days later, on Sunday, September 11th, Reymes 'went ashore at Waymouth, and in the afternoone got home. All ... things safe and well for which God be praysed.'

As he wrote to Fitzgerald, the Colonel arrived in London on Thursday night, September 15th, only to find that

> the King, the Duke, my Lord Fitzharding, Mr. Secretary Bennet that morning gon to Bagshot to hunte the stagg, where they stayed so as they cam not home till Satterday night. As soon as they returned I wayted on Sr H. Bennet, by whom I thought to be presented to the King ... who very kindly went with me to Whitehall ... But the King, being weary and suping privately, I was apoynted to attend in the morning.
>
> In the morning I went againe to Mr. Secretary who ... being then in bed, and fearing he should not be reddy time enuf ... desired me to use some other of my bedchamber acquaintances ... and he would be there time enuf before I

could fall upon anything matteriall. So away went I to my Lord Fitzharding ... who, although he was also then in bed, rise presently and carried me to the King to whom I presented yor letter ... who seemed very joyfull at my return ... Hee, being then going to Prayers, put your letter in his pocket and commanded me to attend in the afternoon at 3 o clock.

At 3, I came, and, as soone as he sawe me, he went into his drawing roome ... where were assembled onely the Privie Counsell. And, being set, as he uses to doe when in Counsell there ... the d. of Yorke, Prince Rupert, the D. of Albemarle, my Lord Archbishop of Cant:, Mr. Vice Chamberlain, and both the secretarys, all set round, and Sir H. Bennet with pen, inck and paper by him.

I was called in. Then his Matie began, saying 'Well Reymes, let me heare now how things stand in Tanger. Give us an account of your Imployment there.' So, beginning my story from our first arrivall there, I proceeded as orderly as my memory would give me leave. But I told the King ... I did humbly desire the letter you sent ... might be read ... to which the Duke hearing, stept to the dore and called for that letter from Mr. Coventry, then in the Bed Chamber.

At which they were all very well satisfyed, makeing now and then som interuption of Commendations ... as when that artickell was read that expressed you did intend to joyne som of the townsmen to the officers in judging matters concerning the marchants. And when the artickell was read that you had payd all the non effectives to avoyd the Clamor of widdows and children, the King and all cryd twas very well done ... In fine, the relation was so satisffactory, and the King was so well pleased with my booke, which he held in his hand and perused all the time, as ... all of them confesed, they never had so good an account ... in all their life.

And I overheard the King say to himselfe, as he was turning over the booke, 'Indeed, indeed, it was very well done and playne' ... And when they rise, the King commanded me to attend the Comitte for Tanger next day ...

There is no copy of the letter read at this meeting, but it probably contained complimentary references to Reymes, for, in a letter to

MISSION TO TANGIER

Bennet, Fitzgerald extolled the Colonel's industry, ability, and grasp of the situation at Tangier, suggesting that he be entrusted with the purchasing of supplies for that city.[8] Nor, unfortunately, is there any extant copy of Reymes's 'booke' which the King found 'so exact and playne'. But to turn back to the letter.

> So having desired all yor friends and mine to be present, I came [to the Tangier Committee] at which was his Royall Highness [the Duke of York], Prince Rupert, the Duke of Albemarle, the Lord Fitzharding, and Vice Chamberlain, Mr. Coventry, Coll Legg, Sr Will Rider, Sr Rich Ford, and Mr. Peeps, Mr. Povee etc. Being sett, I was cald for and to them I gave a shorte repetition ...

It was of this committee meeting that Pepys, on September 19th, 1664, writes:

> ... to White Hall to a Tangier Committee, where Colonell Reames hath brought us so full and methodicall an account of all matters there, as that I never have nor hope to see the like of any publique business while I live again.

This was signal praise from Mr Pepys, usually so critical of the ineptness and dishonesty with which Tangier affairs were conducted.

Reymes goes on to tell Fitzgerald that

> My Lord Archbishop rec'd your letter very kindly and sayd ... he did believe you would make good the high Comendations the Duke of Yorke gave of you to him ... no man ever had greater comendations nor stands higher upon the hopes ... of well doeing than you doe at present. Therefore goe on and Prosper, and be most confident of my fayth, care and industry to serve you.

Bullen was as good as his word and worked hard to have his friend named Governor of Tangier. But his efforts were to prove futile, for Bennet was privately urging the King to appoint Sir John Belasyse.

Reymes's long letter to Fitzgerald is full of news and gossip. 'I wish I were neere your eare for one howre ... to whisper ... things ... but I hope hereafter we shall have an opportunity ... '

He recounts the friction between Lady Teviot, who had returned on the *Swallow*, and her late husband's kinsman, Lord Rutherford, who 'will hardly get there horses together ... He, by vertue of the Laws here, pretends to the whole estate ... ' Then the Colonel turns to

> the other sort of newse. The Dyett at Court goes up againe the first of October ... a littell from every table, beginning even on the Kings, and so downward to the very Dudg [drudge?] of the Courte. Sr Winston Churchill is put into Sr Grove Barkers place of Clarke Controler and one of the Greene Cloth ... But O poore Clunn is killed, he that acted the Alcamist, the French Lawyer and Hugo de Petre so rarely as I believe he will hardly be imitated. 4 men murdered him after they had robd him, goeing to his Country house one evening, whereof 3 were Irish, one English. The English was prest, 2 of the Irish hangd, and the 3rd escaped.

Fitzgerald did not get the post he coveted — Lord Belasyse was appointed Governor of Tangier in December of 1664 — and Reymes was not made purchaser of supplies there. But the Colonel's reputation was so enhanced by his capable handling of the Tangier mission that before the year was over, he was appointed to another and even more important post.

CHAPTER SEVENTEEN

SERVANT OF THE SICK AND WOUNDED

There had been talk of war with Holland long before Reymes left for Tangier. The old jealousy of Dutch maritime power which, during Cromwell's regime, had led to the First Dutch War, still burned. Already in control of trade in the Dutch East Indies, Holland was threatening English commerce in every quarter. In 1614, Parliament, in response to the complaints of the English merchants, voted for protection of English trade, and many of the country's leaders urged immediate action. Although war was not to be officially declared until the following February, preparations were well under way by the autumn of 1664.

Colonel Reymes was to have an important role in the Second Dutch War. On November 11th, 1664, he, along with Sir Thomas Clifford, Sir William Doyley and John Evelyn, was made one of the Commissioners 'for sicke & wounded Seamen & Souldiers and Prisoners etc.' with a salary of £300 a year. It was a challenging assignment, for these four men were virtual pioneers in the humanitarian side of warfare. They did much to alleviate suffering, but they might have accomplished more had they been given adequate funds. They were unusually able men and, with the possible exception of Doyley,[1] of unquestioned integrity. Moreover, they were powerful enough to bring pressure to bear on the Privy Council and get what funds were available. But do what they would, there was not enough money to provide adequate food or care for their own sick and wounded or for the Dutch prisoners. In desperation, the Commissioners were to strain their credit, to dig into their own pockets, angry at their helplessness in the face of the suffering on every side. They fell short of their goal, yet thanks to their efforts, England was far ahead of the rest of the world in her care of the victims of warfare.

Each of the four men was assigned a special district (Reymes was given Hampshire and Dorset), but each also served as a member of the Board of Commissioners which, during November and December of 1664, met three times a week at Painters' Hall in Little Trinity Lane. Later the meetings were less frequent, and after Reymes left for his headquarters at Portsmouth, he was seldom able to attend.

During his first year in Portsmouth, the Colonel wrote and kept copies of ninety-two letters relating to his duties as Commissioner. In alternate moods of hope, fury, frustration and amusement, these letters tell the story of the trials of a Commissioner of the Sick and Wounded. Beneath their pervasive irony and outspoken vexation, two facts stand out sharp and clear — Reymes's determination to perform his duties to the best of his ability, and his deep concern for the unfortunate ones allotted to his care.

About the middle of November Reymes had gone to Portsmouth to make the necessary preparations for the task ahead. He had engaged his assistants — doctors, nurses, clerks; found living quarters and office space in the home of his surgeon, Grantham Wyan; made arrangements for quartering the sick and wounded at Portsmouth, Gosport, Fareham, and Cowes on the Isle of Wight; persuaded the Mayor of Winchester to house the Dutch prisoners in the jail there; had given the Earl of Sandwich a packet of printed papers indicating where the sick and wounded were to be sent, and had explained to him what quarters he had 'designed for each qualification of distempers'. By the end of the year everything was in shipshape order, and the Colonel was congratulating himself on the speed and efficiency with which he had completed his preparations, when he ran into a snag — the cantankerous Sir Philip Honywood.

Out of a clear sky, Honywood, the Deputy-Governor of Portsmouth, announced that neither sick nor wounded men would be allowed in that city. And when Reymes, trying to mollify him, promised that 'noe infectious' persons, but only the wounded, would be brought in, he was unimpressed, insisting that 'ye smell & stink of their wounds would cause some disease.' Dismayed by this turn of events, Colonel Reymes wrote to his friend Fitzharding for advice and help. Lord Fitzharding, the obliging Bedchamber Gentleman who had got up that Sunday morning in September and conducted him to the King to make his report on Tangier, apparently approved of Reymes's new plan for appeasing Honywood — 'to quarter both the sick and wounded at the point ... a place without the town.'² But Honywood refused to be appeased, declaring that 'noe manner of sick persons ... be sett a shore' even at the point outside the city. And so the matter rested, leaving the Colonel 'somwhat in the briers'.

Reymes also wrote to his close friend, Sir Thomas Clifford, regaling him with an account of the difficult Honywood. This, like all the letters to Clifford — he wrote nine within the space of six weeks — is frank, informal and long. After explaining the situation in some detail he says:

> It seems we have counted all the while without our Host. And must call in all printed papers wch ... I sent L:d Sandwich and he distributed throughout the fleet. I must also find new Chirgeons and a new Clerke and, in short, undoe all I have done, wherein I tooke so much delight, because it was so well settled, and did agree with the order of the Councell and yor Instructions ... Indeed I must confesse I began to be a little proud at my good success in putting things into so good a posture in so short a tyme. But now my Babell must doune, and I must begin all anew ...

The passage is revealing, showing as it does the characteristic enthusiasm with which Reymes had undertaken his new task, and the industry and care, perfectionist that he was, in completing it so quickly and, as he thought, so successfully. It sounds a little like the eager young Bullen of the 1630s, but the touch of rueful amusement at the blow to his self-satisfaction belongs to the detachment of maturity. The next paragraph continues the ironic mood.

> Sure we ought to have another title to our Imployment — or leave out sick and wounded — else we shall loose our Prattique ... and be forsed to make quarantine ere admitted into the House of Commons. At Winchester the townes women were struck Dumb at the reports of the Prisoners coming there ... And until I had assured them no infectious persons should enter their Gates, they all got to the windward of me ... I think you must move the King that we may walke

with white staves, as the searchers do in tyme of Plague. If you thinke they will ever grow to be Controllers and Treasurers staves pray doe, that we may a little vie with our Brother Churchill in his preferment.

Sir Winston Churchill's appointment as 'Clarke Controller and one of the Greene Cloth' had apparently annoyed some of his fellow M.P.s. The fanciful picture of the white staves of the Commissioners growing into the staffs of office of Controller and Treasurer is interesting, in view of the fact that Clifford was later to hold those very positions.

The rest of the letter is in a more serious vein. Reymes is troubled by the rumour that the 'Sessions and Assizes' will be moved from Winchester because of the prisoners, 'a sad requittal unto the poore Citty for their cheerfull obeying the King ... and I think you will do very well to move my Lord Chiefe Justice ... about it.'

A few days earlier Reymes had written to Clifford thanking him for 'the little parcell of news' (the announcement that Sir Thomas had been made Sub-Commissioner of Prize Goods) and adding:

Pray if there be sub-Commissioners for Counties or Ports, lett not me be forgotten ... in which imployment I have some insight alredy, and had a promise from his Matie for the same before I went to Tanger. One word from Mr: Secretary [Bennet] doth the business, & I hope it will not be inconsistent with my present imployment, since it obligates me to the same station. Pray, when you see a fitting tyme, give me your assistance therein.

Only once was Reymes away from Portsmouth for any length of time. On January 12th he left 'for South Hampton, so to Poole and thence to Waymouth' and then on to London. There were several reasons for his journey — business connected with his office of Vice-Admiral of Dorset (the pressing of seamen); a brief visit at Waddon, and, in London, conferences with the Commissioners and attendance at Parliament. While he was at Poole 'about the pressing', welcome news came from Clifford. Sir Thomas had spoken with Bennet and secured from him the promise of the post of Deputy-Treasurer of Prizes at Portsmouth for his friend.[3] In his letter of appreciation Reymes says:

SERVANT OF THE SICK AND WOUNDED

I know not which way to expresse my thankfulnesse, my language being to slender for my heart. But if you please ... let him know I doe accept of the favors & will make it my business to deserve his smiles, by my faith and Industry, for I really honor him ...

Late on Friday night, February 24th, Reymes was back in Portsmouth, ready to resume his old and undertake his new duties. With his more than three years' experience as Vice-Admiral of Dorset, he was well qualified for his new position, and soon won the respect of Baron Ashley, the Treasurer of Prizes. As Commissioner, his old trouble, lack of money, was waiting for him, as his letter to Doyley reveals:

It was high tyme I came ... to appease ye Clamor of our Nurses ... Pray then send me ... 600 lb ... send to Capt. Cock ... to send it by Thursdayes wagon ... Ye people and the imployment will require my constant aboad amongst them, or else indeed we shall beggar ye Croune, for I find little Artifices in allmost every body, which if not early nipt, will speedily swell to a great sume ... Hasten away money in specie else we perish.

War had been officially declared on February 25th, 1665, but as yet no engagements had taken place. More English ships, however, were going to sea, prepared to seize Dutch prizes or to take part in possible skirmishes. Seamen were desperately needed, and there was a concerted effort to round up all those who had recovered from wounds and disease. Pressure had been put on the Colonel to send such men back to their ships, and on March 5th he writes to Clifford:

I doe sweep hous every day of all such as are fitt to send on board, and have brought ye number from almost 500 ... to less than fifty.

He is thankful that they have no cases of smallpox or other infectious diseases, but is distressed at the suffering due to the 'terrible cold winter'.

The men ... want bedding ... And so, lying up & doune ye Deck, contract such desperate numnes in their limbs ... their limbs scarce moveable, so as many of their feet & legs doe gangreen ... I heare nothing of mony ... Pray hasten Capt. Cocke ...

Later, in response to the continuing insistence that all malingering seamen be returned to their ships, Reymes wrote to the Commissioners:

> I dare say there is not 3 men now on shore that are well enough to be sent on board. Nay ... we have been chid for sending men too soon ... by my Lord Sandwich ... So our Condition is like ye poore Dog, who was beat till he stunk, and then beaten for stinking. But let them [the critics at Court] talke what they will ... I doe the best of my skill, and doubt not to be able to Justifie my proceedings as well to his Matie, as to my oune conscience, or to any Juditious person that will give himselfe ye trouble to looke into it.

There were two horns to the dilemma which confronted Reymes, a dilemma made more acute by the imminent arrival of the King at Portsmouth. One was the necessity of clearing the city and vicinity of as many seamen as possible, so that the royal visitors and their entourage might not be offended by the sight or smell of the ill-clad sailors; the other was the need to still the clamour of the unpaid nurses, lest their complaints reach the ears of the King. To avoid the latter contingency Reymes paid them out of his own pocket.

King Charles arrived at four on Tuesday afternoon, March 7th, and stayed until Thursday evening. As soon as he had gone, Reymes wrote to the Commissioners:

> Be pleased to know I did so bestir my stumps, as I gott so much money upon my oune credit, as stopt ye mouths of all Complaints before ye King came ... The King ... went abord severall shipps, & is ye most pleased with ye Royall Oake of any Ship he hath, in so much as he hath appointed just such another to be built, with the expression, 'pray lett it not be better.' She cost 6000 lb, less than the Katherine, & is 10000 lb better. All our Learned Gressam Colledge Artists, as my Lord Brunckart [Brouncker], Sr Robert Murry etc ... doe yield her to be ye finest Man of Warr in all weathers and in all seas.

SERVANT OF THE SICK AND WOUNDED

Reymes's need for money was growing more acute. To meet emergencies he used what cash he had, and borrowed wherever and from whomever he could, turning often to Constance Pley, who managed to supply him with considerable amounts — as much as £400 at a time. Eventually the money borrowed from Mrs Pley was repaid. With his own affairs Reymes was less successful.

The other Commissioners were also in difficult straits, but they were often in London and could appeal to Captain Cocke in person for whatever funds he had. He never had enough. There was not enough money to keep the ships in proper repair or to pay the seamen, and far from enough to take care of the increasing numbers of the sick and wounded, to say nothing of the Dutch prisoners. The situation was aggravated by an inadequate system of credit. This worked a particular hardship on Reymes who, when he finally received an order for money, found it well-nigh impossible to cash. Hence his constant plea for 'specie'.

Writing to Cocke on March 18th, the Colonel says:

> Let me intreate you to find out som more certen way of payment then the bills you send, or tis Impossible I shall be able to stay here, being reddy to be torne in pieces with herds of ugly, old, wild women, as I goe up and doune the streets ... Pray hasten away 600 lb more ... even by the next Portsmouth waggon, whose Master will secure your mony and paye it at his coming cheaper then I can get it here, with all my wayting ... Before God, if you doe not send som more, and that spedely, I must be forced to leave all ...

In spite of all his dramatic pleas, Reymes could never get enough money to pay off old debts and meet current expenses. For the shortage of funds Cocke was not to blame, but why he refused to send it 'in specie' by the heavily guarded money wagon is not clear. The whole procedure must have reminded Bullen of the letters he wrote to his father in the early 1630s, letters full of cogent, unanswerable arguments for sending his allowance in a more convenient fashion. The letters to Cocke proved just as futile.

There were other troubles besides money. When the number of Dutch prisoners began to increase, the authorities at Winchester began to worry. The men, crowded into a jail near the centre of town, might, so the townspeople feared, become a source of infection. They wanted them moved to Magdalen College, an almshouse on the east side of the river Itchen and about a mile beyond the city wall. The Mayor agreed and, at long last, the Privy Council agreed, stipulating that the Mayor and Aldermen make the hospital 'fitt for reception of Prisoners' and provide 'for the old people which shall be removed therupon'. Then, just as Reymes was congratulating himself on having been able to help the good people of Winchester, the good people, unwilling to bear any of the expenses, decided they wanted none of it. In vain Reymes pointed out 'that if you will have the Rose you must have the Prickle with it' — they still refused.

The care of the prisoners was a source of endless contention between the Dutch and English, each accusing the other of ill treatment.[4] In late February, Sir George Downing, to advertise the treatment accorded the Dutch, suggested a 'voluntary' manifesto from the prisoners at Colchester. But the resulting declaration painted so rosy a picture as to make its spontaneity suspect.

There is no evidence that Reymes knew of the Colchester manifesto, but during the King's visit to Portsmouth, Bennet (Lord Arlington now) had told him of the 'ill treatment of the English prisoners in the low Countries under pretense that their prisoners were not well used in England'. As a result of this conversation, Reymes, on April 2nd, wrote to Arlington that he had composed and had translated into Dutch 'a little manifesto' for the prisoners at Winchester 'to subscribe to'. Several of them, he says, read it and wanted a few things changed, so 'I bid them take it home & alter it as they pleased, so they pursued what I intended and spake nothing but truth.'

The 'little manifesto' is certainly no spontaneous document, nor does Reymes pretend that it is. In fact he admits his authorship so frankly that one is inclined to believe him when he says he told the men to make what changes they wished, as long as they spoke the truth and followed the spirit of what he had written. The manifesto reads:

> For as much as wee ... are credibly informed (made to beleeve) that the English prisoners ... are very ill used as to

their dyet, and ... beaten and loaded with chains ... under pretense that now their Countrymen were as ill dealt with at Winchester ...

Now know ... that we ... declare the contrary and acknowledge to have received ... five pence every day ... and have as good wholesome provisions ... as that money will buy ... That we have all friendly ... usages ... here, both from the Marshall & his men ... The Commissioner ... often visiting & inquiring how wee doe & what we want, Comanding, in case any abuses be offered ... wee should acquaint him therewith, & he would see it righted ... He hath provided an able ... Chirugion ... Therewith, wee have been pretty well, there having been but only 4 dead out of near 300 prisoners ...

The declaration presents, it is true, a far from gloomy picture of life in a Winchester jail, and undoubtedly the prisoners realized that acquiescence was the politic course. At the same time, it is not quite fair to discount completely the essential truth of the manifesto. There are too many references to visits to the prison, and to conferences with the authorities in Winchester, to doubt Reymes's concern about the welfare of these men. Moreover, when it was suggested that certain of the prisoners be moved to 'Chelsey House', he was in complete accord, telling Evelyn,

If the Removing of the Prisoners from Winchester to Chelsey (wch will be so much nearer there friends & where possibly they may have a Chamber & Bedd to themselves) will any wayes answer your [wishes?], I shall joyne with you in it ... since the gentler wee use them ... ye more for the King's Honor ...

But even better evidence of the Colonel's sympathy for some of his sick and weary Dutchmen, was his dismay at the order of November 15th, reducing the prisoners' rations to bread and water, an order which he refused to obey as long as the men were on the march.

One spring day, Reymes, just back from a trip to Winchester, found his men angry and resentful. After a period of relative calm, Sir Philip Honywood had seen fit to raise new objections. The Colonel had made every effort to smooth the feathers of this belligerent gentleman, and when Sir Philip had insisted 'that nor sick nor wounded should be brought into the towne, and that the Poynt should be for wounded only', he had not only acquiesced, but had gone a step farther in his efforts to keep peace. 'For,' he wrote to the Commissioners, 'notwithstanding I was left to have wounded men at the Poynt, yet I removed all and every man from the toune and Poynt ... '

Yet, in spite of all these concessions, Governor Honywood now decided to object to a small handwritten sign hung over the door of the clerk's office at the 'Poynt'. Reymes bowed even to this bit of malicious officiousness, but gave vent to his anger in a letter to his 'honored Deare Brethern', the Commissioners:

> For God Sake, Quiet me in my Possession, or else send me a Habias Corpus to remove [me] once for all, for I find the very name and Titell of our Imployment offend Sr P.H. there remayning now nothing but that upon the Place ... Yet he is so displeased ... as he threatens to doe, the lord knows what, if we keepe a thing calld an Office here, which is onely a littell, low empty roome, at the Poynt neere the water side, for your Clarke to keep his books in, and where he doth attend all day, to distribute tickets for quarters, and tickets for the recovered to go aboard ... And that they might know where to find the office, ... had got written upon a littell board, 'Here is the Office for the Sick and Wounded,' and hung it over the Dore mornings & tooke it in at nights. Which Inscription is so greate a trubble to him [Honywood], as he sayes, if your Clarke continues there, he will clap a gard of souldiers into the Roome ... I told him since the board offended him, it should be taken doune, and so it is ... Hee still remaynes angry and thretning ...
>
> My humble desire ... is that you would all three goe in a boddy to my Lord Fitz: and ... not come from him till you have his order in writing (for I have had it in promise alreddy) ... I love not Contraversy, and ayme at nothing ... but the well doeing of our duty and performing our trust ...

Apparently the Commissioners 'in a boddy' persuaded Fitzharding to reprimand the Deputy-Governor, for Reymes had no further difficulties with Honywood.

SERVANT OF THE SICK AND WOUNDED

The last recorded letter sent to Clifford was dated March 23rd, shortly before Sir Thomas joined the fleet. Henceforth Reymes was to write most frequently to John Evelyn. On April 16th, 1665, replying to Evelyn's request that he come to London, so that there might be three Commissioners to decide matters of policy, Reymes explains that he dare not leave until the nurses are paid.

> The people have torne one of our chirugeons cloakes off his backe already & I am afraid will doe the Like by mine shortly, & I should come away before they are payd ... Pray had not wee a Privy Seale for 5000 lb more? What is become of all that? ... Why then doth not Cap. Cocke pay my bill drawne for Winchester for 100 lb ... I beseech you looke a Little after the Credits or we must bid good night, & so much for that ...

A week later Reymes wrote again, thanking Evelyn for

> your Promise of endeavoring to get me all I demand ... I have till of late boyed up ye nurses spirits by fair words & now and then a little money ... borrowing (upon my oune acct:) ... but espeacially by promising that I would not goe hence till I had made all even. Those honest Arts ... have hitherto kept my skin whole, for Billingsgate hath not such another Pest of Scolds ...
>
> It seemes they had got a whisper ... as if the Com:ere (meaning me) were goeing to London ... This did so alarm them, as betimes the next morning my door was so beset, as when I came doune the stairs ... my Entry was Baracaded with 20 or 30 of the sharpest tongued women, charging me with an outcry or rather a Jangling (for in an outcry there may be a Harmony) ... they must have their money ... before I went, & that I should not thinke to steale away to London ... That they were sure the Good King (God Blesse him) allowed us money to pay them & wee kept it ... & a 1000 other such Complaints wch another Squadron of them, yt stood without doore in the street, tooke up as an Eccho, & redoubled backe againe, & I ... in the midst of them, crying ... patience ... But all would not serve till I vowed ... I would not stirre hence till they were payd ... their wants

indeed being great & the time Long, since they have ben out of their money ... & so much for that.

Another letter to Evelyn, dated April 26th, has to do with Captain Cocke, suddenly grown super-sensitive. It seems Evelyn had shown him Reymes's letter inquiring about the Privy Seals, and Cocke, construing the question as an aspersion on his honesty, had sent Reymes an angry letter. Reymes writes to Evelyn:

> I find by Capt Cocke, as well as I can hammer it out (I wish he would keep a Clerke) that you have showed him my Letter to you & that therein are some oblique Reflections on him, as if he should rec[eive] our money ... & make use of it himselfe. I hope I have not ... said so ... for I know I doe not beleeve so ...
>
> Possibly I might [have] enquired after the 2 Privy Seales ... supposing ... both ... rec[eived]. But, since they are not, & I in the hands of the Harpyes, wanting food for them, tis likely may speake a Little more concerned then at other times, but not reflecting on him ... If the words will bear it in the Least, I aske his Pardon ... As you have ben Instrumental to make Capt Cocke mistake me, you will doe me the Right to settle him of haveing his wonted good opinion of me, wch I very much desire.

The good opinion of Cocke was imperative if one wanted one's share of the little money available. But Reymes seems to have liked the hard-drinking, talkative Captain. The letters he wrote him — more than a dozen — in which he alternately teased, cajoled, and scolded, bespeak the good-natured, informal relationship between the two men. That of April 30th is typical:

> Did you know the affection & esteeme I have really for you, you would not have taken what I write to Mr. Evelin with the left hand, &, by too much jealousy of yor Honor, create oblique reflections, when I will sweare none was ment ... However, to clear all at once. If the words doe but leane that ways, it was not intended. So, I beg your Pardon for it, as I have reason to doe (I am afraid) for many other slips my pen makes, being neither Scholler nor Scribe. Doe but you pardon my sense, & I will pardon yor Caracter [handwriting]. Yet, for yor comfort now I have a clerke that can pretty well

decipher it ... Pray excuse me that I presse so upon you for money after you have told me how scarce it is.

In May, something more frightening than war was casting its shadow before it. Cases of the plague were beginning to appear. Reymes's earliest reference to this dread disease was on May 4th, when he wrote to Evelyn:

> It seems you have a Report at London as if the Plague were here. But (God be praysed) here is no cause for that Report. Those are the Artifices of the Fanatickes to distract us.[5]

But forces more sinister than the 'Fanatickes' were to blame. The accumulated filth of London, plus a hot, breathless summer, was proving a fertile ally to the fleas which infested London's thriving population of rats. It was the bubonic plague, the old Black Death of Chaucer's day, which, with each advancing summer month, mowed down its victims in steadily increasing numbers. There were 40 deaths in May, 30,000 in September.

In one respect Reymes was fortunate: the plague was making slow progress at Portsmouth, and he, unlike Evelyn and Doyley, had no cases either among the seamen or among the prisoners at Winchester. But householders in Gosport and Fareham were understandably frightened, and refused to take any more of the sick and wounded seamen into their homes. It was only when the Council, at Reymes's request, sent an order to the towns for 'yor assistance ... in providing quarters ... in this sad time of sickness' that he was able to find shelter for his men.

May had come and gone and there was still no money to pay the nurses or the prisoners at Winchester. And there was no London visit for the Colonel. Once more explaining to Evelyn the reasons for his delay, Reymes says:

> Methinks I am Like a man with 2 wounds. I know not wch to dresse first, lest whilst I am dressing one, ye other is bleeding to death. Both mine are in the Belly wch craves incessantly. That at Winchester seemes to be most pressing because [they are] strangers — prisoners; this here is most pittyfulle because sick, because Natives. One large Plaster may doe both. Pray prepare salves and I will spread it to the best of my skill.

Then referring to the prisoners who were to be moved from Winchester to 'Chelsy Colledge', he tells Evelyn that some had been too weak to make the long march. They 'came but to the Top of the Hill without the Towne & were ready to faint ... so as, it had ben an inhuman thing to have forced ... weake and languishing men to have done that ... '

Like everyone else, Reymes had heard rumours of an impending battle, and had been moving his sick to Fareham, 'so our quarters at Gosper [Gosport] may be more free to rec: that glut of wounded men, that may come after an engagement as the more convenient place.' He was wise to be so provident. On June 3rd the first engagement of the war took place off Lowestoft on the Suffolk coast. The English, under the Duke of York, had managed to get the windward position, and by six in the evening the Dutch were in flight. There were heavy losses on both sides, but it was a clear victory for the English. Unfortunately they failed to pursue the flying Dutchmen.

Reymes seems to have respected and admired Evelyn who, perhaps more than the other Commissioners, shared his deep concern for the plight of the men in their charge. But once the two came close to a misunderstanding. In August the Colonel wrote to Cocke about a report being circulated that the nurses in Evelyn's district were promptly paid. This, he said, made his nurses

> so mad, as they curse & Rave ... and have petitioned the King against us, telling it about ... I keep back their money to buy sayle cloth. And 100 other Reproaches ... because you are not sensible of my condicion, as appeares by paying Mr. Evelin his money but lately due, when mine hath been due this 9th of this year ...

Cocke showed this letter to Evelyn. And Evelyn, whose turn it was to have his feelings hurt, seems to have written expressing surprise that Reymes should so resent a kindness to a fellow-Commissioner. Although Reymes was conciliatory in his reply he did not retract what he had written to Cocke.

> I am very sorry you should thinke I am troubled by Capt. Cockes kindness to you. I hope my words will not bear it.

SERVANT OF THE SICK AND WOUNDED

> Nay, I am sure if he were not kind to you I should be much more sorry. If I thinke it a little Injustice that some rec. money & I none, it is because I rec. none, not that they rec. any. And so pray take it. Moreover, my debt is double the age, double the sum & double more troublesome to the King ... These are such reasons as I thought nobody could have taken any exception to ... And because in this extremity I am a little earnest, I am presently misunderstood, misrepresented, so that I am almost afraid to write. I doe not remember in all my life time I have had so much exception agt [against] what I write as I have had of late. I hope I do not deserve it, & so much for that.

Much of Reymes's time in the late summer and early autumn was taken up with the transfer of prisoners. On August 14th a group was moved from 'Chelsy Colledge' to Portchester Castle. They were to be used as day labourers, thus paying for their own keep. At the moment, however, they were proving an additional drain on the Colonel's already depleted purse. Where, he asks Lord Arlington, is he to get the money to feed and clothe them? 'There are 7 score sicke, all contracted by the cold, most of them being, as it were, starke naked ... '

Reymes was genuinely concerned about the prisoners in his care. When, in spite of Arlington's promises, no money came, he wrote to the Duke of Albemarle, saying that he had not only advanced the money for transporting the men, and 'much more, out of my oune purse', but also that he owes over £1,000 to the nurses and surgeons.

> Whereof ... I acquainted the King & the Council a month since, who sent us to my Lo: Treasurer & my Lord Ashly, from whom we were sent to Mr. G. C. [Carteret], thence to Sir Phill. Warwicke[6] ... But at this hour cannot rec. a farthing, so that the poor women are groun raving mad.[7]

The need for money grew even more acute when the prisoners from Portchester Castle were ordered to Bristol, where they were to be employed on boats going to the plantations. On November 12th Reymes wrote to Albemarle:

> This serves to acquaint your Grace that tomorrow ... I send

200 Duch Prisoners to Bristow ... I have given strickt orders to pay all they take in their way ... I have orders to alow them but bread and water after the 15th ... I conceave it is not intended on those that march, nor ... sick.

The new year, 1666, dawned ominously with the news that France had entered the war on the side of the United Provinces. Yet it was not until June that there was another engagement. Again the Dutch escaped, but with few casualties compared to the tremendous losses by the English. The cause of this disappointing turn of events was held to be the unnecessary division of the fleet, and the subsequent failure of Rupert to rejoin Albemarle quickly enough to avert the disaster. Later, however, the English sank twenty enemy ships and made a daring raid on the Dutch coast with the loss of only twelve British sailors.

Then there was another turn of Fate's wheel. On Sunday morning, September 2nd, fire broke out in a baker's house in Pudding Lane. It raged for five days. Most of old London lay in ruins and all would have burned had not the King insisted on blowing up the buildings that lay in the path of the flames.

What with the plague, the fire, the unpaid seamen and the whispers of mismanagement, England was thoroughly sick of the war. By early 1667 peace seemed close. Louis XIV had reached an agreement with Charles and plans for a treaty with Holland were under way. Crews were paid off and only a few ships were kept manned and repaired — economy was the watchword!

Another June came round, and the Dutch, taking advantage of England's frugal unpreparedness, sailed up the Medway to Chatham; destroyed three of the ships lying in the dock — the *Royal London*, the *Royal James* and King Charles's beloved *Royal Oak* — and sailed away towing behind them the *Unity* and the *Royal Charles*. On July 21st, less than six weeks after this ignominious spectacle, a treaty was signed at Breda and the war was over.

By the end of the summer Reymes's role as Commissioner was at an end. It had been a challenging and rewarding experience. In the face of overwhelming difficulties he had done much to alleviate the suffering of those committed to his care; he had served his King and country with energy and intelligence; and had managed to emerge from a struggle, which had often tried his temper and patience, on friendly terms with his fellow-Commissioners and with the many men with whom he had worked. Even the differences with Sir Philip Honywood had been ironed out. That Colonel Reymes took a justifiable pride in his accomplishments is understandable; that his ability and industry were recognized is evidenced by the new honours and responsibilities that crowded the last five years of his life.

CHAPTER EIGHTEEN

THE CROWDED YEARS

1. F.R.S.

On October 10th, 1667, John Evelyn nominated his friend Colonel Bullen Reymes as a Fellow of the Royal Society. A week later Reymes was elected to membership, and on November 7th he was taken by the hand by Sir William Brouncker, the President of the Society, and admitted as a Fellow.

Reymes was not a scientist, but neither were the majority of the Fellows. There were almost three times as many 'non-scientific' as 'scientific' members, a curious phenomenon in a Society which is the symbol of scientific achievement. These so-called 'outsiders' included men of varied occupations, but whatever their occupations and interests, they had, or were supposed to have, three things in common — curiosity, open minds, and a healthy respect for experimental knowledge.

The Royal Society was one of the most forward-looking achievements of the seventeenth century. With its emphasis on empiricism and distrust of petrified tradition, it was the true child of Bacon. At the same time it was not insular, but part of a new climate of opinion which was spreading throughout Europe. In Paris there was the French Academy, and in Florence the Academia del Cimento which, under the sponsorship of Prince Leopold, 'the Patron of all Inquisitive Philosophers of Florence', was interested in facts rather than theories. With both of these groups, as well as with various individuals in Germany and the Low Countries, the Royal Society was in correspondence. It prided itself on its international character. Its members might be of any religion, any country, or any profession, for, says Sprat, it was to be 'the General Banck and Free-port of the world'.[1]

The Society met at Gresham College until 1667, then at Arundel House, one of the old palaces on the Thames. It was there that the Colonel, on Thursday afternoon, November 7th, promised 'to promote the good of the Royal Society' and to be present at as many meetings as he conveniently could, 'especially at anniversary elections and upon extraordinary occasions'.[2] At the weekly meetings (every Thursday afternoon) the Fellows listened to 'Letters, Reports and other Papers', and then watched one of the members perform and explain an experiment. There were experiments on the injection and transfusion of blood from one animal to another; on 'refaction, refraction and condensation'; and on the hatching of chickens by means of lamps — a wide range, for the most part utilitarian.

As a young lad in Paris, Bullen had sat through many a winter night 'discoursing' on medicine and natural phenomena with whomever he could entice into his 'chamber with a fireplace'. And in Florence he had often visited the home of Northumberland, the famous shipbuilder and naval engineer, who had drained the swamp between Pisa and the sea, to listen to the talk of the 'scientists' who foregathered there. 'Restless curiosity' Reymes certainly had; whether he possessed a 'mind free of false images', another of the requirements for a 'non-scientific Fellow', is not so clear. His eyes may have been turned towards the future, but many of his ideas belonged to the past. He bridged a century marked by great changes. In its early decades he had received a training reminiscent of the feudal atmosphere of Chaucer's day; now, thirty years later, he was a Fellow of the Royal Society.

From across the centuries, the step from feudalism to the age of reason and science seems dramatic and sudden. For Bullen it had been a slow and almost imperceptible journey. Just as his attitude towards the role of King and Parliament had altered, almost without his realization, so had other of his views. Not that he discarded all his early precepts. On the contrary, he clung to many of them, some at complete variance with his new outlook. He could listen with interest on Thursday to a scientific discussion on tides, currents and weather disturbances, and hear with approval on Sunday a sermon blaming the unseasonable rains on London's dissolute life. Either he kept his religious beliefs in a compartment sealed off from secular speculation, or, like many of the Fellows, he found little discord between the truths of science and the Anglican faith.

Contrary to popular belief, the Restoration was not irreligious. Though not as dramatic as it had been earlier in the century, religion was still a pervasive influence. Even to such men as Robert Boyle, Christopher Wren, and Isaac Newton, science seemed not an enemy of religion but a new proof of its truth.[3] With such an opinion Reymes would probably have agreed, while with the Society's distrust of excess, he was in complete accord.

The young Royalist Society may seem conservative enough today, but to many in the seventeenth century it was a hotbed of radicalism; to others, the resort of ridiculous crackbrains. There were the conservative groups at Oxford and Cambridge who both feared and despised the empirical emphasis of the Society; there were the emotional enthusiasts among the Dissenters who considered its reliance upon experiment irreligious; and there were the scoffers, who gloried in their cynical pose, the most dangerous of all, according to Sprat, 'For they ... by making it Ridiculous ... may do it more injury than all the ... frowning ... Adversaries.'[4]

To belong to the Society at such a time was a tribute to a man's intelligence, tolerance and courage. Reymes may well have been proud of his new honour. As a Fellow of the Royal Society he was a part of the vanguard of progress.

II. *Surveyor of the Great Wardrobe*

1667 was a good year for Reymes. On November 22nd, some two weeks after his election to the Royal Society, he was appointed Surveyor of the Great Wardrobe at an annual salary of £300. This new post was due in part to his loyal and now powerful friend, Sir Thomas Clifford, who within the space of twelve months had been made Comptroller of the King's Household, a member of the Privy Council, and one of the Commissioners of the Treasury. But it was also due to the reputation for honesty and financial acumen which the Colonel's able performance as Commissioner for the Sick and Wounded and as Deputy-Treasurer for Prize Goods had won for him. There was a crying need for a man of integrity and ability, for the King's Wardrobe Office was suffering from mismanagement and graft.

The Earl of Sandwich, who had been Master of the Great Wardrobe since 1660, involved as he was in other duties, had relied on the honesty of one Mr Townsend.[5] This gentleman was not worthy of the trust. According to Pepys (December 30th, 1667), Townsend was unable to give the Commissioners of the Treasury 'an account of his money received by many thousands of pounds'. As a result, the Commissioners (two of them, Clifford and Coventry, were among Reymes's closest friends) appointed two new officers, Comptroller, Andrew Newport, and Surveyor, Bullen Reymes, who, between them, were to be responsible for the management of the Wardrobe.

Before two months were over, the Colonel had justified the expectations of his friends. On January 29th Pepys records a conversation with Sir William Coventry:

> He tells me that Townsend of the Wardrobe, is the veriest knave and bufflehead that ever he saw in his life, and wonders how my Lord Sandwich came to trust such a fellow and that Reames and —— [i.e. Newport] are put in to be overseers there, and do great things, and have already saved a great deal of money in the King's liverys, and buy linen so cheap, that he will have them buy the next cloth he hath, for shirts.

Although Reymes was supplied with an able clerk, his task was exacting. Literally hundreds of people had to be supplied with liveries and sundry items commensurate with their respective ranks: the royal coach and the royal yachts had to be properly equipped; new hangings had to be purchased, and all the tailors, seamstresses, and artisans supervised and paid. The Colonel had to know his market — when and where to buy; he had to gauge the honesty of the merchants; judge the quality of his purchases, and see that nothing slipped through the fingers of the many underlings who cluttered the halls of the Savoy Palace where the Great Wardrobe was located. The prevention of graft demanded eternal vigilance.

None of Reymes's own letters having to do with his duties at the Wardrobe has survived. But among his papers are three large volumes relating to that office, which give some notion of the many details which took up so much of his time and energy. They also give some idea of life in a King's household.

A typical entry is a letter signed E. Manchester[6] and addressed

To the Right Honble Earle of Sandwich, Master of his Majesties great Wardrobe.

These are to signifie his Maties pleasure to yor Lor: that you provide and deliver to Mr. Thomas Killigrew, Master of their Ma: Comedians, 8 yds of Bastard Scarlett & half yd Velvet for his Livery ... for 1668.

Following this are similar orders for crimson and scarlet velvet for the liveries of the eight 'women Comedians' and the thirteen 'men Comedians',[7] and an order for the stage of the Cockpit: 'Six Turkey chaires, 6 little tyn candlesticks, 1 grt Chair ... as much green bayes as will cover stage. All these perticulers being for his Ma: in his Theatre att Whitehall,' also 'as much greene Bayes as will cover the turning door in the theatre ... and strings to draw it round.'

Elaborate and costly outfits were ordered for the choir-boys, but for the lads whose 'voyces are Changed ... and are to goe from Chapel', merely two suits of plain cloth. Hundreds of liveries were purchased every year. There were liveries for '46 watermen,' for '27 footemen, 10 Coachmen, 26 Groomes and a Kettle Drummer', and for '100 Yeomen of the Guards'. There were even liveries for Bridgett, 'the Strewer of Hearbes', for Randolph Holen, His Majesty's 'Rattkiller', and for Steven Whiffen, the royal 'Corncutter'. Practically all the people at Whitehall went about in liveries — and all of them red!

For the purchase of all those yards of scarlet cloth Reymes was responsible, as well as for the scores of other items that were constantly needed in that elaborate household: 'One suite of hangings, of the story of Donquickzot'; 'a sky colored taffety to cover bird cage & 24 yds of cloth to lay upon stares for her Majesty going down into St James Parke' and so, on and on, for over a hundred folios. Little wonder if, from this relentless record of man's possessions and struggle for place, Reymes sought escape every Thursday afternoon in the sanctuary of the Royal Society in near-by Arundel House.

III. *Privy Chamber, Politics and Parliament*

His residence at Portsmouth had, for a number of years, precluded Reymes's regular attendance at Court, but by April of

THE CROWDED YEARS

1668 he was once more one of the twelve 'Midsummer Quarter Gentlemen' waiting on the King. In spite of the huge sums of money doled out each year to the inhabitants of Whitehall, some were neglected. The Privy Chamber itself was a large, elaborately furnished room, its walls adorned with frescoes by Holbein. But the private quarters allotted to the Gentlemen were in so sorry a state — much of the furniture broken or stolen — that they had decided to buy new furnishings at their own expense. For some reason, either because he had suggested the plan or because he was known to be dependable and willing, the double burden of collecting and purchasing fell on the Colonel's shoulders. Finally, after weeks of prodding, he had received the promised twenty shillings from thirty of the forty-eight gentlemen and had purchased the necessary items, including: '12 Turkey worke Chayers'; '3 Pewter basons & 3 Chamber pots', 'a looking glass', and 'the lent of 7 hangings for 6 weeks'. Some of the men, including Ambrose Pudsey and John Seymore in Reymes's own quarter, never did pay.

Reymes spent as much time as he could spare at Whitehall. The Court was not only a place of idle gossip, but a listening post for the intrigues which sometimes threatened the very existence of Charles's government. Not that the Colonel didn't enjoy gossip. With all his driving sense of duty, he found time to listen to the latest bit of scandal about Lady Castlemaine and *la belle* Stuart, and he could drink and bandy stories with the best of them. He had many friends at Whitehall who kept him abreast of what was going on, and, most important of all, he had a chance to talk informally and frequently with Charles, who was usually so hard to corner when he thought business was in the offing.

The Wardrobe Office at the Savoy, the Court at Whitehall, and, when Parliament was in session, the House of Commons, took their toll of Reymes's time and energy. Although in the five years prior to his death the House sat for less than eighteen months, it included one of the most important periods of the Colonel's Parliamentary career, the long session of October 1667 to May 1668.

Even before it had been prorogued in February of 1667, the temper of the Commons had changed. The one-time House of

Courtiers was turning into a 'House of Critics'.[8] Months before the Medway disaster there had been disenchantment with the administration, and after that June day when the Dutch sailed up the river, there was a constantly increasing demand for a new session of Parliament to investigate the country's finances and the management of the war.

Pepys, on June 25th, 1667, was delighted with the rumour that the King, against the advice of York and Clarendon, had decided to call 'Parliament in thirty days ... pray God it hold though some of us go to the pot.' The next day, near Westminster Hall, he 'met with Colonell Reames'. As the two walked together the Colonel briefed his friend on the latest news from Court: there had been a misunderstanding between the King of France and Lord St Albans [Henry Jermyn] 'which Colonell Reymes tells me, puts them into new melancholy at Court, and he believes hath forwarded the resolution of calling Parliament.'

On October 17th, 1667, just ten days after Parliament had convened, Reymes was appointed to the committee 'to inquire into the miscarriage of affairs in the late war'. This was the most important committee of the session. Both the fiscal policy and the Navy were on trial, and many besides Pepys were fearful lest they 'go to the pot'.

Since Reymes was, in all probability, a government nominee on this committee, he was likely to be sympathetic to the problems of the administration. As for the Navy, he had been in close contact with it for years and was on friendly terms with many of the commissioners and officers. Not that he considered them all blameless. He was well aware that there was a certain amount of graft and a good deal of inefficiency within their ranks. He had had too many struggles trying to get money for sailcloth; he had stumbled upon too many questionable practices in the sale of prize goods, and he had seen too many under-nourished and unpaid seamen wandering about the streets of Portsmouth to brush aside all the charges as inconsequential. At the same time he realized that the chief fault lay not in the mismanagement of funds, but in the lack of funds to manage. Who was to blame for that? The King? Yes, because of his personal extravagance, which roused the animosity and tightened the purse strings of his people. Parliament? Also yes, for their failure to realize how much

THE CROWDED YEARS

it cost to run a government in time of peace, let alone during a war.

Samuel Pepys and Sir William Coventry were under special scrutiny. Although Reymes may have guessed that the hardworking Clerk of the Navy was not averse to an occasional gift on the side, he apparently liked Pepys and felt at ease with him. The two men had several things in common: industry and orderly minds; enjoyment of good company, of music and the theatre; distress over the King's extravagance and neglect of duty, and a deep affection and respect for Coventry.

The Colonel did what he could for his two friends. On October 31st Pepys writes:

> Colonel Reames and cozen Roger Pepys ... do tell me how the Duke of Albemarle and Prince [Rupert] have laid blame on a great many and particularly our Office in general; and particularly for want of provisions, wherein I shall come to be questioned ... Reames did tell me of a fellow last night ... did say he did see one of the Commissioners of the Navy bring in three waggon-loads of prize-goods into Greenwich one night ... but this is me, and I must expect to be called to account, and answer what I did as well as I can.

A few days later, Reymes managed to get copies for him of the 'Narratives' of Albemarle and Rupert 'very cheaply ... of which,' says Pepys (November 4th, 1667), 'I am mighty glad, both for my present information & ... my future satisfaction.'

It must have been a great satisfaction for Colonel Reymes to see his friend, on March 5th, 1668, stand before the bar of the House of Commons and, for three uninterrupted hours, defend himself and the Navy with eloquence and logic. Pepys, who, to begin with, knew far more about the Navy Office than anyone else, had been working hard on his defence for a good four months. He had also been worrying, though no one would have guessed, from his air of calm assurance, that he had slept but three hours the night before, or that he had just fortified himself with a half-pint of mulled sack and a dram of brandy.

Pepy's speech was so convincing that little action was taken against the Navy.[9] There was, however, a condemnation of the division of the fleet in June of 1666. Sir William Coventry, as one of the Navy Commissioners, was implicated. For the delay in sending the order for Rupert to rejoin Albemarle he was held responsible. When the question 'That the not timely recalling the Order for Division of the Fleet ... was a miscarriage' came up for a vote, Reymes was against it. He acted as teller for the 'noes' who, however, received only 99 of the 221 votes. Although, as Admiralty official and government supporter, he would have been expected to vote against the resolution, Reymes would have been glad to do so, for he counted Coventry, along with Clifford and Robert Napier, one of his three closest friends. As it turned out Coventry managed so conclusively to prove his innocence that all charges against him were dropped.

Sir William Coventry was an anomaly in the political arena of the seventeenth century. He dared to say what he honestly thought, and to do what he considered best for the country, regardless of consequences to himself. As he told Pepys, 'He himself was the only man, he thinks, at the council-board that spoke his mind clearly, as he thought to the good of the King.'[10]

A vivid and appealing picture of Sir William emerges from the pages of Pepys's diary. In his admiration and affection for Coventry, and in his effort to set down his friend's words exactly as he spoke them, Pepys anticipates Boswell.

Of Reymes's conversations with Coventry there is no such record. Very probably he discussed with him, as he did with Pepys, the sorry state of the country. Certainly he shared Coventry's dismay at the King's extravagance, though he probably would not have dared to tell Charles to his face, as Sir William once did, that were he King, he 'would eat bread and drink water ... and this day discharge all the idle company about me, and walk with only two footmen.'[11] With Coventry's tolerant attitude towards religion Reymes was in general accord, while his friend's famous definition of an 'Upright Trimmer — One who would sit upright & not overturn the boat by swaying too much on either side'[12] was close to his own mature concept of a stable government in which King and Parliament acted as mutual checks.

Membership in the hard-working 'miscarriage of the War' committee was itself enough to keep a man busy, but the Colonel, during the 1667-8 session, served on more than twenty others. The concerns of many of these committees — 'monies due the crown', the repair of the harbours and piers of Great Yarmouth,

THE CROWDED YEARS

the use of prize ships for 'the encouraging of trade', the rebuilding of London, the care of indigent Royalist officers, the relief of poor prisoners, and the release of those in debt — reflect Reymes's particular interests. Nor did the Colonel forget his own county of Dorset. He was always, as one Mayor of Weymouth put it, 'friendly in toun affairs'. He secured an order permitting Weymouth to demolish 'the jeaty fort' and use the stones 'for the benefit of the town', and promoted the erection of a new bridge, apparently making the initial contribution, for in his letter of thanks the Mayor does not doubt 'that our other Parliament Burgesses will follow your liberal example'.[13]

As a Member of Parliament, Reymes may well have felt that he was playing an important part in the development of the machinery of government. But something happened in the year of 1669 to make the King less dependent on Parliament. Associated as he was with men in power, Reymes must have sensed much that was going on in the worlds of politics and religion. He probably knew nothing of the Secret Treaty of Dover, but he could not have failed to hear whispers of the King's and the Duke of York's conversion to Catholicism, and of some sinister plot with France. And, as the year advanced, he, like others, may have been disturbed by the rumour that Parliament was to be dispensed with and an arbitrary government set up.

Many of the rumours were well founded. Soon after the fall of Clarendon in 1667, the King had taken the initiative in government, although he had admitted to his counsels five men, Clifford, Arlington, Buckingham, Ashley and Lauderdale (easily remembered because their initials spell the world Cabal). Clifford and Arlington knew more about Charles's plans than any of the other five, and Reymes was too close to Clifford not to have guessed something of the struggle going on in that young man's heart. By the spring of 1671, even the unworldly Evelyn had suspected Sir Thomas of 'a little warping toward Rome'.[14] Bullen had probably guessed it as early as 1669 when his friend began collecting Catholic books.

Something, perhaps the fear that his association with both open and cryptic Catholics had put the finger of suspicion on him, or some experience which had stirred old doubts and disturbing memories, roused in Bullen the need to justify himself. Dismayed

P

at the thought of disloyalty to the Church of England, and seemingly driven by some obscure sense of guilt, he protests his innocence not in a letter, but in a will! This long, rambling, unfinished document, written some time before the summer of 1672, after directing that his body should be buried in the aisle of Portesham church, launches into a declaration of faith which, no doubt, served to still his own doubts as well as those of posterity.

> ... because thes are times of greate Pretended Nicetys in Religion, even to the begetting of general unreconsilable oppinions ... to the almost ruen and distruction of the most Orthodox and best reformed Church in the world, I think good to declare, I dye a Protestant and in the fayth of Christ, according to the profession of the Church of England as it is now established by Law. In which as I was Baptised, Catekised, Confirmed, and allways communicated in, so I thanke God, I never so much as (in thought) Inclyned to any other, neither to Popish superstition on the one hand, nor to any of those ungovernable sects of the Phanatticks, on the other hand, (And because ingovernable, therefore enimyes to Government, and Peace) witnes the death of the late King Charles the first, and best Prince, that ever Reigned, for whose cruell murder, God forgive them ...
>
> I charge all my Children ... That they doe not departe from the Doctrine, and Diseplyne of the Church of England, as they love their oune soules and me; And as God shall blise them with children of there oune, that they see them also taught, and Catechised in the same fayth, leaving it as a Command to there Children and so, from one Generation to another, for ever. And not trust schoole-Masters and others to teach them, but ... to make it there oune proper busines to see them well Grounded in the church catechise, and to learne it perfitly by harte ...
>
> And in which Catechise I was so well grounded my selfe, (I thank my parents) as I have hetherto (by God's greate mercy) withstood the shock and batterys of all opinnions, beyond sea, and at home to my present satisfaction, and soul's content at this time. Amen.

THE CROWDED YEARS

A third war against Holland had long been expected, but it was not until March 17th, 1672, that the official declaration came. In December, Evelyn, Doyley, and Reymes had again been named Commissioners for the Sick and Wounded (Clifford's place was taken by Sir Henry Ford).[15] Conversant though he was with a Commissioner's duties, the new task proved a drain on the Colonel's waning energy.

A few weeks after June 4th, when he had accompanied Evelyn to Rochester to act as pallbearer at the funeral of a French Commander,[16] mortally wounded at the battle of Solebay, Reymes became seriously ill. He stayed on at his lodgings in the Savoy, doing what he could to direct the affairs of his two offices. By early autumn he was able to be up and about, though he was still weak, and, if the purchase of 'a paire of the finest large Blanckets' and 'a Green Woolen Rug' is any indication, suffering from the cold. But a letter to the Navy Commissioners, written on October 12th in reply to what he considered an unreasonable request, is still full of the old spirit:

> Gentlemen
>
> My long & tedious sickness as also the great weaknesses upon mee of late ... hath prevented ... constant ... writing ... However the inclosed are the severall lists & Copies of ... all the Ships sent on shore at Godsport, & places adjacent ...
>
> But now gentlemen, as for your Alphabeting, as we have it not in or [our] Instructions ... nor indeed is it possible to bee done ... without neglecting some more material thing ... For pray whoe in the meantime shall quarter sick and wounded, when they come in sometimes by hundreds day & night: whoe shall transcribe our foule books into the ledger; ... whoe shall make enquiries after run awaies; whoe shall pacify mutinies ... Whoe have wee to doe all this & much more but one poore Deputy, & hee without a Clarke ... wheras I conceive you have Clerkes not a few ... It is true the last warre, I in my district (& I only) ... then upon the place in person ... did ... with mine own hand ... make you the return in that forme, without being first required ... But found the lab[or] soe Herculean, & soe little thanks for it ...

as I must begg your pardon for the time to come, unlesse ... yor Clerks prove more kinde, then they have been ...

Savoy 12th October 1672   Yor most humble servant REYMES[17]

For two more weeks after this peppery letter, Reymes stubbornly tried to perform the duties which daily grew more 'Herculean'. Then, on October 25th, he wearily turned his back on London and all he had striven for, and returned to Dorset and his family.

CHAPTER NINETEEN

YE MARINERS OF WEYMOUTH

Reymes had never been one to take his duties lightly. When he married young Elizabeth Gerrard in 1640, he had been ready with all his native earnestness to shoulder the full responsibilities of a household. But war intervened, and it was almost ten years before there was a household to manage. During all the time he and Elizabeth lived with her grandmother, he was little more than a guest, too wise to interfere with the redoubtable Amy Coker's well-run establishment.

When the two finally had a home of their own, Bullen seems to have assumed the major share of its management. He enjoyed managing things, but he probably remembered his mother's admonition that industry and efficiency must go hand in hand with consideration for others. And, striving to live up to his own belief that a man should give his wife 'reall love and kindness', he, no doubt, 'lived lovingly' with Elizabeth, as he once said 'a good husband ought to do'. At any rate theirs seems to have been a happy marriage. Bullen always speaks of his wife with affection — and he never remarried.

After Elizabeth's death, Reymes took over even more of the responsibility for his son and two daughters. None of the correspondence with his children has survived, but in the hints found in letters from friends and relatives, in his wills (he made two), and in a dozen or more sundry papers, the story of his affection and concern for them can be read. Hester Clinch, whom they all loved, took good care of the house and the children, but Bullen must have found Waddon lonely, for he was constantly taking Hester and the three young Reymeses down to Weymouth to stay with the Pleys, or with his sister Mary and her easy-going husband, John Wheatley, whose debts he periodically paid.

The Colonel was fond of the girls, of dependable Tabitha and pathetic little Mary, but his chief interest was his son. Yet there seems to have been a lack of understanding between the two.

Perhaps young Bullen resented the way his father set about arranging his life. Reymes was determined that his son should have two things he had missed — a university education and a training in law. Lack of legal knowledge, he felt, had been a great handicap in his own career. His son should not be so hindered.

Actually, all we know of young Bullen's childhood is a reference to a fall into a heap of lime when he was a little fellow of three or four, which was said to have ruined his eyes; and his attendance at the school of one Mr Clinch of Chilton. Evidently the lime was not as injurious as reported, for, on December 14th, 1666, when he was eighteen, Bullen Reymes of Waddon, Dorset, matriculated at Merton College, Oxford, and two years later received his B.A. degree. From 1668 until his father's death he was a desultory student at the Middle Temple. To Reymes's distress his son was not interested in law. Nor was he interested in much else. Unlike his energetic, friendly father, whose quenchless curiosity filled all his days with zest, young Bullen seems to have been apathetic, self-centred, and bored. Apparently he was not even interested in women — to the Colonel a completely incomprehensible state of affairs.

As for Tabitha, her life too was carefully blue-printed. In the spring of 1666, Bullen and Constance Pley, both of them great organizers, arranged the futures of their respective children, Tabitha and George.[1] The young people must have agreed, for a few months later the new Mrs Pley left for Weymouth, taking with her Hester Clinch and her sister Mary.

Mary, about five years younger than Tabitha, had been born with some physical defect. Whether she was mentally retarded is not made clear. Bullen had agonized over this unfortunate child for years, his pity sharpened by the conviction that he was in some way to blame for her handicap. For Mary's future Reymes felt a grave responsibility, the provisions for her taking up a good third of the long will he had begun early in 1672. He leaves her the same portion (£1,000), he had given Tabitha:

> onely with this difference (in regard to her weakness and Infirmity) that it shall not be payd her untill she bee married, and have a child, nor then neither, unless she have a joynter ... settled on her ...

For my feare is ... her Portion may prove her undoeing, and she be made a Praye to some unworthy person, and then slight her, and lay her aside, which I would willingly prevent, if I could. And, therefore, doe perticulerly recommend her ... to my Executor's love ...

Meanwhile, and untill she be married, and have a Child ... my will is ... she be payd an anuety of eight and forty pounds per annum ... And in case she dye without any Child liveing ... my will is that her husband be payd ... five hundred pounds ... out of the portion ... Allways provided, he love her, and be kind to her ... Hoping her virtue, discression, obedience, and love to him, will compensate her outward misfortune, (layd on her, for my sins) ...

And as I leave her free to make her oun choyce in marriage ... yet I hope she will ... be mindfull of her oune Condition, which in the eye of the world, is not so fitt to marry, as if she were of a stronger Constitution ... Marriage may shorten her life ... However, I ... hope she will not requite me so ill, as to cast herself away. To remedy which I have onely this curb, that if she marry without a Competent Joynter ... that she have not a farding to her portion ...

After Tabitha's marriage Reymes seldom went to Waddon, deserted now by all but the servants and the tenant. Young Bullen showed no interest in the beautiful estate he was some day to inherit. He preferred London to rural Dorset. The Colonel himself must have been lonely there, for he moved many of his books and pictures to his house in Weymouth.

Weymouth was a pleasant town, and Reymes, who had worked hard on its behalf, was widely known and highly regarded. He had many friends and relatives close at hand: his sister Mary and her husband; Captain Pley and Constance; Tabitha and George; Mary and the faithful Hester Clinch. When he could, he went to Weymouth. But there was so little time. With each year and each step up, the Colonel had assumed more responsibilities. In addition to his public duties, he had undertaken to look after not only his immediate family but many of the Reymes and Gerrard kin as well.

There was trouble in Overstrand. Early in 1670, Reymes had

taken time off to travel to this Norfolk village to do what he could to stave off threatened ruin. The once-prosperous and prominent Reymes family there had fallen into hard ways. What little property they had left, brought in so small an income, that the twenty-year-old heir, William Reymes, after paying his grandmother's jointure and the annuities due to his sundry aunts and cousins, had a yearly income of only £34. 16s. to take care of his 'dyet, clothing, and all dutys, taxes and reparations'. The young man was at his wits' end when the Colonel arrived and brought order out of chaos by persuading each person involved to 'abate a third part of his income'.

Then there were the Gerrards and the Cokers, Elizabeth's sisters, cousins, aunts, and uncles. One or another of them was periodically turning to Reymes for help — an errand to run, business in London that needed attention, legal advice, or just sympathy. And he gave unstintingly of his time and effort and, if need be, of his money. Elizabeth's second cousin, Charles Brune of Puckle Church,[2] when his wife died, wrote to the 'Honorable Colonel':

> To think of being a housekeeper by my selfe, it will make an end of me ... having allways lived in famelys where there has ben a great deale of company ... and now to live by my selfe and to converse with none but servants is a sad story ... and what to doe I know not. Therefore, if you can tell wch way to advise me for ye best, youle give me an additional obligation to ye number of yor favours ...

The answers to Cousin Brune and to the dozen or more letters from Elizabeth's hapless sister Etheldread, and her feeble husband, Edward Hyde, have disappeared. But Reymes must have given them wise counsel, for they continued to write letters of appreciation, asking for more favours and more advice. 'Brother Hyde' left his estate in such a muddle that it took the combined efforts of Bullen and his brother-in-law, Francis Wyndham, to retrieve enough for Etheldread to live on.

Etheldread was a problem in herself. In spite of all Reymes's warnings, she couldn't and wouldn't economize. Although what was left of her inheritance was tied up in a formidable bundle of legal lets and hindrances, the Colonel, after much manoeuvring, had managed to extricate £33, enough, he thought, to pay for his sister-in-law's most pressing needs. He sent this with another plea for frugality, only to receive from the plaintive Etheldread:

> Trewley for my oun healths sake I shall be forced to make use of that [£33] spedeyly, for I must ... goe to make use of the Bath, wheare my doctar would have had me goe a month since ... & I shall be forced to take the doctar thither with mee, & then how longe that will last me theare you may Imagen ...

Another time, when she wanted to buy mourning drapes for her bed, Etheldread asked Reymes to get some samples of black baize for her, which the busy Colonel apparently did, for Anne Wyndham, relaying her sister's thanks, wrote:

> Shee disires me to give you thankes for yor care in sending doune patternes ... to her, & also directions for her Bed ... & if shee can furnish herselfe in the Countrye as well ... then sheele give you noe further trouble in this, haveing but to many occasions greater then this, she sayes, to trouble you withal.

One of the greater occasions had to do with 'Sister Hyde's' tenements at Wells, which some 'cropp-eared priest' was trying to get hold of. Wyndham and Reymes together managed 'to wrest it out of his Jawes', but the affair took days of Bullen's precious time.

There is nothing among Reymes's papers to suggest that he was ever involved in any dishonest enterprises. Of even so common a practice as the buying and selling of offices, there is no evidence. But that he expected and got favours from his powerful friends, and that he, in turn, 'planted' friends and relatives in lucrative posts, there is little question.

As Vice-Admiral of Dorset Reymes had named Captain William Ellesdon his deputy at Lyme, and Captain Pley at Weymouth; as Commissioner for the Sick and Wounded, he had 'planted' his kinsman Robert Reymes as Provost-Marshal at Winchester, and his brother-in-law, John Wheatley, as one of his clerks at Weymouth. And early in 1669, the Colonel had used his influence to have his son-in-law 'nominated & appointed by the

Lords Commissioners of the Treasury ... to the Office of Collector of Lyme Regis ... ' He was not only a co-signer of Pley's bond for £2,000, but undertook to supervise his activities, writing out a long list of instructions, prescribing the books to be kept and warning him never to lend any money, nor order any to be paid, without first obtaining his, Reymes's, permission in writing.

Although ready cash may at times have been hard to lay his hands on, never since the Restoration had Reymes been in serious financial straits. There are no expense accounts for his years in London, but the bills of his tailor, Mr Little, show that, during 1670 and 1671, he made four elaborate suits and coats for the Colonel, a 'black shut & cot' for his boy, a 'Livery shut for Futman', and a 'shut, coat and clok' for his coachman. So Bullen had a coach of his own with liveried attendants. His other expenses are less ostentatious. He continued to add to the collection of books and pictures he had started when a lad in Paris. In fact, the last recorded purchase before the Colonel left for Weymouth was for three books and four pictures. Neither the names or the prices of the books are given, but for the pictures, painted by Andrea Vankessell — 'one was of the Circumcision, another of Diana and her nymphs bathing ... and the other two were sea skips' — he paid £6.

Reymes seldom did mention the titles of the books he bought. The *Arcadia*, the folio volume of Shakespeare's plays, the *History of the Turks*, the unnamed books on music, most of the French and Italian comedies, and scores of other books, have disappeared. But the more than two hundred volumes remaining from his once extensive library show the breadth of Reymes's interests. There are plays, essays, romances, sermons, grammars; there are books on medicine, law, religion, history, philosophy, government, mathematics, music, travel, architecture; and among the many authors represented are St Augustine, Bacon, William Byrd, Belleforest, Cicero, Florio, Froissart, Sir Thomas More, Guazzo and Piccolomini.[3]

Perhaps when he ordered the books and pictures to be sent to Weymouth, the Colonel looked forward to days of convalescence in the midst of friends and family, with leisure to read and relax. Instead, soon after his arrival, he grew much worse. Realizing the gravity of his illness, or, as he put it, finding himself 'much decayed in the state of body', Reymes, on October 29th, 1672, made another will, short and to the point. The long discussion of religion is omitted and the even longer section devoted to Mary is cut to the bare essentials, while only a few lines are devoted to Hester Clinch, in contrast to the page-long 'item 20' of the unfinished will in which Reymes tells so much about his devoted friend and servant:

> For as much as Hester Clinch hath been bred up from hir youth ... im my house and family (refusing many better places ... to live with us) and for that she hath ever behaved herself very Modestly, Soberly and faythfully to her Mrs and exceeding careful of her, in all her Sicknesses and lyings-in, and also in weaning my children, and loveingly looking after them, I think myself bound ... to leave her a subsistence ... The first payment to begin as Mary's annuety doth, with whome I would have her live, (if they two so like) ... but I doe not Injoyne, I onely recomend it ... Not that they should remove from my daughter Pleys (where now they ar) ... I thinke they cannot doe better, anywhere ... I could wish, they may still be with her, or with my Sonn, in case he marry, that so they may always live lovingly, and friendly together, as hither to they have done. And I do desire all my Children to be kind, loveing, and frendly to her, as one whom there Mother did very much love and esteeme ...

Another section of the discursive first will, missing from the later document, makes elaborate provisions for Reymes's funeral.

> I give to the Minister that shall bury me, twenty shillings ... and a payre of white Gloves ...
>
> I give to the Poore Inhabitants of Portesham Parish, Tenn graye Gounds of Cloth, to be made long and large, to keepe them warme in the winter, all to be suitable and alike, which sayd poor people ... I desire may goe before my corps, from my house to the church, two and two, in a grave and decent manner, as the occasion and solemnity requires ...
>
> I give to the Grave Maker (because he may be at som littell charge ... in remoouving the Grave stones etc) ten Shillings.

> I give to 8 Bearers that shall carry my corps to the Grave (by 4, at a time, in turns) to each of them, halfe a croune.
> I give to the Ringers at Portesham, tenn shillings.

Instead of this final touch of pomp and circumstance, the last will simply states:

> I give my body to the earth to be privately and decently buried neare my dear wife in the vault I made in the Isle in the church att Possum.

Had Reymes completed the earlier will, he might have revealed much about his son and about Constance Pley. The references to them in the October will are comparatively brief. To his 'very intimate dear friend' Constance, he gives his 'great Dyamond Ring ... ' as a testimony of his 'Thankfulness to her ... ' and he leaves

> all the rest of my estate ... unto my sonne Bullen Reymes whom I make sole executor ... charging him not to leave the study of the Lawe untill hee bee called to the Barre, hoping that by that time hee will have seene enough to invite hym further in that noble calling ... [4]

During the last two months of his life Bullen was surrounded by friends and, save for his son, by the members of his family who were closest to him, Tabitha and Mary and his sister Mary Wheatley. To Constance Pley he was bound now by another interest — their three grandchildren, Tabitha and George Pley's young sons.[5] But the person who was with him most constantly was Hester Clinch, who had moved into his house to take care of 'the Master'.

Except for the frequent references to his weakness and for a remark of one of his friends that 'Col Reymes ... is not like to hold out long, now winter is coming,'[6] there are no hints as to the nature of the Colonel's illness. Since the early days in Paris when Bullen went into such pathological detail about his attacks of fever, the only allusions to his health are to the continuing migraine headaches. Reymes was only fifty-eight, comparatively young, even in the seventeenth century. But, a perfectionist, he had driven himself for years, striving to do all that was expected of him and to provide for every exigency that might befall him or his children.

On Wednesday afternoon, December 18th, Bullen called Hester Clinch into his bedroom and, to his old and faithful friend, spoke his last words and gave his last message. Before the day was over he was dead. Of the many documents relating to Colonel Reymes, the most poignant is a torn sheet of paper on which, in Hester's laborious hand, is written:

> What things were left in charge to bee done by me when he lay on his death bed. Taken by Mrs Hester Clinch.
> My Master bid me tell Mr Reymes that he will have him to keepe faire with Mrs Pley and paye all her accounts for he sayes he is sure she will not wrong him. He charged me to put Mr Reymes in mind often that he follow his buisnes to be a lawer and that he live humbell.
> My Master will give Mary Baker 40s besides her wages and her wages is 3 lb a yeare. He will give Jeane Langman 20s besides her wages ... he will give Mr Capen of Possum 20s and to the pore he will give 40s.
> He desires Mr Reymes to burne all Woamans letters that he finds amongst my Masters papers and he bid me tell Mr Reymes that he doth recommend him to Sir William Coventry, to Mr Naper[7] and Sir Thomas Clifford as his cheifest frinds, unto whome he maye, if he please, make presents of the greate glase, the great Cabinet or what else he please, if he hathe a mind to it.
> My Master desires him not to marry yet unles he be sure with a greate fortune. And he desires him againe to follow his buisnes at the Tempell and to paye all my Master debts.
> He bid me tell Coll. Windham and his lady, Mr Brune and Mr Husey that he dothe beg them to be kind unto his sone.

To serve well his King and country had been Reymes's youthful ambition. He came nearer to attaining this goal than did many more prominent men, for he belonged to a small but significant group of Restoration public servants who gave stability to their own era, while carrying on the best of the traditions of the past and shaping their country for the demands of the future. In public and in private life he had tried very hard to do what he thought was right. He had had his share of happiness and success, but he had been hounded by a sense of guilt which, at the end, was merged with his worry over Mary and young Bullen. His last hours clouded by his concern for his son, Reymes reluctantly dropped the threads he had been holding and left Bullen and Mary and Tabitha, and their children, and theirs — on through the unfolding years — to manage as best they could.

Fortunately Reymes was given one of God's greatest gifts to mankind — ignorance of the future! Young Bullen did not heed his father's charge to 'follow his buisnes at the Tempell' and to 'live humbell'. Instead, he continued his idle and aimless life, and, once the estate was settled, was seldom at Waddon, though Hester had gone there to look after him and, no doubt, to remind him of her dead Master's wishes. Whether he kept 'faire with Mrs. Pley' we do not know, but he apparently did not with her son, for within the year he and his brother-in-law were quarrelling bitterly over who should pay the mourning expenses, and over a diamond ring which the Colonel had left poor Mary. Mary, at least, would have soon ceased to worry her father, for by August of 1673 she too was dead, leaving as a legacy the controversial ring.

One of the Colonel's hopes for his son was, however, realized. Bullen did eventually marry. And he married a girl of whom his father would have approved, Anne Coker, a ruddy-cheeked, determined-looking young woman with reddish blonde hair, the daughter of Robert Coker of Mapowder.[8] But he waited until June of 1691, when he was forty-three years old, and when, deep in debt, he was probably in need of Anne's ample fortune. Perhaps they were happy, though the manner of Bullen's death in the autumn of 1695 scarcely suggests that he had mended his ways. He was found lying wounded on a street in Weymouth (possibly as the result of a tavern brawl) and brought home by coach to his house at Waddon, where he died of gangrene in a wound in his foot. He left everything to his wife — the couple had no children.

Apart from the marriage with 'a great fortune' and the burning of 'all Woamans letters', Bullen Reymes the third had fulfilled none of his father's last wishes. He did not 'have a mind' to give to the Colonel's three 'chiefest frinds' either the 'greate glase' or the 'great Cabinet', and he kept for himself the sundial which his father had dedicated to the seamen of Weymouth.

YE MARINERS OF WEYMOUTH

For more than a decade, Reymes, as Vice-Admiral of Dorset, had been closely associated with the seafaring men of Weymouth. During his last weeks in London, in spite of his 'great weaknesses', he had supervised the construction of a sundial. Deeply incised in the bronze octagonal dial, made by Helkiah Bedford in Fleet Street, is the inscription:

> The Gift of the Honble Coll Bullen Reymes, Vice Admiral of the County/ of Dorset to ye Ingenious Artists/ Navigators & Seamen/ of Weymouth and Melcomb Regis, Calculated by his order purposely/ for the meridian by a Person of Learning Ano Dom, 1672.

Today the sundial stands, not in a harbour of Dorset but in the forecourt of Zeals House in Wiltshire. However, it is no less a tribute to the shipwrights and sailors for whom the donor felt so deep a respect and affection. It is no less a timeless memorial to a man who, in the perilous seas of his age, tried to sail a true course.

ABBREVIATIONS USED IN NOTES

S.P.	State Papers
P.R.O.	Public Record Office, London
H.M.C.	Historical Manuscript Commission
Cal. S.P. Domestic	*Calendar of State Papers, Domestic*
Cal. S.P. Venetian	*Calendar of State Papers, Venetian*

All quotations and allusions not identified in the notes by citations of sources are in Reymes's papers, i.e., diaries, letters, and other manuscripts.

NOTES

CHAPTER ONE (pages 13-25)

[1] The data on the Reymes lineage are derived from Alwyn Leslie Raimes, 'Reymes of Overstrand', *Norfolk Archaeology*, XXX, 1947, pp. 15-64.

[2] Elizabeth, daughter of Sir Edward Boleyn, married Thomas Payne of Itteringham.

[3] This is the first Bullen Reymes. Both he and his son originally spelled the Christian name 'Bulleyn' but later dropped the 'y'.

[4] Tobie Matthew, *A True Historicall Relation of the Conversion of Sir Tobie Matthew* ... 1640 MS., abridged by Rev. Alban Butler, 1795, p. 7.

[5] Sir Ralph Winwood, *Memorials of Affairs of State in the Reigns of Elizabeth and James I*, London, 1725, II, p. 441.

[6] Transcript of the register of the Holy Trinity Church, made by the Rev. F. Nesbitt, 1931.

[7] John Chamberlain, *The Letters of John Chamberlain*, ed. Norman McClure, Philadelphia, 1939, II, p. 275, Letter 341.

[8] See G. E. Aylmer, *The King's Servants*, London, 1961, p. 229, and Lawrence Stone, 'The Inflation of Honours', *Past and Present*, XIV, Nov. 1958, pp. 45-65.

[9] Chamberlain, II, pp. 576-8, Letter 457.

[10] Deeds of Bargain & Sale, Exeter, Roll 58, April 4th, 1628, records a sale of 'March 9, 1627, by Sir George Petre of Hayes, Knight, to John Petre of Bowhay ... for £500 paid to the Earl of Dorset by John who has given security to the Earle ... to pay £1400 ... for the ... debt of Sir George ... The properties sold include the manor of Peter Hayes in St Thomas ... '

[11] T. W. Horsfield, *History of Sussex*, Lewes, 1835, I, p. 393, gives the ground plan. The hall was 55' × 40'; the chapel 40 feet square, and the tennis court 55 feet long.

[12] P.R.O., R6/32, 1629, 'An Inventorie of the goods Chattels and debts of Sr George Petre'.

CHAPTER TWO (pages 26-35)

[1] It was the second Duke who, when he sold the estate in 1672, made the stipulation that the streets built on the site be given these names.

[2] A drawing of Old York House by Anthony von Wyngaered, in the Bodleian, shows a structure with six pointed turrets; Hollar's drawing of 'New' York House, in the Pepysian Library, is of a long building parallel with the river, with a battlemented parapet and projecting wings at either end; and Jacob Esselens' drawing, in the Graphische Sammlung Albertina, Vienna, shows the east side of York House with a square tower and, to its north, an even higher structure, probably the thirty-five-foot-square room said to have been built by Gerbier.

[3] Rawlinson MS. A. 341:30 includes a copy of the indenture of May 11th, 1635, made 'between Randall Macdonell and his wife, the Duchess of Buckingham, on the one part, and the Earl of Pembroke and Sir Robert Pye of the other part' by which the pictures, statues, furniture, etc. at York House and 'Chelsea House' were assured to the 2nd Duke of Buckingham. Among Reymes's papers is an earlier inventory, probably made soon after the first Duke's death, which lists the gems, the pictures beginning with number 279 and ending with 387 (the first part of the inventory is missing), and the furnishings of two rooms, the red and green closets, which are omitted from the 1635 inventory. With the exception of these two rooms, all the furnishings and pictures referred to are from the 1635 inventory. A later inventory, *A Catalogue of the Curious Collection of Pictures of George Villiers*, ... made by Brian Fairfax

NOTES

in 1649 and published in 1758, contains only 215 pictures, those sent to Antwerp to be sold.

[4] Henry Peacham, *Peacham's Compleat Gentleman*, 1634, ed. G. S. Gordon, Oxford, 1906, p. 108.

[5] Bishop Goodman, *Court and Times of James I*, London, 1839, II, pp. 342-3.

[6] Maréchal de Bassompierre, *Journal de ma Vie*, Paris, 1875, II, p. 274.

[7] Goodman, II, 370-1.

CHAPTER THREE (pages 36-44)

[1] P.R.O., S.P. France 78/79, f. 142.

[2] Ibid., f. 179.

[3] The gentlemen listed in S.P. France, 78/79, f. 179, are:

Mr. Augier	Mr. Wilkinson	(My Lords Nephew)
Mr. de Vic	Mr. Smith	Secretary
Mr. Conway	Mr. Morton	Secretary
Mr. Windham	Mr. Browne	Secretary
Mr. Lenton	Mr. Stiles	Chaplain
Mr. Reames	Mr. Jacob	Gent. of Chamb.
Mr. Trevalany	Mr. Cawles	steward

[4] Ibid.

[5] Giles was a younger brother of Endymion Porter.

[6] A loose wrap which women threw about their shoulders.

[7] Philip Burlamachi, an English capitalist, with correspondents in Paris and other European cities, was employed by his government to transmit money abroad for the use of its ambassadors.

CHAPTER FOUR (pages 45-56)

[1] The Protestant church in near-by Charenton was built *c.* 1623.

[2] Jan. 7th, 1632, N.S., which Reymes was using, corresponded to Dec. 28th, 1631, O.S., still used in England in the seventeenth century. 'Bullin' was christened, according to the parish register of St Thomas the Apostle, '1 Jan. 1613/14', when he was four days old.

[3] A pistole according to Reymes, was worth 18 shillings.

[4] There were 44 cards, 12 to each player, the remaining forming a common stock. The 'gleek' was 3 of a kind.

[5] Sir Thomas Wharton (1615-84) of Edlington, Yorkshire.

[6] H.M.C. Fourth Report, Part I, p. 259.

[7] P.R.O., S.P. France, 78/91, f. 62, Wake to Dorchester, Feb. 16/26, 1632.

[8] Dorchester died Feb. 15th, 1632.

[9] Sir Thomas Roe (1581-1644) was himself a candidate for the Secretaryship. It was given to Sir Francis Windebank, June 15th, 1632.

[10] P.R.O., S.P. France, 78/91, Part I, f. 66.

[11] Henry Wilmot (1612-58), 1st Earl of Rochester, fought in Holland and in the Civil War. He was with Charles II after Worcester, masquerading as Bullen Reymes.

[12] William Legge (1609?-70), according to a letter Reymes wrote to him, Jan. 8th, 1632, was in the 'king of Sweds army'. He fought in the Scots Wars and in the Civil War.

[13] William Villiers (1614-43) succeeded his father, Sir Edward Villiers, as Viscount Grandison in 1626.

[14] P.R.O., S.P. France, 78/90, Part II, ff. 246, 249.

NOTES

CHAPTER FIVE (pages 57-66)

[1] Occasionally the quotations from the diaries are given in French or Italian, as the case may be. Usually they are in translation.

[2] William Davison (*fl.* 1631-60), chemist and physician to the King of France, attended the members of the English embassy.

[3] Sir Richard Browne (1605-83) had been Wake's secretary since 1628. He was later secretary to Amb. Scudamore, and Resident in Paris, 1641-60. His daughter married John Evelyn.

[4] Sir Robert Anstruther, Privy Councillor to Charles I, was ambassador to Denmark in 1620 and to Germany in 1627, 1629, and 1630.

[5] Reymes must mean Francesco Gentileschi, who came to London in 1621 where, for 20 years, he was a painter in the Court of Charles I. He was a relative of Orazio Gentileschi.

CHAPTER SIX (pages 67-80)

[1] *Chaucer's Poetry*, ed. E. T. Donaldson, New York, 1958, *Canterbury Talés*, General Prologue, 11. 91-6.

[2] Pluvinel died in 1621. His academy was taken over by his manager, M. Benjamin.

[3] Peacham, p. 77.

[4] Charles Howard, Earl of Berkshire and Viscount Andover (1615-79), Gentleman of the Bedchamber to Charles II in 1669.

[5] Arthur, Lord Chichester, first Earl of Donegal (1606-75), captain in the Irish army and Governor of Carrickfergus, 1643-4 and 1661-75.

[6] Sir Robert Slingsby (1611-61), cousin of Sir Henry Slingsby, sent on mission to Paris in 1644, was Comptroller of the Navy, 1660-1.

[7] Sir Henry Frederick Thynne, 1st baronet, of Longleat, Wiltshire, died in 1680.

[8] Sir Thomas Lyttleton, 1st baronet (1596-1650), M.P. for Worcester.

[9] Without further identification, it is impossible to say whether Mr Digbie refers to Sir Kenelm Digby (1603-65), author, diplomat, and naval commander; to George Digby, 2nd Earl of Bristol (1612-77), Royalist commander; or to his brother, John Digby, a colonel in the Royalist forces.

[10] Sir Robert Dallington, *A method for Travell: Showed by taking the view of France as it stood ... in 1598*, London, 1606, as quoted by Dorothy Carrington, *The Traveller's Eye*, London, 1947, p. 11.

[11] Mme de Montbazon was a relative of Mme Chevreuse.

[12] Guillaume du Vair, dismissed as Keeper of the Seals, was of the anti-Richelieu party.

[13] Mme Saint-George was the governess of 'Mademoiselle', Gaston's young daughter.

[14] Mountjoy Blount, Baron Mountjoy and Earl of Newport (1597?-1666), natural son of Charles Blount by Penelope, Lady Rich, daughter of Walter Devereux, and subject of Sidney's *Astrophel and Stella*.

[15] John Belasyse (1614-89), fought for Charles I, was Governor of Hull and later, of Tangier, and Lord Commissioner of the Treasury in 1687.

[16] *Cal. S.P. Domestic*, May 6th, 1633, and S. R. Gardiner, *History of England*, London, 1899, VII, p. 339.

CHAPTER SEVEN (pages 81-9)

[1] Sir Henry Blount (1602-82), travelled to Constantinople and in Egypt. He published *Voyage to the Levant* in 1636.

[2] Walter Montagu (1603?-82), son of Sir Henry Montagu, first Earl of Manchester, was sent by Buckingham on a secret mission to France, 1624 and 1625, continuing in the secret service there from 1627 to 1633. He announced his conversion to Catholicism in 1635, was exiled in 1649, and became Abbot of St Martin near Pontoise.

NOTES

[3] Robert Dormer, Earl of Carnarvon in 1628, commanded a regiment in the second Scottish war, effected the submission of Dorchester, and fell at the first battle of Newbury in 1643.

[4] According to Reymes, a Jacobus (coined under James I) was worth about a guinea; a piece of eight was worth 8 réales, and a réal was worth 1s.; an Italian livre was valued at 1 franc or 1s. 9d.; a gazet, or gazetta, at about 1d. and a sòldo at ½d. or less.

[5] K. M. Lea, 'Sir Aston Cokayne and the Commedia dell' Arte', *Modern Language Review*, XIII, 1928, pp. 47-51.

CHAPTER EIGHT (pages 90-100)

[1] This is probably Robert Slingsby whom Reymes met in Paris, although it may be Sir Henry Slingsby, whose *Diary* (1638-48) was published in 1806 and 1836.

[2] Mr Fitton may be Sir Alexander Fitton, Lord Chancellor of Ireland, who fled to France after the abdication of James II.

[3] Mr Twisden may be Sir Thomas Twysden (1602-83), Royalist and Judge of the King's Bench.

[4] *The Diary of John Evelyn*, ed. E. S. de Beer, London, 1955, Feb. 28th, 1644/5.

[5] The letter was sent from Paris on Nov. 21st, 1635. It was printed in 1641, but the quotations are from the copy Montagu gave to Reymes.

CHAPTER NINE (pages 101-12)

[1] Zante or Zakintos, one of the Ionian Islands lying south of Cephalonia, was under Venetian rule from 1485 until 1797.

[2] *The Memoirs of Sir George Courthop* (1616-85), ed. Mrs S. C. Lomas, *The Camden Miscellany*, London, 1907, XI, p. 116: '... we were so often becalmed, that we were thirteen weeks ... going from Messina to Smyrna, which voyage Sir Sackville Crow performed with a fair wind in thirty-five days.'

[3] The ruler in 1634 was Murad IV, hence the history Reymes was reading must have been published before 1622, the date of Oman's death.

[4] A *fede* or *bulletino di sanità*, as Reymes sometimes calls it, contained a description of the bearer and the proper signatures. It had to be renewed at stated intervals.

[5] The three quotations are from a letter from Harvey to Lord Feilding, dated Treviso, August 6/16, 1636, H.M.C., *Denbigh Papers*, vol. 68., Part V, pp. 31-3.

CHAPTER TEN (pages 113-19)

[1] 'Signor Julio Cesero' may have been related to Sir Julius Caesar (1562?-1636), Chancellor of the Exchequer under James and Master of the Rolls, 1614-36; possibly a son by his second marriage, or a nephew.

[2] John Tracy, son of Robert Tracy, second Viscount Tracy, was born in 1617 and succeeded his father as third Viscount in 1662.

[3] Dudley married his cousin at Lyons by Papal dispensation. They had thirteen children.

[4] See Logan Pearsall Smith, *Life and Letters of Sir Henry Wotton*, London, 1907, I, p. 434.

CHAPTER ELEVEN (pages 120-31)

[1] According to K. M. Lea, *Italian Popular Comedy*, vol. I, pp. 295-301, Gabrielle, the original Scappino, belonged to a branch of the *Confidenti*, a *commedia dell' arte* company. His troupe was disbanded in 1636.

[2] Windebank was a son of Sir Francis Windebank, joint Secretary of State with Sir John Coke. John Reeves and Hyde were Feilding's secretaries.

NOTES

[3] *Cal. S.P. Venetian*, Oct. 8th, 1645.
[4] H.M.C., *Denbigh Papers*, vol. 68, Part V, pp. 10-11.
[5] According to Reymes's calculations, a Venetian ducat was worth about 4s. 6d.; a scudo was worth 5s. 6d., and a grosee amounted to less than 1d. He says that 1691 lbs. (Venetian) and 12 soldi were worth 50 lb. sterling.
[6] *Cal. S.P. Venetian*, 1632-6, no. 430, p. 338.
[7] H.M.C., *Denbigh Papers*, vol. 68, Part V, p. 14.

CHAPTER TWELVE (pages 132-42)

[1] Thomas Coryat, *Coryats Crudities*, Glasgow, 1905, I, pp. 401-6. The book was first published in 1611.
[2] *Cal. S.P. Venetian*, 1637, no. 190, p. 178.
[3] When this post, left vacant by the death of the Earl of Carlisle, was given to Lord Holland, Lady Denbigh did her best to have Basil sent as ambassador to France.
[4] *Cal. S.P. Venetian*, 1637, no. 206, p. 195.

CHAPTER THIRTEEN (pages 143-57)

[1] Sir John Scudamore served as ambassador from 1635-6, and as joint ambassador with Robert Sydney, 2nd Earl of Leicester, from 1636-9.
[2] The three letters are in H.M.C., *Denbigh Papers*, vol. 68, Part V, pp. 47, 49, 50.
[3] Elizabeth married John Chapman; Mary married John Wheatley; and Judith married Paul Stevens.
[4] All speeches of the King are from P.R.O., L. C. 5/135, Warrants for Swearing Servants to the King. The other information and quotations are from Edward Chamberlayne, *Angliae Notitia or the Present State of England*, London, 1674, 8th ed., pp. 172-4.
[5] Although many of his friends fought at Edgehill, there is no evidence that Reymes was there. The first reference to his activities in the Civil War is a receipt signed by him on May 8th, 1643, for 'Back one, Brest one, Hand guard one, Gorgett one' (the normal armour of the seventeenth-century 'harquebusier') for the use of 'Liut Generall Willmot'. See P.R.O., Royal Ordnance Papers, W.O. 55/458, vol. 65, f.l, dorso.
[6] C. V. Wedgwood, *The King's War*, London, 1958, p. 194.
[7] Edward, Earl of Clarendon, *The History of the Rebellion and Civil Wars in England*, Oxford, 1731, vol. II, Part I, Book VII, pp. 26-242; S. R. Gardiner, *History of the Great Civil War*, London, 1893, I, 128-31; Wedgwood, *The King's War*, pp. 193-4.
[8] *Journal of Sir Samuel Luke*, ed. I. G. Philip, *Oxfordshire Record Society*, 1950-2, vol. 28, pp. 78, 90, 104.
[9] *Thomason Tracts* E, 70 (13), London, Oct. 11th, 1643, pp. 1-2.
[10] In an order dated Dartmouth, Nov. 9th, 1643, Maurice appointed William Holloway Clarke 'chaplin to Colonel Bullen Reymes regiment of Foot'.
[11] R. N. Worth, *History of Plymouth*, Plymouth, 1890, p. 107.
[12] Another letter from Wagstaff, undated, also refers to the 'hill' and was probably written at the same time: 'Sr. I desire you to cause the tents to bee brought upon the topp of the hill & to draw the men off to their old posts with as much privacy as may bee, & there to stay, and before day I shall send you greater strength, only you are to leave Centenells in fitting places ... '
[13] It was in connection with their departure that Wagstaff, on Dec. 24th, wrote to Reymes: 'To bee with yor Regimt at Compton Hill by eight of the clock in the morning with the bags and baggage, there you shall receive further orders ... '
[14] John Leland, *The Itinerary of John Leland, 1535-1541*, ed. Lucy Toulmin Smith, London, 1907, Parts 1-3, p. 244.
[15] A. R. Bayley, *The Civil War in Dorset*, Taunton, 1910, p. 137.

NOTES

[16] Clarendon MS., 23, no. 1738 (8), f. 106; Bayley, p. 186.

[17] Among Reymes's papers are six lists relating to his military activities: 'A Rowle of my officers' gives the names of Phillips, Richard Williamson, his sergeant-major, and of six captains, nine lieutenants, and eight ensigns; another 'Rowle' gives in their respective columns, the names of his fifteen sergeants, fourteen corporals, and eleven drummers (the column headed 'Soldiers' is left vacant). Under the heading, 'Paye for the Armye by the Kings Rowle', are four other lists which give the daily pay of the personnel, ranging from £10 for the 'Lord Generall' and £1. 10s. for 'A Colonell of Futt', down to a fraction over 10d. a day for the common soldier.

[18] Lt-Col. Alfred H. Burne and Lt-Col. Peter Young, *The Great Civil War*, London, 1959, p. 234.

CHAPTER FOURTEEN (pages 158-75)

[1] The *Calendar of Proceedings of Committee for Compounding*, p. 1368, states that Reymes, on June 27th, 1646, compounded on Exeter Articles for Delinquency; on July 16th was fined £100, and on July 22nd was allowed to go into the country 'for 3 weeks to raise it'.

[2] *A Narration/Of severall passages betwixt His/Maiesty/and/Master B. Reymes, at/New Market/Concerning the Army*, London, printed for John Wright at the Kings Head in the old Bayley, 1647.

[3] *A Vindication* was 'printed for John Benson, and are to be sold at his shop in Chancery Lane neere the Rouls, 1647'.

[4] *Memoirs of Sir John Berkeley*, London, 1699, included in *Select Tracts Relating to the Civil Wars in England*, London, 1815, Part II, pp. 355-94.

[5] Ibid., p. 377.

[6] Etheldread married Edward Hyde of 'Westhatch', Wiltshire; Frances married John Wynter of Dyrham, Gloucestershire.

[7] A True and perfect Inventory of all, and singlar goods and Chattels of Mrs. Amy Coker ... the 22nd of July 1648.'

[8] The parish register of Mapowder began in 1598, but the portion prior to 1654 has been lost.

[9] Anne Wyndham, *Claustrum Regale Reseratum or the Kings Concealment at Trent*, London, 1681, as reproduced in Allan Fea, *After Worcester Fight*, London, 1904, Tract no. IV, p. 191. Fea's *Flight of the King*, London, 1908, includes an account by a Captain Alford, which (pp. 257-8) says, 'The Colonel advised that one Captain Alford ... might be a fit person to be entrusted, or if he were not to be found, then he knew of no other but one Mr Ellisdon that lived in Lime.' Since Alford was in Portugal in September of 1647, he probably knew less about the matter than did Anne Wyndham. Fea admits that his (Alford's) account is full of errors.

[10] Wyndham, p. 204.

[11] Ibid., p. 196.

[12] 'Mr Ellesdon's Relation of the King's escape from Lyme', in a letter to the Earl of Clarendon, ('Clarendon State Papers' II, 563, 571) as reproduced in *After Worcester Fight*, pp. 211-35.

[13] Ibid., pp. 232-3.

[14] Ibid., p. 233.

[15] The parish registers at Portesham were lost during the war and not resumed until several years after the Restoration.

[16] A picture of Waddon made between 1700 and 1704, the year the west wing was destroyed, reveals through the trees a glimpse of a two-storey structure to the west of the house. According to the outline on the west side of the present house, the wing was only twenty-one feet wide. (Pictures and an account of Waddon appeared in *Country Life*, Nov. 14th, 1931.)

NOTES

CHAPTER FIFTEEN (pages 176-89)

[1] General Montagu, who had been elected to serve for both Weymouth and Dover, elected to serve for Dover. Pepys, *The Diary of Samuel Pepys*, ed. H. B. Wheatley, New York, 1892-9, on June 2nd, 1660, says that Montagu, now the Earl of Sandwich, 'being ... to sit in the House of Peers ... endeavours to get Mr. Edward Montagu for Weymouth ... '

[2] The combined borough of Weymouth and Melcombe Regis was a burgage borough in which the franchise belonged to a limited number of burgage owners. The members from this combined borough, elected to serve in the second Parliament, were Sir John Strangways, Sir William Penn, Winston Churchill, Esq., and Colonel Reymes. Churchill sat for Weymouth and Reymes for Melcombe Regis. In accordance with the procedure then in vogue, the first two candidates sat for Weymouth, the next two for Melcombe Regis.

[3] 'The Diary of Col. B. Reymes, 1661', Egerton MS. 2043, British Museum, was purchased from Rev. J. C. Jackson, to whom it had been given by Mr Chafyn-Grove, an ancestor of the present owner of the Reymes papers.

[4] James Butler, Marquis and Earl of Ormonde, was one of the Privy Councillors and Lord Steward of the Royal Household.

[5] Sir Charles Berkeley, created Viscount Fitzharding in 1643 and Earl of Falmouth in 1665, was a favourite of the King.

[6] The King's proclamation of June 6th repeated the promises at Breda.

[7] Dated Nov. 23rd, 1665, this letter is in Pepys's Official Correspondence, National Maritime Museum, Greenwich, no. 304; most of the letters quoted are in the *Cal. S.P. Domestic* from June 2nd, 1660, to Aug. 25th, 1672; some are among the Reymes papers.

[8] *Cal. S.P. Domestic*, Aug. 20th and Sept. 3rd, 1665.

[9] *Cal. S.P. Domestic*, Feb. 1st, 1666 and Sept. 3rd, 1665.

[10] *Cal. S.P. Domestic*, Feb. 27th, 1666.

[11] *Cal. S.P. Domestic*, Jan. 16th, 1666.

[12] Captain George Cocke was made Receiver for the Sick and Wounded in 1664.

[13] Sir George Carteret was Treasurer of the Navy from 1660 to 1670.

[14] Of these more than 900 were deprived for refusing conformity to the new Prayer Book; some 800 others had already been ejected, since the Restoration, for other reasons.

[15] The Conventicle Act prohibited assemblies of five or more persons for religious reasons.

[16] *Angliae Notitia*, 8th ed., Part I, p. 175.

[17] Pepys, Feb. 17th, 1666/67. Pepys refers to other walks and conversations with Reymes: May 22nd, 1664; May 29th, 1664; June 26th, 1667, and Oct. 31st, 1667.

[18] *The Complete Works of George Savile* ... , ed. Walter Raleigh, Oxford, 1912, 'A Character of King Charles II', pp. 189-90.

[19] Reymes continued to serve as Gentleman of the Privy Chamber until his death. In June of 1664 his place was temporarily filled by Owen Martin. P.R.O., L. C. 3/24 lists the 'Gent of Privy Ch' for 'Midsummer Q', naming various substitutions.

CHAPTER SIXTEEN (pages 190-8)

[1] For an overall picture of Tangier see Enid M. G. Routh, *Tangier, England's Lost Atlantic Outpost*, London, 1912.

[2] Pepys, Aug. 10th, 1663; Jan. 27th, 1662-3; June 3rd, 1664.

[3] P.R.O., S.P. 104, Foreign Entry Book, 174 B, pp. 32-3.

[4] Pepys, Sept. 19th, 1664.

[5] P.R.O., C.O., 279/3, April 5th, 1664.

[6] P.R.O., C.O., March, 1664.

NOTES

⁷ P.R.O., S.P., 94/46. On the back of the letter from Wescombe to Bennet, 'Martin Wescombe without date by Coll. Rheims, Rec'd Sept. 17'.
⁸ P.R.O., C.O., 279/3, Aug. 13th, 1664.

CHAPTER SEVENTEEN (pages 199-215)

¹ J. J. S. Shaw, 'The Commission of Sick and Wounded and Prisoners, 1664-1667', *Mariner's Mirror*, XXV (1939), p. 314, says that in the Third Dutch War, Doyley 'overcharged the Crown two days maintenance per man' and that later Clifford suspended him from his duties as Teller of the Exchequer for fraudulent practices.
² The 'point' was at the end of Broad Street, just across the water from Gosport.
³ Reymes's salary began on Feb. 11th; on Feb. 16th, 'Robert Napier of Puncknoll, Dorset' went on his bond for £5,000 'to Act. Ld. Ashly', and on Feb. 20th, 'Instructions to Collonel Bullen Rhemes Deputy Treasurer for Prizes at Portsmouth ... ' were signed by Ashley.
⁴ Sir George Downing, Resident at the Hague at various times, was a Teller of the Exchequer and ministerial spokesman upon finance in the House of Commons.
⁵ Throughout the war and during the plague and fire, there was fear that the extremists among the Dissenters might start a revolution.
⁶ Sir Philip Warwick managed the Treasury for the Earl of Southampton from 1660 until 1667.
⁷ This is the last letter relating to Reymes's duties as Commissioner. There is, however, a correspondence with Coventry, Ashley and others, concerning the offices of Vice-Admiral and Sub-Treasurer of Prizes. There are also a volume giving the 'Alphabet of every Ship and its respective Cargo'; a 'Day Book' which lists 276 ships with a description of and prices paid for each; an outsize folio volume, inscribed 'Register of Sick and Wounded, Portsmouth 1664-1667', giving on each of its page openings sixteen specific details about each of the seamen listed; and, at the end of the 'Letter Book', containing letters having to do with the sick and wounded, there are numerous 'Warrants and Orders' connected with the same office.

CHAPTER EIGHTEEN (pages 216-28)

¹ Thomas Sprat, *The History of the Royal Society of London for the Improving of Natural Knowledge*, London, 1667, ed. Jackson I. Cope and Harold Whitman Jones, *Washington University Studies*, St Louis, Missouri, 1958, p. 64.
² Reymes's signature, along with that of John Locke and thirty-five other Fellows, is on p. 8, Part II, of the Charter Book in *Signatures in the First Journal Book and the Charter Book of the Royal Society*, London, 1912.
³ Evelyn, vol. I, pp. 110-11, and note 1, p. 110.
⁴ Sprat, p. 417.
⁵ Mr Townsend was possibly a relative of Sir Horatio Townshend, sent to the Hague as deputy in 1660.
⁶ Edward Montagu, brother of Walter Montagu, was the Earl of Manchester and Lord Chamberlain of the King's Household. Most of the letters are signed by Manchester or Albemarle, a few by Buckingham, Master of the Horse. They are addressed either to Sandwich, Reymes or Newport.
⁷ The women were Mesdames Quin, Marshall, Carey, Rutter, Givin, Frances Davenport, Elizabeth Davenport and Jane Davenport. The male actors were Charles Hart, Mich. Mohun, John Lacy, Nicholas Bert, Wm. Wintersell, Wm. Cartwright, Edw. Kinaston, Robt. Shatterell, Marmaduke Watson, Th. Handcocke, Tho. Loveday, Th. Gradwell and John Bateman.
⁸ David Ogg, *England in the Reign of Charles II*, Oxford, 1934, p. 321.
⁹ Pepys, July 25th, 1667.
¹⁰ Pepys, Oct. 28th, 1667.
¹¹ Ibid.

NOTES

[12] 'The Character of a Trimmer' by Coventry's nephew, George Savile, Marquis of Halifax, incorporated many of Coventry's ideas and was often attributed to him. Writing to another nephew, Thomas Thynne, Coventry denied the authorship, but admitted himself to be a 'Trimmer', enclosing the definition quoted.

[13] *Cal. S.P. Domestic*, Jan. 1664.

[14] Evelyn, May 18th, 1671.

[15] Sir Henry Ford, Irish Secretary, was M.P. for Tiverton.

[16] M. des Rabesnières Treillebois, Commander of the French Squadron at Southwold Bay. See Evelyn, May 31st and June 5th, 1672.

[17] *Cal. S.P. Domestic*, Oct. 12th, 1672.

CHAPTER NINETEEN (pages 229-39)

[1] George Pley Jun. was considerably older than Tabitha. His parents, George Pley Sen. and Constance Wise, had been married on June 2nd, 1635. See *Hutchins*, 3rd ed., II, p. 459.

[2] Puckle Church was 3 miles east of Margotsfield, Gloucester. Brune's wife was Mary Coker, Elizabeth's aunt.

[3] There were three sales of Reymes's books by Sotheby: July 27th, 1925, lots 172-93; Dec. 14th, 1925, lots 1-105; and June 27th, 1927, lots 492-524. A number of the 158 lots include more than one volume, some as many as eleven. Hence the actual number of books sold plus 38 books still at Zeals House add up to considerably more than 200.

[4] The October 29th will was granted probate on Feb. 5th, 1672/3, London, P. C. C.

[5] The sons' names were Reymes, George and Benjamin. A daughter Mary was born later. Both Reymes and Mary Pley died without issue.

[6] *Cal. S.P. Domestic*, Dec. 7th, 1672, Nath. Osborne to James Hicks.

[7] Robert Napier (1611-86), second son of Sir Nathaniel Napier, in 1637 was called to the Bar from the Middle Temple, being seated at Puncknowle, Dorset, less than 10 miles from Waddon. He collected money for the King during the Civil War and was at Exeter while Reymes was there. He went on Reymes's bond for £5,000 in 1665 (see note 3, Chapter Seventeen).

[8] A portrait of Anne Coker, with that of Colonel Bullen Reymes, reproduced as frontispiece, and two 'sea skips' by Vankessell hang on the walls of the late Major G. V. Troyte-Bullock's home, Zeals House, Wiltshire.

After the death of her first husband, Anne Coker Reymes married Henry Chafyn of Zeals, Wiltshire. They had no children, and, after Anne's death in 1721, Chafyn married Tabitha's daughter, Mary Pley. She too died childless, and Chafyn willed all of Reymes's property (with the exception of West Chelborough which, in 1696, after a bitter lawsuit, had been given to the Pleys) to his sister Jane, who married John Grove. From the Chafyn-Groves the property of Colonel Bullen Reymes descended to the late Major Troyte-Bullock.

INDEX

Adams, Patience, 19, 53, 59, 79
Adams, Richard, 19, 59
Albemarle, Duke of, 196, 197, 213, 214, 223, 224
Alchemist, The, 187
American Philosophical Society, 10
Andover, Lord, 72, 73, 77
Anstruther, Sir Robert, 64
Arcadia, 51, 71
Arlington, Lord, *see* Bennet, Sir Henry
Ashburnham, Sir John, 165, 188
Ashley, Lord, 203, 213, 225
Aston, Sir Arthur, 148
Athens, 108
Augier, M., 74
Aumont, Marie, 78

Bacon, Sir Francis, 26
Bartlett, Mr, 94, 96, 101, 106, 107, 110, 115
Bassan, 28, 94
Bassett, Major-General Thomas, 153
Bassompierre, 29
Beaumont, 187
Bedford, Earl of, *see* Russell, Lord William
Beer, Dr E. S. de, 10
Belasyse, Sir John [Mr Bellas], 77, 197, 198
Bennet, Sir Henry (later Lord Arlington), 186, 193, 194, 195, 196, 202, 206, 213, 225
Berkeley, Sir Charles, 179
Berkeley, Sir John, 150, 151, 154, 156, 157, 164, 165, 170
Blake, Colonel Robert, 155, 156
Blount, Sir Henry, 81-2, 84, 90
Blount, Mountjoy, *see* Newport, Earl of
Boleyn, Elizabeth, 15
Boleyn, Mary (wife of William Reymes), 15
Bologna, 92
Boyle, Richard, *see* Dungarvan, Viscount
Boyle, Robert, 64, 218
Bridges, Sir Tobias, 192, 193, 194
Brouncker, Sir William, 204, 216
Browne, Major-General Richard, 162-3
Browne, Sir Richard, 57, 61, 74
Buckingham, the Duchess of, 13, 25, 29, 30, 39, 46, 47, 58, 62-3, 66, 74, 79, 120, 130, 131, 187

Buckingham, the Duke of, 19-22, 25, 26, 29, 48, 49, 99, 120
Burlamachi, Philip, 43
Burrowes, Mr, 137
Burton, Dr I. F., 10

Cabal, the, 225
Cademan, Dr, 137
Canada, 50
Carleton, Sir Dudley, 22, 40
Carnarvon, Earl of, 82, 85, 94, 95, 97, 107, 118, 149-50, 187
Castlemaine, Lady, 188, 194, 221
Catherine, Charles II's queen, 179, 190
Chafyn-Grove, William, 9, 249
Chamberlain, John, 22
Charles I, 21, 22-3, 30, 40, 41, 48, 50, 77, 130, 141, 144, 146, 147, 148, 155, 156, 161, 161-2, 162-4, 165, 166, 168, 226
Charles II: as King of Scotland, 168; escape after Worcester, 169-72; restored, 175, 176, 177, 178-9, 180, 185, 188, 189, 190, 195, 196, 204, 214, 221, 222, 225
Châteauneuf, the affair of, 74-5
Chaucer, 67
Chevreuse [Chevereux], the Duchess of, 28, 49-50, 73, 74ff., 99
Chichester, Lord, 73
Cholmley, Sir Hugh, 192
Chudleigh, Colonel James, 151
Churchill, Sir Winston, 198, 202
Clarendon, Earl of, *see* Hyde, Edward
Clifford, Sir Thomas, 186, 199, 201, 202, 209, 218, 219, 224, 225
Clinch, Hester, 165, 179, 229, 230, 235, 236, 237
Cocke, Captain, 204, 205, 209, 210, 212
Cokain, Sir Aston, 88
Coke, 54, 55, 77
Coker family, 14, 232
Coker, Amy Molford, 145, 165, 229
Coker, Anne (married Bullen Reymes the third), 238
Coker, Robert, 145, 148, 159, 160, 162, 166
Coker, William, 130, 145, 147, 159, 160, 165
Compleat Gentleman, 67, 69
Condé, Prince of, 42
Coningsby, Mrs Julian, 170

251

INDEX

Constantinople, 105-6
Cooper, 186
Corbett, Mr and Mrs, 10
Cornwallis, Sir George, 18
Cotterell, Sir Charles, 64, 73, 76, 188
Cotterell, Sir Clement, 18, 20
courtesans, Venetian, 135-6
Coventry, Sir William, 182, 186, 188, 191, 196, 197, 219, 223, 224
Cromwell, 157, 162, 164, 165, 169, 174, 175, 199
Cromwell, Robert, 175

DALKEITH, LADY, 156
Dallington, Sir Robert, 74
Davenant, 187
David, John, 192, 193-4
Delos, 103
Denbigh, the Earl of, 33, 48, 147, 187
Denbigh, Lady, 20, 33, 48, 120, 131, 133, 140, 141, 143, 187
Desmond, the Earl of, 33, 73, 75, 77, 78, 84, 85, 111, 120, 123, 131, 132, 135, 136, 137, 138, 141, 143, 187
Desmond, Lady, 48
Digbie, Mr, 73
Digby, George, 147
Digby, Colonel John, 152, 153
Digby, Sir John, 18
Dorchester, Lord, 13, 33, 34, 36, 39, 40, 50
Dormer, Robert, *see* Carnarvon, Earl of
Dorset, the Earl of, 18, 23-4
Downing, Sir George, 206
Doyley, Sir William, 199, 203, 211, 227
Dryden, 187
Dudley, Robert, *see* Northumberland, Duke of
Dungarvan, Viscount, 64, 73, 76

EDGEHILL, BATTLE OF, 148
Ellesdon, John, 165
Ellesdon, Captain William, 165, 169, 170, 171, 233
Essex, Lord, 148, 155
Evelyn, John, 199, 207, 209, 210, 211, 212, 216, 225, 227
Exeter, 14, 19, 150, 155-6, 157

FAIRFAX, GENERAL SIR THOMAS, 156, 157, 158, 187
Feilding, Anne (wife of Basil, Lord Feilding), 128-9
Feilding, Basil, Lord, 33, 48, 48-9, 67, 77, 113, 120, 122, 123, 124, 126, 128, 129, 133-4, 134-5, 136, 137, 138, 139, 140-1, 143, 147, 148, 187
Feilding, Lady Elizabeth, 33, 48, 78
Feilding, George, *see* Desmond, Earl of

Feilding, Captain Richard, 123, 125, 126-7, 128, 129, 133, 137, 148-9
Feilding, Sir William, *see* Denbigh, Earl of
Felton, John, 25
Ferrara, 83
Fielding, Cuthbert, 26-7
Fitzgerald, Colonel John, 191, 193, 194, 195, 196, 197
Fitzharding, Lord, 195, 197, 200-1, 208
Fletcher, 187
Florence, 114-19
Fontainebleau, 42
Ford, Sir Henry, 227

GAYLAND (Moorish leader), 190, 192
Gazette, 52, 70
Gentileschi, Orazio, 33, 34, 72
Gerbier, Balthazar, 27, 28, 29
Gerrard family, 232
Gerrard, Anne, 145, 165
Gerrard, Elizabeth (wife of Bullen Reymes II), 145, 179, 229
Gerrard, Etheldread, 145, 165, 232-3
Gerrard, Frances, 145, 165
gleek, game of, 47, 48
Golding, Peter, 30, 32-3, 34, 79
Gondomar, 20, 21, 22
Goring, George, 156
Gournie, M., 73-4
Grandison, Lord, 51
Guise, Duke of, 116

HAMILTON, MARQUIS OF, 140, 144
Hamilton, Sir James, 144
Hammond, Robert, 165
Harvey, Dr William, 112, 152
Henrietta-Maria, Charles I's queen, 23, 48, 50, 74, 99, 147, 156, 164, 187
Hertford, Marquis of, 149
Hill, Mistress Priscilla, 13, 27, 33, 51
Holbein, 28, 221
Holland, Earl of, *see* Rich, Sir Henry
Honywood, Sir Philip, 200, 201, 207-8, 215
Hopton, Sir Ralph, 149, 156, 157
Howard, Charles, *see* Andover, Lord
Hulton, P. H., 10
Hyde, Edward (later Earl of Clarendon), 176, 186, 187, 222, 225

IRETON, 164

JACOB, ROBIN, 57, 78, 81f., 83, 85, 88, 90
James I, 16-17, 18, 21, 22, 30
Jermyn, Henry, 76-7, 222
Jesuits, 18, 21, 81, 82, 93, 94, 95, 97, 106
Jonson, Ben, 187
Joyce, Cornet George, 162, 164

INDEX

Kempson, Antony, 152
Killigrew, Thomas, 188

Lane, Jane, 169
Lanier, Nicholas, 28
La Pearce, 45
Legge, William, 51, 165, 188, 197
Little French Lawyer, The, 187
Loreto, 92
Lostwithiel, battle of, 155, 156
Louis XIII, 23, 40, 42, 47
Louis XIV, 214
Lyme Regis, siege of, 154-5
Lyttleton, Sir Thomas, 73

Macdonnell, Randall, 130
Malamocco, 89, 110-12
Manners, Lady Katherine, *see* Buckingham, the Duchess of
Mantua, 91
Mapowder (Dorset), 14, 144-5, 165
Marrane, Signor Francesco, 30, 59ff., 63, 65, 72
Marston Moor, battle of, 156
Martin, Robert, 120
masters, drawing—, music—, dancing— etc., 30, 52, 58, 64, 68, 69, 114, 115
mathematics, as part of the art of war, 69-70
Matthew, Tobie, 17, 18, 21, 22, 93
Maurice, Prince, 149, 150, 151, 152, 153, 154, 155, 156, 161
Medici, Marie de, 40-1
merchants, 60, 63, 82, 89, 96, 98, 101, 102, 103, 104, 111, 112, 121, 125, 126, 127-8, 138
Messina, 98
Middleton, Mr, 134
Middleton, Thomas, 22
Milan, 91
Milles, Sir John, 110
Milos, 103
Monk, General, 175, 176
Montagu, Walter, 50, 82, 85, 94, 95, 96, 97, 98, 99-100, 114, 116
Monteverdi, Claude, 86
Mordaunt, Henry, Earl of Peterborough, 190
Mosly, Mistress Frances, 27, 33-4, 51, 79
Mosly, Michael, 118, 119, 120, 121
Mountjoy, Mrs, 59
Mullins, E. L. C., 10
Mytens, 27

Napier, Robert, 224
Naples, 96-7
Naseby, battle of, 156
Naudine, M., 37, 48, 49
Newport, the Earl of, 77

Newport, Andrew, 219
Newton, Isaac, 218
Northumberland, the Duke of, 116, 117, 217
Notestein, Professor Wallace, 10
Nottingham, the Earl of, 17

Old Buckhurst, 14, 23-5, 143
Overstrand, 14-15, 231-2
Oxford, 148

Padua, 90
Paris, 36-80 *passim*, 133; particular references to, 43, 78
Parker, William, 57, 61
Peacham, Henry, 67, 69-70
Pepys, Samuel, 88, 182, 183, 187, 188-9, 190-1, 193, 197, 219, 222, 223, 224
Petre, Sir George, 13, 17-18, 21, 22, 23-4, 93, 160
Petre, John (Mary's great-grandfather), 15
Petre, John (elder brother of Sir William), 16
Petre, John (cousin of Mary), 160
Petre, Mary, *see* Reymes, Mary
Petre, Robert, 13, 23, 24, 34, 38, 43, 52, 53-4, 66, 160
Petre, Sir William, 15
Petre, William (father of Mary), 16
Petre, Hayes, 16, 19
Philip IV (of Spain), 22, 41
Phillips, Lieutenant-Colonel William, 155
Pickering, Mr, 115, 132
plague, the, 17, 23, 85, 109, 111, 145, 211, 214
Pley, Constance, 182-4, 205, 230, 236
Pley, Captain George, 182
Pley, George (son of Constance), 230, 231-2
Plutarch, 71
Pluvinel, M. Antoine de, 67
Plymouth, siege of, 152-3
Porter, Endymion, 33, 34
Porter, Giles, 39, 51, 78, 81f., 83, 85, 87, 88, 92, 94, 96, 97, 107, 116, 120, 187
Porter, Olive, 33
Portland, the Earl of, 120, 130
Pym, John, 146, 147

Raimes, A. L., 10
Rames, Roger de, 14
Raphael, 27, 94
Reymes, Barnaby (Barney), 15, 71, 76
Reymes, Bullen (the first), 15, 18-19, 20, 21, 25, 33, 34, 38, 43, 44, 55, 60, 71-2, 125, 130, 131, 143, 144-5, 173

INDEX

Reymes, Bullen (the second):
introductory remarks, 13-14
ancestry, 14-16
early years, 23, 25
at York House, 29, 30-5
career:
in Paris: journey there, 36; in lodgings, but member of ambassador's household, 37-40; at embassy, 41-56; in lodgings, 57-80
journey to Italy, 77-8, 79, 81-2
in Venice, 83-9, 113-14; as member of ambassador's official family, 123-9
trip to Greece and Constantinople, 89-112, *via* Rome, 93-6, and Sicily, 98
visit to Florence, 114-19
sent to England to bear news of Lady Feilding's death, 129
in Venice as Lord Desmond's guardian, 132-42
in London, 130-1, 143, 161, 167, 174, 175, 178, 186, 195, 202, 227
military career, 144, 149-57; becomes colonel, 151
marriage, 145, 229
Gentleman of the Privy Chamber, 146, 148, 221
at Oxford, 148-9
in the west country during First Civil War, 149-57
under virtual house-arrest, 158ff.
visits Charles I at Newmarket, 162-4; publication of his report, 164
role in escape of Charles II, 169-72
squire at Waddon, 172-5
Member of Parliament, 177, 178-81, 185-6, 221-5
Vice-Admiral of Dorset, 181-2, 202, 203, 233
merchant, 182-4
mission to Tangier, 189, 191-8
Commissioner for the sick and wounded during Dutch Wars, 199-215, 227-8, 233
Deputy-Treasurer of Prizes, 202-3
Fellow of the Royal Society, 216-18
Surveyor of the Great Wardrobe, 218-20
financial affairs, 34, 38, 43-4, 46-7, 54, 58, 60, 64, 107, 125-6, 131, 160, 234
expense accounts, 37, 39, 44, 57, 73, 74, 80
sequestration of estates, 158-60, 166
wills, 226, 229, 230-1, 235-6
learns French, 52-3, 69, Italian, 83, 114, Spanish, 134, and other accomplishments, 68-9, 114
as lutenist, 39, 40, 42, 43, 46, 47, 51, 55, 64, 68, 102, 115, 124, 129, 133

Reymes—*contd*
appreciation of the theatre, 88, 187
relations with women, 51, 75, 77, 78, 87, 135, 136, 184-5
character and views, 72, 177, 201, 217-18, 221
attitude to Catholicism, 79-80, 85-6, 93, 98-9, 117, 225-6
illnesses, 60-3, 139, 227, 234-5, 236
death, 237
diaries, comments on, 9, 38, 45, 52, 58, 120, 129, 132, 142, 178, 191
letters, comments on, 9, 38, 45, 80; excerpts from: to his mother, 40, 46 57-8, 79-80; to his father, 41, 42, 43-4, 46, 52, 54, 55-6, 61, 63-4, 64-5, 65, 72; to other members of his family, 52, 71, 79; to friends, 39, 47, 58, 63, 76-7, 79; to the Duchess of Buckingham, 47, 62-3, 75; to Patience Adams, 53, 53-4, 59; to Pepys, 193; to Bennet, 193; to Fitzgerald, 195-6, 197, 198; to Clifford, 201-2, 203, 209; to Doyley, 203; to Commissioners, 204, 208, 227-8; to Cocke, 205, 210-11, 212; to Evelyn, 207, 209, 210, 211-12, 212-13; to Albemarle, 213-14
Reymes, Bullen (the third), 165, 229-30, 236, 237, 238
Reymes, Clement, 15, 18
Reymes, Elizabeth: i) sister of Bullen II, 19, 79, 144; ii) wife of Bullen II, *see* Gerrard, Elizabeth
Reymes, Francis, 15, 19, 20
Reymes, John (d. 1411), 14-15
Reymes, Judith, 19, 79, 144
Reymes, Mary: i) mother of Bullen II, 15, 19, 21, 24, 25, 35, 38, 46, 53, 57, 79-80, 93, 130, 143, 160-1, 166-7, 173, 175; ii) sister of Bullen II, 19, 79, 144, 229, 236; iii) daughter of Bullen II, 173, 229, 230-1, 235, 236, 238
Reymes, Robert, 168, 173
Reymes, Tabitha, 165, 179, 229, 230, 236
Reymes, William: i) father of Bullen I, 15; ii) brother of Bullen II, 19, 71; iii) son of Bullen II, 166, 173
Rich, Sir Henry, Earl of Holland, 45, 48, 50
Richelieu, 40, 49, 50, 71, 74, 99-100
Robbins, Professor Caroline, 10
Roe, Sir Thomas, 50
Rome, 93-5
Roundway Down, battle of, 149
Rowlandson, Thomas, 84, 85, 110, 113-14, 122, 123-4, 126, 127, 128, 132, 134
Royal Society, 216-17, 218
Rubens, 27, 28, 29, 31

INDEX

Rupert, Prince, 148, 156, 161, 191, 196, 197, 214, 223, 224
Russell, Lord William (later Earl of Bedford), 64, 68, 73, 77, 147
Rutherford, Andrew, *see* Teviot, Earl of

SACKVILLE, EDWARD, *see* Dorset, Earl of
Sackville, Richard, 18
Sackville, Thomas, 23
Sandwich, the Earl of, 200, 204, 218, 219
Sarto, Andrea del, 28
Seneca, 71
Shakespeare, 71, 137, 187
Slingsby, Mr, 93, 94, 99
Slingsby, Robert, 73
Smedley, Mistress Anne, 33, 34, 47, 58, 63
Smyrna, 104
Soissons, the Duchess of, 42
Somerset, the Earl of, 19-20
Soranzo, Giovanni, 49
Southcott, Cecily, 16
Southwell, Elizabeth, 117
Spicer, Grace, 16
Sprat, Thomas, 216, 218
Stamford, the Earl of, 150
Stanhope, Bridget, *see* Desmond, Lady
Stanhope, Sir Michael, 48
Strangways, Colonel Giles, 169, 170
Suckling, Sir John, 51

TABARIER, M., 81, 96, 97
Tangier, 190
Taunton, siege of, 156
tennis, 73-4
Teviot, the Earl of, 190, 191, 192-3
theatre, 87-8, 95, 121, 139, 187
Thomason Tracts, 9, 151
Thynne, Henry Frederick, 73, 94, 96, 97, 110, 132
Tibbut, H. G., 10
Tintoretto, 28
Titian, 27, 28
Tor Newton House, 15-16, 23
Townsend, Mr, 219
Tracy, John, 115
Trent manor house, 165, 166, 167, 168, 169, 172
Troyte-Bullock, Major G. V., 9, 10, 249
Tuke, 187
Turin, 82
Turner, Sir Edward, 179

VAIR, GUILLAUME DU, 75
Van Dyck, 27
Vane, Sir Henry, 51
Venice, 84-9, 113, 120-9, 133-41
Verona, 90-1
Veronese, Paul, 28, 29
Vic, de, 54, 74
Vicenza, 90
Villiers, Eleanor, 76-7
Villiers, Francis, 59
Villiers, George, *see* Buckingham, Duke of
Villiers, George, 2nd Duke of Buckingham, 34, 58, 59, 187
Villiers, Lady Mary, 33
Villiers, Susan, *see* Denbigh, Lady
Villiers, William, *see* Grandison, Lord

WADDON MANOR, 10, 168, 172-3
Wagstaff, Joseph, 153
Wake, Sir Isaac, 13, 36-7, 39-40, 41, 42, 43, 47, 49, 50, 52, 53, 54-6, 62, 74, 124
Waller, 149, 155
Wardlaw, Colonel, 152, 153
Warr, Ned, 120, 121
Wedgwood, Dr C. V., 10
Wescombe, Martin, consul at Cadiz, 194
Weston, Benjamin, 123, 128, 134
Weston, Richard, *see* Portland, Earl of
Weymouth, 178, 182, 186, 229, 231, 239
Whalley, Major-General, 162, 163
Wharton, Sir Thomas, 45, 48, 57
Wheatley, John, 229, 233
wigs, 74
Wilkinson, 54, 57, 61
Wilmot, Henry (later Earl of Rochester), 51, 169, 170, 171, 172
Wilson, Mr J., merchant in Tangier, 192-3
Wotton, Sir Henry, 40, 117
Wren, Christopher, 218
Wych, Sir Peter, 105
Wyndham, Colonel Francis, 165, 168, 169, 170, 232

YORK, THE DUKE OF, 196, 197, 212, 222, 225
York House, 13, 26-35, 187

ZANTE, 102-3, 109-10
Zeals (Wiltshire), 9, 249